Mississippi Reflections

A Collection of Recipes Seasoned with Memories
from Hospice of Central Mississippi

Hospice
of Central Mississippi, Inc.

The unending circle, coupled with the three leaf motif, is the symbol of Hospice of Central Mississippi. The circle depicts the unbroken commitment to those we serve while the leaves represent the three facets encompassed in hospice care . . . care for the body, mind and soul.

Dedication

Mississippi Reflections is lovingly dedicated to the volunteers of Hospice of Central Mississippi. You continue to give and give. Let us never fail to reflect upon your unselfish devotion to this special calling.

This cookbook is a collection of favorite recipes,
which are not necessarily original recipes.

Published by Hospice of Central Mississippi, Inc.

Copyright© Hospice of Central Mississippi, Inc.
2600 Insurance Center Dr., Suite B-120
Jackson, Mississippi 39216-4911
(601) 366-9881
1-800-273-7724
FAX (601) 981-0150

Library of Congress Number: 96-84222
ISBN: 0-9652150-0-8

Edited, Designed and Manufactured by Favorite Recipes® Press
P.O. Box 305142
Nashville, Tennessee 37230
1-800-358-0560

Manufactured in the United States of America
First Printing: 1996   5,000 copies

Cover photograph by David Keeney. Fog rising off the lake at early morning,
Holmes County State Park, Durant, Mississippi

Foreword

Reflections offer us a glimpse at our pasts—who we were, our heritage, our ancestors, our backgrounds. Reflections of our pasts bring to mind sights, sounds, smells, sensations, and thoughts of those we have known. Some of our memories give us warm, wonderful, happy feelings. Other memories may make us sad. Still others are bittersweet. All in all, reflections of our pasts are a collection of memories, thoughts of people who touched our hearts, events that shaped our lives, places we'll remember forever.

Remembering the best often makes us long to go back. While that is impossible, we offer *Mississippi Reflections . . . A Collection of Recipes Seasoned with Memories* as a look back at all the best of our pasts, the delectable food we have enjoyed, and the fine hands that prepared the wonderful dishes.

Each of the recipes in this special collection is a reflection of someone. As you flip through the pages of this cookbook, we hope that our memories will bring to mind some of your own. Remember Grandmother's scrumptious cake and how special she made you feel when she baked it just for you. Remember the first meal you prepared as a young bride, how you burned that expensive roast that he ate anyway. Remember the first time you ever cooked in home economics, the pie that won the blue ribbon at the county fair, the cookies you made with your children every Christmas and you now make with their children. Remember that special time your husband told you "This is even better than Mama's."

Just as the beautiful waters of Mississippi lakes and rivers roll on, we must also move on. As we go along the way, we will gather together more memories upon which to reflect. Our lives are blessed with our memories of special days, special times, special people, our *Mississippi Reflections*.

Hospice of Central Mississippi, Inc.

As recently as 1989, most people in Mississippi were unfamiliar with the hospice concept of care. Thankfully, there were those around with a great deal of insight and foresight who recognized that family members needed assistance caring for their terminally ill loved ones who chose to remain at home.

These individuals spent months researching the need for hospice care in the central area of Mississippi and, in 1989 opened the Jackson office of Hospice of Central Mississippi, Inc., with a staff of six. Before the first year had passed, the average daily census had reached 35 and 150 patients had been served in their homes. Because of the small, but committed staff, more and more physicians began finding out about Hospice of Central Mississippi. They discovered the compassionate care demonstrated by the HOCM team of caregivers, and many became strong hospice advocates.

Over the years, HOCM has progressed into an agency that is well respected and recognized in the community for its accomplishments. HOCM has signed contracts with area hospitals to offer inpatient hospice care. Staff members worked long hours to get the Mississippi legislature to pass the Hospice Licensure Law and a law providing hospice benefits for Medicaid patients. HOCM is also honored to operate as a community service affiliate of the Mississippi Health Network, a consortium of Mississippi Baptist Medical Center, Rankin Medical Center, and St. Dominic/Jackson Memorial Hospital. HOCM is also an active member of the Mississippi Hospice Organization.

Today, in addition to service in Hinds, Madison, and Rankin Counties, HOCM has a branch office in Brookhaven, serving Copiah and Lincoln Counties and a fifty-mile radius of that office, and also serves patients in Yazoo County out of the satellite office in Yazoo City. Staff members currently number 65, and in 1995 census reached 123. Currently, there are over 2500 hospices in all fifty states and Puerto Rico. In 1994, these hospices served over 340,000 patients and their families. Over the past five years, annual growth in the number of hospice patients nationwide has averaged 16 percent. In spite of the rapid growth of hospice in every state, far too many people confront the tragedy of a terminal illness alone, fearful, and in pain. With hospice, death does not have to be this way.

Hospice is a philosophy of care focusing on improving quality of life, not extending life. The major emphasis is on pain management and symptom control. A team that includes physicians, nurses, home health aides, social workers, counselors, clergy, therapists, pharmacists, and volunteers strives to meet the physical, emotional, psychosocial, and spiritual aspects of pain.

At Hospice of Central Mississippi, a message of hope is offered to individuals who feel they are in hopeless situations. Hospice is dedicated to ensuring that individuals die with dignity, without pain, and in a loving environment. Hospice provides care for the patient and the family—care for the body, mind, and soul.

Hospice of Central Mississippi, Inc., is a nonprofit organization serving patients regardless of their ability to pay for services. The proceeds from the sale of this cookbook will go directly into the patient fund to meet the needs of these individuals.

Contents

Contributors

Becky Adams
Dot Allen
Theresa Allen
Rebecca Askew
Ruby (Mrs. Woodie)
    Assaf
Kathy Behan
Faye Bein
Rosetta Belcher
Mary Bell
Patty Bell
Hattie Berch
Jean Berch
Jerry Berch
Elizabeth Black
Marjorie Bobington
Joseph Bonfiglio
Louise "Peggy" Melton
    Bookout
Noreen Botts
Durwood J. (Woody)
    Breeland
Jane Breeland
Marian C. Brewer
Eddie J. Briggs
Beverly Brimer
Cathy Britt
Bob Burst
Mrs. Ralph Calcote
Rev. Ralph Calcote
Ruth Calcote
Dott Cannon
Peggy Castilow
Ann Catt
Amber Clanton
Jerry Clower
Thad Cochran
Alma Graham Conner
Elizabeth M. Covington
Debbie Cox
Pam Cranford
Sue Cunningham
Tommie Darras
Winifred De Jonge
Ron DelBene
Kane Ditto
Susan Dobbs
Linda Ebbers
Nancy Edmonson
Richard Edmonson
Carlton Evans
Donna Evans
Carol Fair
Mary Fair

Beverly Farabee
Helen McClean Fletcher
John C. Fletcher
Sally Fletcher
Perry "Porkchop"
    Florence
Katherine Gales
Dianna Gonzalez
Frances Griffin
Judy Griffin
Jeanette Guice
Mrs. Jeanette N. Haag
Kevin Hale
Jennifer Hane
Scott Hane
Cynthia B. Harper
Mrs. Paul D. (Fay) Harris
Debbie (Mrs. Rickey)
    Hartzog
Elizabeth Helms
Cinda Henderson
Amy Hickman
Kathy Hilton
Hazel Hogue
Paula Honea
Claire Houston
Gerry Ann Houston,
    M.D.
Dena Howington
Beth Huckabee
Thomas Huckabee
Paul Hux
Sandra Hux
Chuck Ivey
LaVerne Jackson
Mrs. Charles R.
    (Patricia) Jacobs
Ann F. Jarratt
Linda Jenkins
Martha Jenkins
Joe Anne Johnson
Betty L. Johnston
Cathy Joiner
Mandy Jones
David Keeney
Melissa Melton Keeney
Martha M. Kenahan
Susan Landrum
Hallie S. Lea
Bart Lee
Bret Lee
Nicky Lee
Sara S. Lee
Roselle Brister Lefferts

Mary Ann Lefoldt
Fannie Lewis
Jan Lingenfelter
Trent Lott
Lou Ella Lowery
Marilyn O. Magee
Martha Makamson
Abe J. Malouf, M.D.
Lynn Manker
Mary M. Manning
Jo Mathews
Hilda May
Kathy May
Mary Helen Mayers
Christie McBroom
Steve McCombs
Doris McDaniel
Donna McGehee
Linda McLain
Myrtis Meaders
Vincent "Snow"
    Mechatto
Louise Brister Melton
Mary Ann Mobley
Sally (Mrs. Dick) Molpus
Congressman G. V.
    (Sonny) Montgomery
Melody Montgomery
Mike Moore
Amy C. Morgan
Joe Myrick
Mildred Myrick
Pam Myrick-Motley
Zahra Noe
Frances Nowell
Frances McRee
    Oberschmidt
Mrs. Bill Oberschmidt
Nan Oestmann
Frances Parker
Sister June Pemberton
Holly Perkins
Patricia A. Perkins
Diana Pias
Donna Powell
Pat Powers
Susan Pratt
Gail Price
Francis Quimby
Helga Reed
Nell Rein
Gene Richerson
Patricia Roper
Jean Marie Rose

Margeret Jo Rose
Linda Russo
Kathie Salley
Winnie Sandifer
Anita Sarabia
Lizzie Sartin
Marjorie Scott
William E. "Scott" Scott
Lee Seehaver
Jennifer Segrest
Mrs. Wm. T. (Jimmie)
    Sistrunk
Elsie R. Smith
Laurie Mason Smith
Opal Smith
Sherra C. Smith
John T. Snook, Jr.
Edith Soup
Cathy Sparkman
Mrs. Ben (Phyllis)
    Spearman
Angie Spencer
David Starns
Sara Melton Starns
Faith Stauss
Darlene Stephens
Judy Stevens
Ruth Stevens
Edith Stewart
Jan Szalay
Mary L. Taylor
Darlene Tenney
Ann P. Townsend
Connie Trask
Delores Ulmer
Mrs. Dwight E. Waddell
Iris Waldrop
Sandra Wallace
Mrs. Bill (Carroll) Waller
Carla Walsh
Loretta Ward
Indy (Mrs. Charles)
    Whitten
Sallye M. Wilcox
Jennifer Wilkinson
Marietta Wilkinson
Rhonda "Chellie"
    Williams
Ron Wojcik
Sandra Wojcik
Delora Woodruff
Cathie Young
Janis Zimmerman

Acknowledgments

*W*e are able to share this cookbook with you for your enjoyment because many generous individuals were willing to share their time and talents in support of the mission of Hospice of Central Mississippi. We are deeply grateful to our volunteers, too numerous to name, who were so faithful to this project. We would also like to extend a special word of thanks to each individual who shared a favorite recipe or a special memory. Our heartfelt appreciation goes out to each one who, in large ways or in small, made the publication of *Mississippi Reflections . . . A Collection of Recipes Seasoned with Memories* a reality.

HOSPICE OF CENTRAL MISSISSIPPI, INC.
COOKBOOK COMMITTEE

Jean Berch
Branch Director
Brookhaven Office,
Hospice of Central Mississippi

Melissa Keeney
Coordinator of
Community Relations,
Hospice of Central Mississippi

Jill Boteler
Volunteer Coordinator
Hospice of Central Mississippi

Cynthia Harper
Chairperson, Board of Directors,
Hospice of Central Mississippi

Elizabeth Thompson
Board of Directors
Hospice of Central Mississippi

Iris Waldrop
Volunteer Coordinator
Brookhaven Office,
Hospice of Central Mississippi

Photography

Steve Colston Commercial Photography, Jackson, Mississippi
Gil Ford Photography, Jackson, Mississippi
David Keeney, Jackson, Mississippi
Sara S. Lee, Terry, Mississippi

Nutritional Profile Guidelines

The editors have attempted to present these family recipes in a form that allows approximate nutritional values to be computed. Persons with dietary or health problems or whose diets require close monitoring should not rely solely on the nutritional information provided. They should consult their physicians or a registered dietitian for specific information.

ABBREVIATIONS FOR NUTRITIONAL PROFILE

Cal — Calories	Fiber — Dietary Fiber	Sod — Sodium
Prot — Protein	T Fat — Total Fat	g — grams
Carbo — Carbohydrates	Chol — Cholesterol	mg — milligrams

Nutritional information for these recipes is computed from information derived from many sources, including materials supplied by the United States Department of Agriculture, computer databanks, and journals in which the information is assumed to be in the public domain. However, many specialty items, new products, and processed foods may not be available from these sources or may vary from the average values used in these profiles. More information on new and/or specific products may be obtained by reading the nutrient labels. Unless otherwise specified, the nutritional profile of these recipes is based on all measurements being level.

- **Artificial sweeteners** vary in use and strength so should be used "to taste," using the recipe ingredients as a guideline. Sweeteners using aspartame (NutraSweet and Equal) should not be used as a sweetener in recipes involving prolonged heating, which reduces the sweet taste. For further information on the use of these sweeteners, refer to package.
- **Alcoholic ingredients** have been analyzed for the basic ingredients, although cooking causes the evaporation of alcohol, thus decreasing caloric content.
- **Buttermilk**, **sour cream**, and **yogurt** are the types available commercially.
- **Cake mixes** which are prepared using package directions include 3 eggs and 1/2 cup oil.
- **Chicken**, cooked for boning and chopping, has been roasted; this method yields the lowest caloric values.
- **Cottage cheese** is cream-style with 4.2% creaming mixture. Dry curd cottage cheese has no creaming mixture.
- **Eggs** are all large. To avoid raw eggs that may carry salmonella, as in eggnog or 6-week muffin batter, use an equivalent amount of commercial egg substitute.
- **Flour** is unsifted all-purpose flour.
- **Garnishes**, serving suggestions, and other optional additions and variations are not included in the profile.
- **Margarine** and **butter** are regular, not whipped or presoftened.
- **Milk** is whole milk, 3.5% butterfat. Lowfat milk is 1% butterfat. Evaporated milk is whole milk with 60% of the water removed.
- **Oil** is any type of vegetable cooking oil. **Shortening** is hydrogenated vegetable shortening.
- **Salt** and other ingredients to taste as noted in the ingredients have not been included in the nutritional profile.
- If a choice of ingredients has been given, the nutritional profile reflects the first option. If a choice of amounts has been given, the nutritional profile reflects the greater amount.

Appetizers, Soups & Salads

Appetizers, Soups & Salads

Beer Batter Pickles, 11
Stuffed Mushrooms, 11
Sausage-Stuffed Mushrooms, 12
Aunt May's Shrimp with Rémoulade Sauce, 12
Tuna Mold, 13
Cheese Log, 13
Pineapple Cheese Ball, 13
Deviled Ham Dip, 14
Pineapple Dip, 14
Sally's Shrimp Spread, 14
Sausage and Bean Soup, 15
Cheese and Vegetable Soup, 15
Hodgepodge Soup, 16
Potato Soup, 16
Corn and Potato Soup, 17
Tomato Soup, 17
Sopa Rosita (Saffron Tomato Broth), 18
Orange Congealed Salad, 18
Watermelon Salad, 19
Frozen Fruit Salad, 19
Italian Fruit Salad, 20
Spiced Peach Salad, 20
Pineapple Salad, 21
Strawberry Salad, 21
Chicken Salad, 22
Chicken Pasta Salad, 22
Zesty Pasta Salad, 23
Tortellini Salad, 23
Beet Salad, 24
Broccoli-Cauliflower Salad, 24
Black Bean Salad, 24
Spinach, Bacon and Apple Salad, 25
Fresh Sweet Potato Salad, 26
Honey Poppy Seed Dressing, 26

Photograph on preceding page by Steve Colston Photography. The bridge over the mighty Mississippi River at historic Vicksburg, Mississippi

Beer Batter Pickles

1 (12-ounce) bottle dark beer
1¹/2 cups flour
¹/2 teaspoon salt
Pepper to taste
¹/8 teaspoon Worcestershire sauce, or
    to taste
12 large dill pickle spears
1 cup canola oil
1 cup flour

- Whisk the beer and 1¹/2 cups flour together in a medium bowl. Add the salt, pepper and Worcestershire sauce, mixing until the batter is smooth; set aside. Drain the pickle spears.
- Heat the oil to 350 degrees in a deep skillet. Dip each pickle in the remaining 1 cup flour and then into the batter. Place pickles carefully into the hot oil. Fry for 3 to 5 minutes or until golden brown. Drain on paper towels. Serve hot.
- Batter can also be used for fish and vegetables or small dill slices.
- Yield: 12 servings.

Approx Per Serving: Cal 272; Prot 3 g;
Carbo 22 g; T Fat 18 g; 61% Calories from Fat;
Chol 0 mg; Fiber 1 g; Sod 341 mg

—*Mrs. Wm. T. (Jimmie) Sistrunk*

Stuffed Mushrooms

8 large mushrooms
4 slices bread, crumbled
¹/2 cup minced onion
¹/2 cup minced celery
¹/2 cup chopped green or red bell pepper
1 (6-ounce) can crab meat, drained
1 (4-ounce) can shrimp, drained
¹/4 teaspoon oregano
¹/2 teaspoon sweet basil
¹/2 teaspoon garlic salt
¹/4 teaspoon white pepper
1 egg
¹/2 cup shredded Cheddar cheese

- Remove the stems from the mushrooms; chop the stems. Wipe the stems and caps clean.
- Mix the stems, bread crumbs, onion, celery and green pepper in a bowl. Add the crab meat, shrimp, oregano, basil, garlic salt, white pepper and egg; mix well. Add 2 tablespoons water if the mixture is too dry.
- Spoon the mixture into the mushroom caps. Place the caps in a 7x9-inch glass baking dish. Bake at 350 degrees for 30 minutes.
- Sprinkle with cheese. May substitute cheese sauce for shredded cheese.
- Yield: 4 servings.

Approx Per Serving: Cal 255; Prot 24 g;
Carbo 21 g; T Fat 8 g; 29% Calories from Fat;
Chol 156 mg; Fiber 2 g; Sod 708 mg

Patricia Roper

Sausage-Stuffed Mushrooms

■ ■

36 medium mushrooms
8 ounces sausage
1 large onion, chopped
1/2 cup herb stuffing mix
1/4 cup (about) mayonnaise
Lemon juice to taste

- Rinse the mushrooms; remove the stems and chop them.
- Brown the sausage, stems and onion in a nonstick skillet; drain well.
- Combine the sausage mixture with the stuffing in a bowl.
- Add enough mayonnaise to hold the mixture together.
- Place the mushroom caps in a baking dish. Fill the caps with the stuffing mixture. Cover and chill until baking time.
- Bake at 450 degrees for 10 minutes.
- Yield: 18 servings.

Approx Per Serving: Cal 63; Prot 2 g; Carbo 4 g; T Fat 5 g; 62% Calories from Fat; Chol 7 mg; Fiber 1 g; Sod 127 mg

—Roselle Brister Lefferts

Snake Dinner with Dad

When I was younger, my dad and I went out to dinner one night at a restaurant that had a floor show. We were very much enjoying the entertainment but found it difficult to talk over the music. I don't remember what I ordered to eat, but I remember my dad commenting on how wonderful his food was. I thought I heard Dad say, "This is the best snake I've ever had. Try some."

Now, I had tried lots of unusual food in my day and I knew some people ate snake, turtle, and alligator, but I didn't think I was ready to try snake for myself. I told Dad "no, thanks," but he kept insisting. Finally, I gave in. I took a bite of the "snake." It wasn't bad. I said, "Dad, don't you think this snake tastes an awful lot like steak?"

I thought Dad was going to fall off his chair, he was laughing so hard. "Snake?" he finally said. "I didn't say snake. I said steak!" I hadn't been able to hear what he had ordered over the live music. We had a great laugh over this for many years to come.

—Robin Lefferts Tanksley

Aunt May's Shrimp with Rémoulade Sauce

■ ■

2 pounds fresh shrimp
3 hard-boiled eggs
2 ribs celery, minced
2 cups mayonnaise
1 teaspoon Worcestershire sauce
2 tablespoons sauterne
3 tablespoons prepared mustard
1/2 cup Creole mustard with horseradish
1 teaspoon salt
1 teaspoon sugar
1/2 teaspoon pepper

- Cook the shrimp in boiling water in a saucepan until the shrimp turn pink. Drain, rinse with cold water and drain well. Peel and devein the shrimp. Chill in refrigerator.
- Mash the eggs in a large bowl. Add the celery; toss to mix.
- Add the mayonnaise, Worcestershire sauce, sauterne, mustards, salt, sugar and pepper; mix well. Chill in refrigerator.
- Add the shrimp to the sauce just before serving; mix until the shrimp are coated.
- Serve on lettuce-lined salad plates as an appetizer, first course or a salad.
- To serve as an appetizer for a buffet table, place the sauce in a bowl in the center of a large serving plate and arrange the shrimp around the sauce.
- Yield: 8 servings.

Approx Per Serving: Cal 561; Prot 20 g; Carbo 9 g; T Fat 50 g; 79% Calories from Fat; Chol 270 mg; Fiber <1 g; Sod 1069 mg

—Dott Cannon

Tuna Mold

2 tablespoons minced dried parsley
1 (6-ounce) can water-pack white tuna
8 ounces cream cheese, softened
1 teaspoon grated onion
1/2 cup chopped pecans
1/2 teaspoon salt
1/8 teaspoon Tabasco sauce, or to taste
6 tablespoons minced dried parsley

- Sprinkle the 2 tablespoons parsley into a lightly oiled mold.
- Combine the tuna, cream cheese, onion, pecans, salt, Tabasco sauce and remaining 6 tablespoons parsley in a bowl; mix well.
- Spoon into the prepared mold.
- Chill the tuna mold until serving time.
- Invert onto a serving plate and garnish as desired.
- Serve with crackers.
- May prepare ahead and freeze. Let stand in the refrigerator for several hours to thaw.
- Yield: 15 servings.

Approx Per Serving: Cal 93; Prot 4 g;
Carbo 1 g; T Fat 8 g; 76% Calories from Fat;
Chol 20 mg; Fiber <1 g; Sod 155 mg

—Frances Nowell

Cheese Log

1 pound Velveeta cheese, shredded
6 ounces cream cheese, softened
1 1/2 teaspoons Worcestershire sauce
1 teaspoon Tabasco sauce, or to taste
1/2 cup chopped pecans

- Combine the cheese, cream cheese, Worcestershire sauce, Tabasco sauce and pecans in a bowl; mix well.
- Shape into two 5-inch logs. Wrap in plastic wrap or waxed paper.
- Chill until serving time.
- Cut into slices. Arrange on a serving plate.
- Yield: 20 servings.

Approx Per Serving: Cal 134; Prot 6 g;
Carbo 1 g; T Fat 12 g; 79% Calories from Fat;
Chol 31 mg; Fiber <1 g; Sod 355 mg

—Frances Griffin

Pineapple Cheese Ball

16 ounces cream cheese, softened
1 cup drained crushed pineapple
1 cup chopped pecans
1/4 cup finely chopped green bell pepper
1/4 cup finely chopped red cherries
1 bunch green onions, chopped
1 teaspoon salt
1 cup chopped pecans

- Combine the cream cheese, pineapple, 1 cup pecans, green pepper, cherries, green onions and salt in a bowl; mix well.
- Shape into a ball. Roll the ball in the remaining 1 cup pecans.
- Chill until serving time.
- Yield: 30 servings.

Approx Per Serving: Cal 113; Prot 2 g;
Carbo 4 g; T Fat 11 g; 81% Calories from Fat;
Chol 17 mg; Fiber 1 g; Sod 116 mg

—Sally Fletcher

Deviled Ham Dip

2 (3-ounce) cans deviled ham
16 ounces cream cheese, softened
1 medium onion, grated
Garlic salt to taste
Mayonnaise to taste

- Mix the deviled ham, cream cheese, onion, garlic salt and mayonnaise in a bowl. Chill until serving time.
- Yield: 20 servings.

Approx Per Serving: Cal 106; Prot 3 g;
Carbo 1 g; T Fat 10 g; 85% Calories from Fat;
Chol 32 mg; Fiber <1 g; Sod 134 mg

—*Paula Honea*

Pineapple Dip

1 (12-ounce) jar pineapple preserves
1/4 cup prepared mustard
1/4 cup horseradish

- Mix the preserves, mustard and horseradish in a bowl.
- Serve hot or cold as a dip or sauce with chicken nuggets.
- Yield: 6 servings.

Approx Per Serving: Cal 149; Prot 1 g;
Carbo 38 g; T Fat 1 g; 3% Calories from Fat;
Chol 0 mg; Fiber 1 g; Sod 163 mg

—*Darlene Tenney*

Sally's Shrimp Spread

2 (6-ounce) packages frozen tiny shrimp
1 lemon
1/2 cup mayonnaise
1/2 cup sour cream
1/2 teaspoon dillweed
1/2 teaspoon sugar
1/2 teaspoon garlic powder

- Thaw the shrimp in a colander under cool running water.
- Squeeze the juice from the lemon over the shrimp; toss to coat.
- Squeeze the excess moisture from the shrimp and pat dry with paper towels.
- Combine the shrimp, mayonnaise, sour cream, dillweed, sugar and garlic powder in a bowl; mix well.
- Serve with butter crackers.
- Yield: 12 servings.

Approx Per Serving: Cal 116; Prot 6 g;
Carbo 1 g; T Fat 10 g; 74% Calories from Fat;
Chol 65 mg; Fiber <1 g; Sod 121 mg

—*Kathy Behan*

Sausage and Bean Soup

1 medium onion, chopped
2 ribs celery, chopped
1 tablespoon butter
8 ounces beef sausage, cut into 1/4-inch slices
3 (16-ounce) cans Great Northern beans

- Sauté the onion and celery in the butter in a skillet. Add the sausage. Sauté until the onion is browned.
- Heat the beans in a large saucepan. Stir in the sausage mixture. Cook for 15 minutes longer.
- Yield: 6 servings.

Approx Per Serving: Cal 278; Prot 15 g; Carbo 38 g; T Fat 8 g; 26% Calories from Fat; Chol 18 mg; Fiber 14 g; Sod 975 mg

Grandmother, Pork and Beans, and the Soap Opera

When I was a kindergarten-aged child growing up in Vicksburg, my maternal grand-mother lived with us. I remember her as almost regal. She was kind and sweet, and she was my best friend. When I would come home from school, she always seemed so glad to see me. She and I would curl up together and watch "Days of Our Lives." Grandmother's maid, Mattie Lee, always fixed us a snack. It seems it was pork and beans every day, although, in truth, I'm sure it varied. My memories of those days spent with Grandmother are especially dear to me.

—Jean Marie Rose

Cheese and Vegetable Soup

2 tablespoons margarine
1/4 cup chopped green onions
1/4 cup chopped celery
1/4 cup chopped green bell pepper
1/4 cup grated carrots
1/2 cup grated potato
1/4 cup margarine
1/2 cup flour
4 1/2 cups chicken stock
1/8 teaspoon Worcestershire sauce, or to taste
1/4 teaspoon cayenne
1/3 cup milk
2 1/2 cups shredded medium Cheddar cheese

- Heat the 2 tablespoons margarine in a skillet until melted. Add the green onions, celery, green pepper, carrots and potato. Sauté until the vegetables are tender; set aside.
- Combine the remaining 1/4 cup margarine and flour in a large Dutch oven; mix well. Add the chicken stock. Simmer for 5 minutes.
- Add the Worcestershire sauce, cayenne, sautéed vegetables and milk; mix well. Simmer for 1 hour.
- Add the cheese gradually, stirring well after each addition. Cook until heated through.
- May blend in a blender at medium speed for 3 to 4 minutes to make cream of cheese soup.
- Yield: 6 servings.

Approx Per Serving: Cal 391; Prot 18 g; Carbo 16 g; T Fat 29 g; 66% Calories from Fat; Chol 51 mg; Fiber 1 g; Sod 1024 mg

—Marilyn O. Magee

Hodgepodge Soup

2 pounds ground beef
1 1/2 cups chopped onion
1 1/2 cups chopped celery
2 (15-ounce) cans ranch-style beans
3 (10-ounce) cans minestrone
1 (10-ounce) can tomatoes with green chiles
2 teaspoons chili powder
Garlic powder and Tabasco sauce to taste
1 1/2 cups water

- Sauté the ground beef, onion and celery in a large saucepan until the ground beef is no longer pink and the onion and celery are tender.
- Add the beans, minestrone, tomatoes, seasonings and water; mix well.
- Simmer for 30 minutes or until heated through, adding more water if needed to make the soup of the desired consistency.
- Yield: 10 servings.

Approx Per Serving: Cal 365; Prot 28 g; Carbo 26 g; T Fat 17 g; 41% Calories from Fat; Chol 68 mg; Fiber 2 g; Sod 1118 mg

—*LaVerne Jackson*

Potato Soup

3 cups chopped peeled potatoes
1/2 cup chopped or sliced onion
1/2 cup chopped celery
2 chicken bouillon cubes
Salt to taste
1 cup milk
1 cup sour cream with chives
1 tablespoon flour
1 cup milk

- Combine the potatoes, onion, celery, bouillon cubes, salt and just enough water to cover in a large saucepan or Dutch oven. Simmer, covered, for 20 minutes or until vegetables are tender.
- Add the 1 cup milk. Cook until heated through; do not boil.
- Mix the sour cream and flour in a bowl. Stir in the remaining 1 cup milk gradually.
- Pour 1/3 of the potato mixture into the flour mixture; mix well. Stir the flour mixture into the soup.
- Cook until the soup is slightly thickened, stirring frequently.
- Serve on a cold night with cheese toast.
- Yield: 8 servings.

Approx Per Serving: Cal 154; Prot 5 g; Carbo 16 g; T Fat 8 g; 47% Calories from Fat; Chol 21 mg; Fiber 1 g; Sod 343 mg

—*Kathy Hilton*

Corn and Potato Soup

2 cups chopped cooked chicken
2 cups chicken broth
2 (10-ounce) cans cream of potato soup
2 (10-ounce) cans cream of chicken soup
1 (16-ounce) can Mexicorn
1 (6-ounce) jar sliced mushrooms, drained
1 1/2 cups shredded Cheddar cheese

- Combine the chicken, chicken broth, cream of potato soup and cream of chicken soup in a saucepan or Dutch oven; mix well.
- Stir in the Mexicorn and mushrooms. Cook until heated through.
- Stir in 1 cup of the cheese.
- Stir until the cheese melts.
- Ladle into individual soup bowls. Sprinkle with the remaining 1/2 cup cheese.
- May add one 4-ounce can green chiles.
- Yield: 10 servings.

Approx Per Serving: Cal 261; Prot 17 g; Carbo 19 g; T Fat 13 g; 44% Calories from Fat; Chol 51 mg; Fiber 1 g; Sod 1468 mg

—Debbie Hartzog

Tomato Soup

1 bunch green onions
1/2 cup butter
1 (49-ounce) can chicken broth
3 (11-ounce) cans tomatoes
3 (10-ounce) cans tomato soup
1/8 teaspoon Tabasco sauce, or to taste

- Chop the green onions as desired.
- Sauté the green onions in the butter in a skillet.
- Heat the chicken broth in a saucepan.
- Add the undrained tomatoes and the canned tomato soup.
- Add the sautéed green onions. Season with Tabasco sauce.
- Heat to serving temperature, stirring constantly.
- Yield: 8 servings.

Approx Per Serving: Cal 260; Prot 11 g; Carbo 22 g; T Fat 15 g; 51% Calories from Fat; Chol 33 mg; Fiber 2 g; Sod 2192 mg

—Susan Pratt

Sopa Rosita (Saffron Tomato Broth)

1 (46-ounce) can tomato juice
2 cups chicken broth
1/4 cup white wine
1 teaspoon grated onion
1 1/2 teaspoons dried basil
1/8 teaspoon ground nutmeg
1/2 to 1 clove of garlic, crushed
1/8 teaspoon cayenne, or to taste
1/8 teaspoon saffron, or to taste

- Combine the tomato juice, chicken broth and wine in a saucepan. Stir in the onion, basil, nutmeg, garlic, cayenne and saffron.
- Simmer, covered, for 25 to 30 minutes or until heated through. Ladle into soup bowls or cups.
- Garnish with thin lemon slices.
- It is important that the saffron not be omitted from this recipe.
- Yield: 8 servings.

Approx Per Serving: Cal 43; Prot 3 g; Carbo 7 g; T Fat <1 g; 8% Calories from Fat; Chol 0 mg; Fiber 1 g; Sod 783 mg

—*Cynthia B. Harper*

Orange Congealed Salad

1 (20-ounce) can crushed pineapple
1 (6-ounce) package orange gelatin
24 ounces small curd cottage cheese
16 ounces whipped topping

- Drain the pineapple, reserving the juice.
- Combine the reserved juice with the gelatin in a saucepan.
- Cook over medium heat until the gelatin is dissolved, stirring constantly.
- Let stand until cooled to lukewarm.
- Add the cottage cheese and whipped topping; mix well.
- Spoon into a serving dish or lightly oiled mold. Chill for 8 to 10 hours or until set.
- Invert molded gelatin onto serving plate.
- Yield: 12 servings.

Approx Per Serving: Cal 269; Prot 9 g; Carbo 33 g; T Fat 12 g; 40% Calories from Fat; Chol 8 mg; Fiber <1 g; Sod 276 mg

—*Paula Honea*

Watermelon Salad

1 (6-ounce) package strawberry gelatin
2 cups boiling water
3 cups chopped seeded watermelon
1 (8-ounce) can crushed pineapple
1 cup coarsely chopped pecans
8 ounces cream cheese, softened
1/4 cup milk
1/4 cup sugar
4 ounces whipped topping
1/4 cup coarsely chopped pecans

- Dissolve the gelatin in the boiling water in a medium bowl. Chill until partially set.
- Add the watermelon, undrained pineapple and 1 cup pecans; mix well.
- Chill until set.
- Beat the cream cheese in a mixer bowl until fluffy. Add the milk and sugar; beat until smooth.
- Fold in the whipped topping. Spread evenly over the gelatin mixture.
- Sprinkle with the remaining 1/4 cup pecans.
- Chill until serving time.
- Yield: 15 servings.

Approx Per Serving: Cal 224; Prot 3 g;
Carbo 23 g; T Fat 14 g; 55% Calories from Fat;
Chol 17 mg; Fiber 1 g; Sod 78 mg

—*Donna McGehee*

Frozen Fruit Salad

2 cups sour cream
1 cup drained crushed pineapple
1 (10-ounce) package frozen sweetened
   strawberries, thawed
2 teaspoons lemon juice
1/2 cup sugar
2 ripe bananas, mashed
1/2 cup chopped pecans

- Spray a 12x12-inch dish lightly with oil or coat it lightly with mayonnaise.
- Combine the sour cream, pineapple, strawberries, lemon juice, sugar, bananas and pecans in a bowl; mix well.
- Spoon into the prepared dish.
- Freeze until firm.
- Let stand at room temperature for several minutes before cutting into squares.
- Yield: 16 servings.

Approx Per Serving: Cal 149; Prot 2 g;
Carbo 18 g; T Fat 9 g; 50% Calories from Fat;
Chol 13 mg; Fiber 1 g; Sod 16 mg

—*Ann F. Jarratt*

Italian Fruit Salad

1 cantaloupe
2 navel oranges
2 plums
2 cups fresh pineapple chunks
1 cup seedless green grapes
3/4 cup peach nectar
1/4 cup honey
2 tablespoons balsamic vinegar
1 to 2 tablespoons lemon juice

- Peel the cantaloupe and cut into bite-size chunks.
- Peel the oranges and separate into sections.
- Pit the plums and slice as desired.
- Combine the cantaloupe, oranges, plums pineapple and grapes in a large bowl.
- Whisk the peach nectar, honey, vinegar and lemon juice in a small bowl.
- Pour over the fruit mixture, tossing to mix.
- Chill for 1 hour, tossing occasionally.
- Yield: 8 servings.

Approx Per Serving: Cal 128; Prot 1 g; Carbo 33 g; T Fat 1 g; 4% Calories from Fat; Chol 0 mg; Fiber 2 g; Sod 9 mg

—*Beth Huckabee*

Spiced Peach Salad

3/4 cup sugar
1/4 cup vinegar
1 cinnamon stick
1/2 teaspoon whole cloves
1 (16-ounce) can peach halves, drained
6 ounces cream cheese, softened
1/4 cup chopped pecans
6 lettuce leaves
6 tablespoons mayonnaise

- Combine the sugar, vinegar, cinnamon and cloves in a saucepan. Simmer for 5 minutes; remove from heat. Strain the syrup, reserving 1/4 cup. Pour remaining syrup over the peach halves in a bowl. Chill for 4 hours.
- Mix the cream cheese, pecans and reserved 1/4 cup syrup in a small bowl. Drain the chilled peaches, reserving the liquid. Place 1 peach on each lettuce leaf.
- Mix the reserved liquid with the mayonnaise in a bowl. Spoon over the peaches.
- Yield: 6 servings.

Approx Per Serving: Cal 372; Prot 3 g; Carbo 39 g; T Fat 24 g; 57% Calories from Fat; Chol 39 mg; Fiber 1 g; Sod 168 mg

—*Winnie Sandifer*

Pineapple Salad

1 (20-ounce) can crushed pineapple
1 (6-ounce) package cherry gelatin
1 teaspoon vinegar
2 cups buttermilk
16 ounces whipped topping

- Combine the undrained pineapple and gelatin in a saucepan.
- Cook over medium heat until the gelatin is dissolved, stirring constantly.
- Remove from the heat; let stand until cool.
- Stir in the vinegar. Add the buttermilk and whipped topping and mix well by hand; do not use a mixer.
- Pour into a serving dish. Chill, covered, in the refrigerator until firm.
- May substitute any flavor gelatin for the cherry.
- Yield: 15 servings.

Approx Per Serving: Cal 182; Prot 2 g;
Carbo 26 g; T Fat 8 g; 38% Calories from Fat;
Chol 1 mg; Fiber <1 g; Sod 71 mg

—Indy (Mrs. Charles) Whitten

Strawberry Salad

2 (3-ounce) packages strawberry gelatin
2½ cups boiling water
1 (10-ounce) package frozen strawberries
3 bananas, sliced
½ cup chopped pecans
1 cup sour cream

- Dissolve the gelatin in boiling water in a bowl. Add the strawberries and stir until the berries have thawed.
- Stir in the bananas and pecans.
- Pour half the mixture into an 8x8-inch dish and chill until set.
- Chill the remaining strawberry mixture just until of pouring consistency.
- Spread the sour cream over the congealed mixture in the dish; top with the remaining gelatin mixture.
- Chill until the entire salad is set.
- Yield: 8 servings.

Approx Per Serving: Cal 244; Prot 4 g;
Carbo 35 g; T Fat 11 g; 40% Calories from Fat;
Chol 13 mg; Fiber 2 g; Sod 71 mg

—Hilda May

Chicken Salad

■ ■ ■ ■ ■ ■ ■ ■ ■ ■ ■ ■ ■ ■ ■ ■ ■

2/3 cup sesame seeds
1 tablespoon butter
2 cups seedless green grapes
3 cups chopped cooked chicken breasts
1 cup cashews
1 cup sour cream
1/2 cup mayonnaise
1 tablespoon sugar
1 teaspoon salt
1 tablespoon tarragon vinegar

- Sauté the sesame seeds in the butter in a skillet until browned.
- Combine with the grapes, chicken, cashews, sour cream, mayonnaise, sugar, salt and vinegar in a bowl; mix well.
- Chill for several hours.
- Serve on a bed of lettuce and sliced fruit for lunch.
- Yield: 10 servings.

Approx Per Serving: Cal 369; Prot 19 g; Carbo 13 g; T Fat 28 g; 67% Calories from Fat; Chol 56 mg; Fiber 2 g; Sod 338 mg

—LaVerne Jackson

Chicken Pasta Salad

■ ■ ■ ■ ■ ■ ■ ■ ■ ■ ■ ■ ■ ■ ■ ■ ■

4 to 6 boneless chicken breasts
2 cups uncooked pasta
1 cup mayonnaise
1 (10-ounce) package frozen tiny peas, thawed
1 cup grated Parmesan cheese
1 (4-ounce) can chopped olives
2 envelopes Good Seasons salad dressing mix

- Cook the chicken breasts as desired until tender. Cool, skin and chop the chicken.
- Cook the pasta using the package directions. Drain, rinse with cold water and drain well.
- Combine the chicken, pasta, mayonnaise, peas, cheese and olives in a bowl; mix well.
- Prepare the salad dressing using the package directions. Pour the dressing over the salad, tossing to coat.
- Yield: 12 servings.

Approx Per Serving: Cal 533; Prot 21 g; Carbo 19 g; T Fat 42 g; 70% Calories from Fat; Chol 54 mg; Fiber 2 g; Sod 735 mg

—Connie Trask

Zesty Pasta Salad

1¹/₄ pounds spaghetti
1 (8-ounce) jar zesty Italian salad dressing
2 cups chopped green bell pepper
1 cup chopped onion
1 (2-ounce) jar Vegetable Supreme
    seasoning or Salad Supreme seasoning

- Break the spaghetti into thirds. Cook using the package directions; drain, rinse and drain well.
- Let stand for several minutes to cool slightly.
- Combine the spaghetti with the salad dressing, green pepper, onion and Vegetable Supreme seasoning in a bowl; mix well.
- Chill until serving time.
- May chop 3 tomatoes and add to pasta just before serving.
- Yield: 6 servings.

Approx Per Serving: Cal 567; Prot 17 g; Carbo 80 g; T Fat 21 g; 33% Calories from Fat; Chol 0 mg; Fiber 3 g; Sod 736 mg

—*Rebecca Askew*

Tortellini Salad

1 pound cheese-filled tortellini
2 red peppers, roasted, peeled, seeded, sliced
¹/₂ cup chopped black olives
¹/₂ cup chopped walnuts
1 cup crumbled feta cheese
Red Wine Salad Dressing

- Cook the pasta using the package directions; drain.
- Combine the pasta, peppers, olives, walnuts and cheese in a bowl. Add half the salad dressing. Cover and chill for several hours.
- Stir in more salad dressing before serving if needed.
- Yield: 8 servings.

Red Wine Salad Dressing

1 cup olive oil
¹/₃ cup red wine vinegar
2 teaspoons Dijon mustard
2 tablespoons chopped parsley
2 tablespoons chopped fresh dill, or
    1 teaspoon dried
1 tablespoon chopped fresh oregano, or
    1 teaspoon dried
1 teaspoon salt, or to taste
¹/₂ teaspoon pepper, or to taste

- Combine the olive oil, vinegar, mustard, parsley, dill, oregano, salt and pepper in a bowl; mix well.

Approx Per Serving: Cal 442; Prot 15 g; Carbo 31 g; T Fat 30 g; 60% Calories from Fat; Chol 54 mg; Fiber 1 g; Sod 764 mg
Nutritional information includes the entire amount of salad dressing.

—*Clair Houston*

Beet Salad

2 (15-ounce) cans sliced beets
2 medium onions, thinly sliced
1 bay leaf
2 cloves of garlic, minced
Salt and pepper to taste
1/2 cup red wine vinegar
1/2 cup olive oil

- Combine the beets, onions, bay leaf, garlic, salt, pepper, vinegar and olive oil in a bowl; mix well.
- Marinate in the refrigerator for several hours. Remove and discard the bay leaf.
- Yield: 8 servings.

Approx Per Serving: Cal 164; Prot 1 g; Carbo 11 g; T Fat 14 g; 72% Calories from Fat; Chol 0 mg; Fiber 2 g; Sod 280 mg

—Francis Quimby

Broccoli-Cauliflower Salad

1 or 2 bunches broccoli, broken into bite-size pieces
1 head cauliflower, broken into bite-size pieces
12 ounces fresh mushrooms, sliced
1 (6-ounce) can small black olives, drained
1 (8-ounce) can sliced water chestnuts
3 tomatoes, cut into wedges
1 (8-ounce) bottle Italian salad dressing

- Mix the broccoli, cauliflower, mushrooms, olives, water chestnuts and tomatoes in a bowl.
- Add the salad dressing; toss well to coat. Chill thoroughly.
- Yield: 8 servings.

Approx Per Serving: Cal 234; Prot 5 g; Carbo 19 g; T Fat 17 g; 65% Calories from Fat; Chol 0 mg; Fiber 6 g; Sod 417 mg

—Kathy Hilton

Black Bean Salad

3 cups canned black beans
2 cups cooked rice
1 1/2 tablespoons olive oil
2 tablespoons cider vinegar
1/4 cup chicken stock
1/2 cup chopped green onions
1/2 cup chopped red onion
1/2 cup chopped red bell pepper
1/4 cup chopped cilantro
1 teaspoon chopped garlic
1 teaspoon salt, or to taste
1/2 teaspoon white pepper
2 tablespoons fresh lime juice

- Drain and rinse the beans.
- Combine with the rice, olive oil, vinegar, chicken stock, green onions, red onion, red pepper, cilantro, garlic, salt, white pepper and lime juice in a bowl; mix well.
- Marinate in the refrigerator for 8 to 10 hours.
- This salad keeps well.
- Yield: 10 servings.

Approx Per Serving: Cal 145; Prot 6 g; Carbo 25 g; T Fat 2 g; 15% Calories from Fat; Chol 0 mg; Fiber 4 g; Sod 511 mg

—Mrs. Paul D. (Fay) Harris

Spinach, Bacon and Apple Salad

■ ■ ■ ■ ■ ■ ■ ■ ■ ■ ■ ■ ■ ■ ■ ■ ■ ■ ■

1/4 cup olive oil
3 tablespoons wine vinegar
1 teaspoon sugar
1/2 teaspoon prepared mustard
Salt and freshly ground pepper
5 slices bacon
1/3 cup sliced almonds
1 pound fresh spinach, torn into bite-size
    pieces
1 red apple, cored, coarsely chopped
3 green onions, thinly sliced

- Combine the olive oil, vinegar, sugar, mustard, salt and pepper in a jar with a tight-fitting lid; shake well. Chill until needed.
- Fry the bacon in a large skillet over medium-high heat until crisp-fried and crumbly; drain well on paper towels. Crumble the bacon and set it aside.
- Drain the skillet, reserving 1 tablespoon bacon drippings.
- Cook the almonds in the reserved bacon drippings in the skillet until lightly toasted, shaking the skillet frequently; remove from the heat.
- Combine the spinach, bacon, apple, green onions and almonds in a bowl and toss lightly. Pour the dressing over the salad and toss again. Serve immediately.
- Yield: 6 servings.

Approx Per Serving: Cal 198; Prot 5 g;
Carbo 9 g; T Fat 17 g; 73% Calories from Fat;
Chol 7 mg; Fiber 3 g; Sod 164 mg

Remembering "Theme" Meals

My best friend, Eryl Aynsley, used to organize "theme" meals. On India Night all of us dressed in native costume, replete with decorations and music, and addressed each other by chosen ethnic names. Jimmy Perkins was particularly grand in his version of Indian attire and headpiece. We each had to share something of the theme culture with the group—a most memorable time for all. Many other "theme" meals were enjoyed with Dr. and Mrs. Aynsley, but there were probably none more unique.

—Patricia A. Perkins

Fresh Sweet Potato Salad

1/2 cup sour cream
1/2 cup mayonnaise
1 teaspoon grated lemon peel
2 tablespoons lemon juice
3 tablespoons honey
1/4 teaspoon salt
1/4 teaspoon pepper
4 cups shredded uncooked sweet potatoes
1 medium tart apple, chopped
1/2 cup drained pineapple tidbits
1 cup golden raisins

- Mix the sour cream, mayonnaise, lemon peel, lemon juice, honey, salt and pepper in a small bowl and set aside.
- Combine the sweet potatoes, apple, pineapple and raisins in a large bowl and mix well.
- Pour the dressing over the sweet potato mixture, stirring well.
- Cover and chill thoroughly.
- May add 1/2 cup chopped pecans.
- Yield: 8 servings.

Approx Per Serving: Cal 388; Prot 4 g; Carbo 65 g; T Fat 14 g; 32% Calories from Fat; Chol 15 mg; Fiber 6 g; Sod 171 mg

Honey Poppy Seed Dressing

1 1/2 cups honey
1/2 cup boiling water
1 1/2 cups Champagne vinegar
1 cup prepared mustard
1/2 cup country-style Dijon mustard
1/2 cup plain Dijon mustard
2 cups safflower oil
4 cups olive oil
1/2 cup (about) slightly toasted poppy seeds

- Blend the honey with the boiling water in a mixer bowl.
- Add the vinegar, prepared mustard, Dijon mustard, safflower oil, olive oil and poppy seeds. Beat at low speed until well mixed.
- Let stand at room temperature for 4 hours to allow the flavor to develop.
- Store the salad dressing in a covered container in the refrigerator.
- Yield: 128 servings.

Approx Per Serving: Cal 110; Prot <1 g; Carbo 4 g; T Fat 11 g; 85% Calories from Fat; Chol 0 mg; Fiber <1 g; Sod 75 mg

—*Winnie Sandifer*

Blue Ribbon Salad

My fresh sweet potato salad will always be special to me. I submitted this recipe the first time I entered a recipe contest, and I won first place! This is an original recipe and is quite unique. I have never heard of, or tasted another, quite like it!

—*Jo Mathews*

Brunch, Breads & Beverages

Brunch, Breads & Beverages

Photograph on preceding page by Sara S. Lee. Autumn morning at
Mayes Lake, Jackson, Mississippi

Breakfast Bake

3 eggs
1¼ cups milk
7 ounces chopped ham
½ cup chopped onion
½ cup crushed saltines
3½ cups shredded Cheddar cheese
Salt and pepper to taste

- Beat the eggs lightly in a bowl.
- Add the milk gradually, beating well after each addition.
- Stir in the ham, onion, cracker crumbs, Cheddar cheese, salt and pepper; mix well.
- Pour the mixture into a greased 9x13-inch baking dish.
- Bake at 350 degrees for 45 minutes or until set.
- Yield: 10 servings.

Approx Per Serving: Cal 252; Prot 18 g; Carbo 6 g; T Fat 17 g; 62% Calories from Fat; Chol 120 mg; Fiber <1 g; Sod 597 mg

—*Sandra Hux*

Breakfast Casserole

4 slices bread
1 pound bulk sausage
1 cup shredded sharp Cheddar cheese
6 eggs
2 cups milk
1 teaspoon dry mustard
1 teaspoon salt
Dash of pepper

- Tear the bread into pieces; place in the bottom of a greased 9x13-inch casserole.
- Brown the sausage in a skillet, stirring until crumbly and cooked through; drain.
- Spread over the top of the bread pieces. Top with the Cheddar cheese.
- Beat the eggs, milk, mustard, salt and pepper in a bowl until well blended.
- Pour over the prepared layers.
- Chill, covered, in the refrigerator for 8 to 10 hours.
- Bake at 350 degrees for 35 to 40 minutes or until set.
- Yield: 8 servings.

Approx Per Serving: Cal 288; Prot 17 g; Carbo 11 g; T Fat 19 g; 61% Calories from Fat; Chol 205 mg; Fiber <1 g; Sod 847 mg

—*Marilyn O. Magee*

Breakfast Ham and Egg Casserole

1/2 cup (or less) butter or margarine,
   softened
14 to 15 slices bread
3 cups chopped cooked ham
2 cups shredded Cheddar cheese
1 teaspoon salt
1/2 teaspoon pepper
6 eggs
3 cups milk

- Spread the butter on both sides of the bread slices; cut the buttered bread into small cubes.
- Combine the bread cubes, ham, Cheddar cheese, salt and pepper in a bowl; mix well.
- Beat the eggs in a bowl until light; stir in the milk. Pour over the ham mixture, stirring to mix.
- Spoon the mixture into a lightly greased 9x13-inch baking pan. Chill, covered, for 8 to 10 hours.
- Bake at 350 degrees for 1 hour or until golden brown. Serve immediately.
- Yield: 10 servings.

Approx Per Serving: Cal 441; Prot 26 g; Carbo 26 g; T Fat 26 g; 53% Calories from Fat; Chol 210 mg; Fiber 1 g; Sod 1292 mg

—*Diana Pias*

Santa Fe Green Chile Torte

2 eggs, beaten
2 tablespoons flour
1/2 teaspoon salt
1/3 cup milk
1 (4-ounce) can chopped green chiles
2 cups shredded sharp Cheddar cheese
2 cups shredded Monterey Jack cheese

- Beat the eggs, flour, salt and milk in a mixer bowl.
- Stir in the chiles, Cheddar cheese and Monterey Jack cheese; mix well.
- Spoon into a greased 9x13-inch baking dish.
- Bake at 350 degrees for 35 minutes or until set.
- Cut into small squares; arrange on a serving plate.
- Yield: 6 servings.

Approx Per Serving: Cal 339; Prot 22 g; Carbo 5 g; T Fat 26 g; 69% Calories from Fat; Chol 146 mg; Fiber <1 g; Sod 862 mg

—*Jennifer Segrest*

Muesli

²/₃ cup rolled oats or quick-cooking oats
¹/₃ cup finely chopped apple
¹/₈ teaspoon cinnamon
¹/₄ to ¹/₂ cup milk
Lemon juice to taste

- Combine the oats with enough water to cover in a bowl.
- Let stand for 8 to 10 hours.
- Strain, discarding the excess water.
- Stir in the apple, cinnamon, milk and lemon juice. Spoon into 2 serving bowls. Garnish with your choice of sliced fresh fruit, nuts, raisins and/or honey.
- Serve warmed or at room temperature.
- May substitute plain or flavored yogurt for the milk.
- Yield: 2 servings.

Approx Per Serving: Cal 153; Prot 6 g;
Carbo 24 g; T Fat 4 g; 22% Calories from Fat;
Chol 8 mg; Fiber 3 g; Sod 31 mg

Memories of Switzerland

I first had muesli in Switzerland and thought it was wonderful. Later, I found this recipe and started preparing it occasionally for Saturday mornings.

—Nancy C. Edmonson

Britt Grits

1 pound sliced bacon
2 green bell peppers, finely chopped
2 medium onions, finely chopped
1¹/₂ cups chopped cooked ham
1 (28-ounce) can whole tomatoes
1¹/₂ cups uncooked grits

- Fry the bacon in a skillet until crisp. Remove the bacon from the skillet; drain, reserving 2 to 3 tablespoons of the pan drippings.
- Sauté the green peppers and onions in the reserved pan drippings in the skillet until tender.
- Stir in the ham; sauté over low heat for 15 minutes, stirring frequently.
- Add the undrained tomatoes; mix well. Cook for 30 minutes longer.
- Cook the grits in a saucepan using package directions. Add the grits to the ham mixture; mix well.
- Spoon into a serving dish.
- Crumble the bacon over the top. Serve hot.
- Yield: 12 servings.

Approx Per Serving: Cal 220; Prot 11 g;
Carbo 21 g; T Fat 11 g; 43% Calories from Fat;
Chol 23 mg; Fiber 4 g; Sod 541 mg

—Cathy Britt

Cheese Toast

▪ ▪ ▪ ▪ ▪ ▪ ▪ ▪ ▪ ▪ ▪ ▪ ▪ ▪ ▪ ▪ ▪ ▪

16 slices white bread
4 ounces bleu cheese, softened
2 tablespoons margarine or butter
2 tablespoons finely chopped fresh basil
  leaves

- Trim the crusts from the bread slices about
  45 minutes before serving time. Roll each
  slice very thin.
- Spread the bleu cheese over 8 of the bread
  slices. Place the remaining bread slices over
  the top, making 8 sandwiches; press gently.
- Melt the margarine in a small saucepan
  over low heat. Remove from heat; stir in
  the basil. Brush the basil mixture over the
  top of each sandwich.
- Cut each sandwich into 4 triangles. Cut
  each triangle into halves. Arrange the
  triangles on a greased large baking sheet.
- Bake at 400 degrees for 12 minutes or until
  golden brown.
- Serve hot or cool on a wire rack.
- Store in a covered container.
- Yield: 64 bite-size servings.

Approx Per Serving: Cal 23; Prot 1 g;
Carbo 2 g; T Fat 1 g; 42% Calories from Fat;
Chol 1 mg; Fiber <1 g; Sod 54 mg

—Kathie Salley

Honey Breakfast Bars

▪ ▪ ▪ ▪ ▪ ▪ ▪ ▪ ▪ ▪ ▪ ▪ ▪ ▪ ▪ ▪ ▪ ▪

1 1/2 cups chunky peanut butter
1 cup honey
3/4 cup packed brown sugar
5 cups cornflakes
1 (6-ounce) package dried fruit pieces

- Blend the peanut butter, honey and brown
  sugar in a large saucepan.
- Bring to a boil over medium heat, stirring
  constantly. Remove from heat.
- Stir in the cornflakes and dried fruit
  quickly; mix well.
- Press the mixture evenly into a 9x13-inch
  dish sprayed with nonstick cooking spray,
  using a buttered spatula.
- Let stand for 15 minutes or longer. Cut
  into bars.
- May substitute bran or crisp rice cereal for
  the cornflakes.
- Yield: 18 servings.

Approx Per Serving: Cal 261; Prot 6 g;
Carbo 40 g; T Fat 11 g; 35% Calories from Fat;
Chol 0 mg; Fiber 2 g; Sod 180 mg

—Christie McBroom

Cinnamon Coffee Cake

¹/₄ cup vegetable oil
¹/₂ cup milk
1 egg, beaten
1 cup flour
¹/₂ teaspoon salt
1 tablespoon baking powder
¹/₂ cup sugar
2 tablespoons cinnamon-sugar

- Combine the oil, milk and egg in a bowl; mix well.
- Sift the flour, salt, baking powder and sugar together several times.
- Add to the milk mixture, stirring just until moistened; do not beat.
- Spoon into a greased 9x9-inch baking pan. Sprinkle with the cinnamon-sugar.
- May also sprinkle with ¹/₂ cup chopped pecans.
- Bake at 375 degrees for 18 minutes or until brown.
- Yield: 9 servings.

Approx Per Serving: Cal 174; Prot 3 g; Carbo 25 g; T Fat 7 g; 37% Calories from Fat; Chol 25 mg; Fiber 1 g; Sod 242 mg

—*Kathie Salley*

Cranberry Coffee Cake

1 cup margarine, softened
1 cup sugar
2 eggs
2 cups self-rising flour
Dash of cinnamon
1 cup sour cream
1 teaspoon almond extract
1 (16-ounce) can whole cranberry sauce
¹/₂ cup sliced almonds
¹/₄ cup warm milk
2 cups confectioners' sugar
¹/₂ teaspoon vanilla extract

- Cream the margarine and sugar in a mixer bowl until light and fluffy. Beat in the eggs. Add a mixture of the flour and cinnamon alternately with the sour cream, mixing well after each addition. Stir in the almond flavoring. Spread in a greased 9x13-inch baking pan.
- Chop the cranberry sauce with a spoon in a bowl. Drop by spoonfuls over the batter. Sprinkle the almonds over the top.
- Bake at 350 degrees for 35 to 40 minutes or until brown.
- Add the warm milk to the confectioners' sugar 1 tablespoon at a time in a bowl, stirring until slightly thickened. Stir in the vanilla. Drizzle over the hot coffee cake. Cut into 2-inch squares.
- May substitute egg substitute equal to 2 eggs.
- Yield: 24 servings.

Approx Per Serving: Cal 244; Prot 2 g; Carbo 34 g; T Fat 11 g; 41% Calories from Fat; Chol 22 mg; Fiber 1 g; Sod 239 mg

—*Nan Oestmann*

Mexican Corn Bread

■ ■ ■ ■ ■ ■ ■ ■ ■ ■ ■ ■ ■ ■ ■ ■ ■ ■

1¹/₂ cups self-rising cornmeal
1 tablespoon flour
2 eggs
1 cup buttermilk
²/₃ cup vegetable oil
1 (4-ounce) can green chiles, drained,
    chopped
1 bunch green onions, chopped
1 small green bell pepper, chopped
1 (17-ounce) can cream-style corn
1¹/₂ cups shredded Cheddar cheese
1 teaspoon salt

■ Combine the cornmeal and flour in a
  bowl; mix well. Add the eggs, buttermilk
  and oil, stirring until blended.
■ Stir in the chiles, green onions, green
  pepper, corn, Cheddar cheese and salt;
  mix well.
■ Spoon into a greased preheated 12-inch
  cast-iron skillet.
■ Bake at 350 degrees for 1 hour or until
  golden brown.
■ Cut into wedges.
■ Yield: 10 servings.

Approx Per Serving: Cal 340; Prot 9 g;
Carbo 28 g; T Fat 22 g; 57% Calories from Fat;
Chol 61 mg; Fiber 2 g; Sod 907 mg

—Pat Powers

Sour Cream Corn Bread

■ ■ ■ ■ ■ ■ ■ ■ ■ ■ ■ ■ ■ ■ ■ ■ ■ ■

1 cup self-rising cornmeal
1 cup sour cream
1 (17-ounce) can cream-style corn
¹/₄ cup vegetable oil
2 eggs

■ Combine the cornmeal, sour cream, corn,
  oil and eggs in a bowl; mix well.
■ Spoon into nonstick muffin cups.
■ Bake at 425 degrees for 25 minutes or until
  golden brown.
■ Yield: 8 servings.

Approx Per Serving: Cal 245; Prot 5 g;
Carbo 25 g; T Fat 15 g; 52% Calories from Fat;
Chol 66 mg; Fiber 2 g; Sod 435 mg

—Hazel Hogue

Hush Puppies

4 cups self-rising cornmeal
2 cups buttermilk
2 eggs
2 large onions, chopped into large pieces
2 large green bell peppers, chopped
1 teaspoon crushed red pepper
1/2 teaspoon salt

- Combine the cornmeal, buttermilk and eggs in a bowl; mix well.
- Stir in the onions, green peppers, red pepper and salt, stirring until well mixed.
- Drop by teaspoonfuls into hot deep 375-degree oil in a deep skillet or deep fryer.
- Deep-fry until golden brown; drain on paper towels.
- Yield: 150 servings.

Approx Per Serving: Cal 16; Prot 1 g;
Carbo 3 g; T Fat <1 g; 9% Calories from Fat;
Chol 3 mg; Fiber <1 g; Sod 61 mg
Nutritional information does not include oil for deep-frying.

—Mrs. Bill (Carroll) Waller
Former First Lady, State of Mississippi

Banana Bread

1/2 cup butter, softened
2 cups sugar
2 cups sifted flour
1 teaspoon baking soda
1/4 teaspoon salt
3 eggs
4 ripe bananas, mashed
3/4 cup chopped pecans or walnuts

- Beat the butter and sugar in a mixer bowl until light and fluffy.
- Sift the flour, baking soda and salt together. Add to the beaten mixture; mix well.
- Add the eggs 1 at a time, mixing well after each addition.
- Stir in the bananas and pecans; mix well.
- Pour into a greased 5x9-inch loaf pan.
- Bake at 300 degrees for 1 hour or until the loaf tests done.
- Yield: 12 servings.

Approx Per Serving: Cal 370; Prot 5 g;
Carbo 58 g; T Fat 14 g; 34% Calories from Fat;
Chol 74 mg; Fiber 2 g; Sod 208 mg

—Hilda May

Blueberry Banana Bread

1/2 cup low-fat margarine, softened
1 cup sugar
Egg substitute equivalent to 2 eggs
2 cups flour
1 teaspoon baking soda
1 teaspoon baking powder
Pinch of salt
3 ripe bananas, mashed
1/2 cup frozen whole blueberries

- Cream the margarine and sugar in a mixer bowl until light and fluffy. Stir in the egg substitute; mix well.
- Mix the flour, baking soda, baking powder and salt together. Add to the creamed mixture alternately with the bananas, mixing well after each addition.
- Stir in the blueberries.
- Spoon into a 5x9-inch loaf pan sprayed with nonstick cooking spray.
- Bake at 350 degrees for 40 to 50 minutes or until the loaf tests done.
- May add 1/2 cup chopped pecans to the batter.
- Yield: 12 servings.

Approx Per Serving: Cal 221; Prot 4 g; Carbo 40 g; T Fat 6 g; 22% Calories from Fat; Chol <1 mg; Fiber 1 g; Sod 160 mg

—*Gerry Ann Houston, M.D.*

Broccoli Bread

1 (10-ounce) package frozen chopped broccoli, thawed, drained
1 medium onion, chopped
3/4 cup light cottage cheese
4 eggs
1/2 cup melted margarine
1 teaspoon salt, or to taste
1 (6-ounce) package corn bread mix

- Combine the broccoli, onion, cottage cheese, eggs, margarine and salt in a bowl; mix well.
- Stir in the corn bread mix.
- Pour into a greased baking pan.
- Bake at 350 degrees for 20 to 30 minutes or until the bread is brown.
- Yield: 8 servings.

Approx Per Serving: Cal 262; Prot 9 g; Carbo 19 g; T Fat 17 g; 58% Calories from Fat; Chol 108 mg; Fiber 3 g; Sod 497 mg

Hates Broccoli, Loves Bread

A co-worker of mine hates broccoli as much as George Bush, but loved this bread.

—*Iris Waldrop*

Orange Walnut Bread

2¹/2 cups flour
1¹/4 cups sugar
2 teaspoons baking powder
¹/2 teaspoon baking soda
¹/2 teaspoon salt
2 eggs, beaten
¹/4 cup melted margarine
¹/2 cup orange juice
2 tablespoons grated orange peel
2 tablespoons water
1 cup chopped walnuts
¹/4 cup margarine, softened

- Combine the flour, sugar, baking powder, baking soda and salt in a mixer bowl.
- Beat the eggs with ¹/4 cup melted margarine, orange juice, orange peel and water. Add to the flour mixture, stirring just until moistened.
- Stir in the walnuts.
- Spoon into a greased and floured 5x9-inch loaf pan.
- Bake at 350 degrees for 1 hour or until the loaf tests done.
- Cool in the pan for 10 minutes. Remove to a wire rack to cool completely.
- Slice the loaf and spread with ¹/4 cup margarine before serving.
- Yield: 12 servings.

Approx Per Serving: Cal 326; Prot 5 g; Carbo 44 g; T Fat 15 g; 40% Calories from Fat; Chol 35 mg; Fiber 1 g; Sod 280 mg

—*Donna Evans*

Strawberry Bread

3 cups flour
1 teaspoon salt
2 cups sugar
1 teaspoon baking soda
4 eggs, beaten
1¹/4 cups vegetable oil
1¹/4 cups chopped pecans
1 tablespoon cinnamon
2 (10-ounce) packages frozen strawberries, thawed

- Combine the flour, salt, sugar and baking soda in a mixer bowl.
- Add the eggs 1 at a time, mixing well after each addition.
- Stir in the oil, pecans, cinnamon and undrained strawberries; mix well.
- Spoon into 2 lightly greased and floured 5x9-inch loaf pans.
- Bake at 350 degrees for 1 hour or until the loaves tests done.
- Cool for 10 minutes in the pans. Remove to a wire rack to cool completely.
- Yield: 24 servings.

Approx Per Serving: Cal 285; Prot 3 g; Carbo 32 g; T Fat 17 g; 51% Calories from Fat; Chol 35 mg; Fiber 1 g; Sod 135 mg

—*Amy Hickman*

Low-Fat Blueberry Muffins

2 cups flour
3/4 cup sugar
1 teaspoon baking powder
1/2 teaspoon baking soda
1/2 teaspoon salt
2 egg whites
1/2 cup fat-free lemon yogurt
1/2 cup applesauce
2 tablespoons canola oil
1 teaspoon grated lemon zest
1 cup blueberries

- Combine the flour, sugar, baking powder, baking soda and salt in a large bowl.
- Mix the egg whites, yogurt, applesauce, canola oil and lemon zest in a bowl.
- Add to the flour mixture, stirring just until moistened.
- Fold in the blueberries.
- Spoon into 12 greased muffin cups.
- Bake at 400 degrees for 25 minutes or until the muffins test done.
- Remove to a wire rack to cool.
- Yield: 12 servings.

Approx Per Serving: Cal 172; Prot 3 g;
Carbo 34 g; T Fat 3 g; 13% Calories from Fat;
Chol <1 mg; Fiber 1 g; Sod 168 mg

—Jennifer Hane

All-Bran Rolls

2 envelopes yeast
1 cup lukewarm water
1 cup shortening
3/4 cup sugar
1 cup All-Bran
1 1/2 teaspoons salt
1 cup boiling water
2 eggs, well beaten
6 1/2 cups unbleached flour

- Dissolve the yeast in the lukewarm water in a small bowl.
- Combine the shortening, sugar, cereal, salt and boiling water in a bowl, stirring until blended.
- Let stand until the mixture is cooled to lukewarm.
- Add the eggs and yeast mixture; mix well.
- Add the flour gradually, mixing well after each addition.
- Chill, covered, in the refrigerator for 2 hours.
- Roll 1/2 inch thick on a lightly floured surface; cut with a biscuit cutter. Fold each biscuit in half; place on a nonstick baking sheet.
- Let rise until doubled in bulk.
- Bake at 400 degrees or until golden brown.
- May bake as loaves in 2 nonstick 5x9-inch loaf pans.
- Yield: 24 servings.

Approx Per Serving: Cal 240; Prot 5 g;
Carbo 35 g; T Fat 9 g; 35% Calories from Fat;
Chol 18 mg; Fiber 2 g; Sod 180 mg

—Susan Dobbs

Refrigerator Rolls

4 cups milk
1 cup shortening
1 cup (scant) sugar
2 cakes yeast
4 cups flour
1 tablespoon salt
1 teaspoon baking soda
1 teaspoon (heaping) baking powder

- Bring a mixture of the milk, shortening and sugar to the boiling point in a saucepan, stirring constantly. Remove from the heat to partially cool. Pour into a mixer bowl.
- Dissolve the yeast in the lukewarm mixture.
- Beat in the flour gradually, mixing well after each addition.
- Let rise, covered, in a warm place for 2 hours. Sift in the salt, baking soda and baking powder; mix well.
- Roll 1/2 inch thick on a lightly floured surface; cut with a biscuit cutter.
- Place on a nonstick baking sheet.
- Let rise, covered, in a warm place for 2 hours.
- Bake at 400 degrees for 15 to 20 minutes or until golden brown.
- May store the dough in an airtight container in the refrigerator.
- Yield: 50 servings.

Approx Per Serving: Cal 101; Prot 2 g; Carbo 13 g; T Fat 5 g; 43% Calories from Fat; Chol 3 mg; Fiber <1 g; Sod 161 mg

—*Edith Stewart*

Katherine's Rolls

1/2 cup sugar
1/2 cup shortening
1/8 teaspoon salt
1/2 cup boiling water
1 envelope yeast
1/2 cup warm water
1 egg, lightly beaten
3 cups flour

- Combine the sugar, shortening and salt in bowl. Pour the boiling water over the top; mix well.
- Dissolve the yeast in warm water in cup.
- Add the egg, yeast mixture and flour to the sugar mixture; mix well.
- Chill, covered, for 8 to 10 hours.
- Knead on a floured surface until smooth and elastic.
- Roll on a lightly floured surface; cut with a biscuit cutter. Place on a nonstick baking sheet.
- Let rise, covered, in a warm place for 45 minutes or until risen to the desired height.
- Bake at 300 degrees for 15 to 20 minutes or until the rolls just begin to brown; increase the oven temperature to 350 to 375 degrees. Bake until golden brown.
- May shape rolls, refrigerate for 8 to 10 hours, let stand at room temperature for several minutes or until risen as desired and bake.
- Yield: 36 servings.

Approx Per Serving: Cal 77; Prot 1 g; Carbo 11 g; T Fat 3 g; 36% Calories from Fat; Chol 6 mg; Fiber <1 g; Sod 9 mg

—*Katherine Gales*

Old-Time Butter Rolls

1 envelope yeast
1/2 cup warm water
5 cups self-rising flour
3 tablespoons sugar
2/3 cup vegetable oil
2 cups milk
1/2 cup sugar
1/2 cup butter, softened
3/4 cup sugar
2 cups milk
1/2 teaspoon vanilla extract

- Dissolve the yeast in the warm water in a cup.
- Mix the flour and 3 tablespoons sugar in a large bowl; make a well in the center.
- Pour a mixture of the oil and 2 cups milk into the well; mix until a stiff dough forms.
- Roll very thin into a 12-inch wide rectangle on a lightly floured surface. Spread a mixture of 1/2 cup sugar and butter over the dough.
- Roll as for a jelly roll. Cut into 2-inch sections; place in a nonstick baking dish.
- Pour a mixture of 3/4 cup sugar, 2 cups milk and vanilla over the top.
- Bake at 375 degrees for 30 minutes or until golden brown.
- May substitute 1/2 teaspoon cinnamon for the vanilla.
- Yield: 30 servings.

Approx Per Serving: Cal 201; Prot 3 g;
Carbo 27 g; T Fat 9 g; 41% Calories from Fat;
Chol 13 mg; Fiber <1 g; Sod 312 mg

—*Louise Brister Melton*

Potato Rolls

2/3 cup shortening
2/3 cup sugar
1 teaspoon salt
2 eggs
1 cup mashed cooked potatoes
2 envelopes yeast
1/2 cup (105- to 115-degree) potato cooking liquid
1 cup scalded milk, cooled
5 to 6 cups flour

- Cream the shortening and sugar in a mixer bowl until light and fluffy. Stir in the salt. Add the eggs 1 at a time, mixing well after each addition.
- Add the mashed potatoes to the sugar mixture.
- Dissolve the yeast in the reserved cooking liquid. Add to the potato mixture. Add the milk alternately with the flour, mixing well after each addition.
- Roll on a lightly floured surface; cut with a biscuit cutter. Place on a nonstick baking sheet.
- Let rise in a warm place for 1 1/2 to 2 1/2 hours or until doubled in bulk.
- Bake at 400 degrees for 15 to 20 minutes or until golden brown.
- May store the dough in the refrigerator in an airtight container for 7 to 8 days.
- Yield: 30 servings.

Approx Per Serving: Cal 168; Prot 4 g;
Carbo 26 g; T Fat 6 g; 32% Calories from Fat;
Chol 16 mg; Fiber <1 g; Sod 80 mg

—*Martha Jenkins*

Chocolate Chip Caramel Rolls

- - - - - - - - - - - - - - - -

1/4 cup packed brown sugar
2 tablespoons butter or margarine, softened
1 tablespoon light corn syrup
1 cup flour
1 tablespoon wheat germ
1 1/2 teaspoons baking powder
3 tablespoons shortening
1/4 cup milk
1 tablespoon melted butter or margarine
2 tablespoons sugar
1/4 teaspoon grated orange peel
1/4 cup miniature semisweet chocolate chips

- Mix the brown sugar, 2 tablespoons butter and corn syrup in a small microwave-safe dish. Microwave on High for 1 to 2 minutes or until the butter is melted and the brown sugar is dissolved, stirring frequently.
- Spoon into six 6-ounce custard cups; set aside.
- Combine the flour, wheat germ and baking powder in a bowl. Cut in the shortening until the mixture is crumbly. Add the milk, stirring just until the mixture leaves the side of the bowl.
- Knead 15 to 20 times on a lightly floured surface. Roll into a 10x16-inch rectangle on a lightly floured surface.
- Brush with the melted butter. Sprinkle a mixture of the sugar and orange peel over the dough. Sprinkle with the chocolate chips.
- Roll as for a jelly roll, pressing the seams to seal. Slice into 1-inch pieces. Place the slices cut side down in the prepared custard cups.
- Arrange the custard cups in a circle in the microwave. Microwave on High for 1 minute. Rotate the cups. Microwave for 1 to 2 minutes longer or until a wooden pick inserted in the center comes out clean.
- Let stand for 1 minute.

- Loosen the rolls from the sides of the custard cups and invert onto a serving plate. Spread any remaining caramel mixture from the bottom of the cups over the rolls.
- Serve warm.
- Yield: 6 servings.

Approx Per Serving: Cal 302; Prot 3 g; Carbo 38 g; T Fat 16 g; 46% Calories from Fat; Chol 17 mg; Fiber 1 g; Sod 154 mg

—Cathy Joiner

Honey Rolls

- - - - - - - - - - - - - - - - - -

2 envelopes yeast
1/3 cup warm water
2 cups milk
1/2 cup butter
1/2 cup honey
3 eggs
1/2 cup wheat germ
5 1/2 cups flour

- Dissolve the yeast in the warm water in a cup.
- Heat the milk in a saucepan until scalded; remove from the heat. Add the butter, honey, eggs and wheat germ; mix well. Let cool to lukewarm. Add the yeast mixture. Add the flour 1 cup at a time, mixing well after each addition. Add additional flour if mixture is too sticky.
- Let rise until doubled in bulk; punch the dough down and let rise again. Punch the dough down. Shape into biscuit-size shapes. Arrange on a nonstick baking sheet. Let rise until doubled in bulk.
- Bake at 400 degrees for 15 to 20 minutes or until brown.
- May substitute a mixture of 3 cups whole wheat flour and 2 1/2 cups all-purpose flour for 5 1/2 cups flour. May bake the rolls in a 5x9-inch nonstick loaf pan at 350 degrees for 45 minutes or until the loaf tests done.
- Yield: 10 servings.

Approx Per Serving: Cal 457; Prot 12 g; Carbo 72 g; T Fat 14 g; 27% Calories from Fat; Chol 95 mg; Fiber 3 g; Sod 140 mg

—Beverly Farabee

Citrus Cooler

2¹/₂ cups sugar
2¹/₂ cups water
1 (46-ounce) can orange juice
1 (46-ounce) can pineapple juice
1¹/₂ cups lemon juice
1¹/₂ quarts ginger ale

- Bring the sugar and water to a boil in a large saucepan. Add the orange, pineapple and lemon juices; mix well. Pour into a 2-gallon container with a lid.
- Chill or freeze until serving time.
- Add the ginger ale just before serving.
- Yield: 32 servings.

Approx Per Serving: Cal 119; Prot <1 g; Carbo 30 g; T Fat <1 g; 1% Calories from Fat; Chol 0 mg; Fiber <1 g; Sod 5 mg

—*Rebecca Askew*

Coffee Punch

1 cup sugar
4 quarts hot strong coffee
1 quart milk, chilled
1 tablespoon vanilla extract
2 quarts vanilla ice cream, softened
1 quart chocolate ice cream, softened
2 to 4 cups whipping cream, whipped
Cinnamon to taste

- Dissolve the sugar in the coffee. Let stand until cool. Stir in the milk and vanilla. Chill in the refrigerator.
- Pour the coffee mixture over the vanilla and chocolate ice creams in a punch bowl. Ladle into mugs.
- Top with dollops of whipped cream and sprinkle with the cinnamon.
- Yield: 30 servings.

Approx Per Serving: Cal 271; Prot 4 g; Carbo 24 g; T Fat 19 g; 60% Calories from Fat; Chol 69 mg; Fiber 1 g; Sod 72 mg

—*Helen McClean Fletcher*

Russian Tea

1 (18-ounce) jar orange instant breakfast drink mix
¹/₂ cup (or more) instant tea
1¹/₂ cups sugar
¹/₂ teaspoon ground cloves
1 teaspoon cinnamon
1 teaspoon dried lemon rind

- Combine the drink mix, tea, sugar, cloves, cinnamon and lemon rind in a bowl; mix well.
- Pour the mixture into a large airtight container.
- Stir 2 heaping teaspoons of the tea mixture into 1 cup boiling water for each serving, stirring until dissolved.
- Yield: 120 servings.

Approx Per Serving: Cal 27; Prot <1 g; Carbo 7 g; T Fat <1 g; <1% Calories from Fat; Chol 0 mg; Fiber <1 g; Sod 1 mg

—*Sandra Wallace*

Main Dishes

Main Dishes

Photograph on preceding page by Gil Ford Photography. Horseback riding
lakeside in Raymond, Mississippi

Best-Ever Beef Brisket

1 (7- to 9-pound) whole beef brisket
2 tablespoons garlic salt
2 tablespoons lemon pepper
1/3 cup lemon juice
1/2 cup A.1. steak sauce
1/2 cup Heinz 57 sauce
1/2 cup Worcestershire sauce
1 onion, chopped
1 1/2 cups brewed coffee

- Rub the brisket with the garlic salt and lemon pepper.
- Mix the lemon juice, A.1. sauce, Heinz 57 sauce and Worcestershire sauce in a bowl. Pour over the brisket; spread the mixture over the beef.
- Place the brisket in a roasting pan. Top with the onion.
- Bake, covered, at 450 degrees just until the onion begins to brown.
- Reduce the oven temperature to 275 degrees.
- Pour in the coffee. Bake, covered, for 2 to 2 1/2 hours longer or until tender and cooked through.
- Yield: 24 servings.

Approx Per Serving: Cal 238; Prot 32 g; Carbo 4 g; T Fat 10 g; 37% Calories from Fat; Chol 96 mg; Fiber <1 g; Sod 986 mg

—*Ann P. Townsend*

Country-Style Pot Roast

1 tablespoon vegetable oil
1 (4- to 5-pound) boneless chuck roast
1 envelope onion soup mix
2 cups water
4 potatoes, peeled, cut into 1-inch cubes
4 carrots, scraped, cut into 1-inch pieces
2 tablespoons flour
1/2 cup water
1/4 teaspoon salt
1/4 teaspoon pepper

- Heat the oil in a Dutch oven.
- Brown the roast in the hot oil. Add the soup mix and 2 cups water. Bring to a boil; reduce the heat. Simmer, covered, for 2 hours.
- Add the potatoes and carrots. Return to a boil; reduce the heat. Simmer, covered, for 30 minutes. Remove the roast and vegetables to a serving platter and keep warm.
- Remove and discard the fat from the pan drippings; return 1 cup of the drippings to the Dutch oven.
- Combine the flour and remaining 1/2 cup water in a bowl, stirring until smooth. Stir into the pan drippings. Bring to a boil over medium heat. Cook until thickened, stirring constantly. Stir in the salt and pepper. Serve with the roast and vegetables.
- Yield: 10 servings.

Approx Per Serving: Cal 597; Prot 43 g; Carbo 15 g; T Fat 40 g; 61% Calories from Fat; Chol 164 mg; Fiber 2 g; Sod 224 mg

—*Cathie Young*

Sauerbraten (Sour Roast Beef)

Salt and pepper to taste
1 (5- to 6-pound) rump roast
5 cups vinegar
5 cups water
3 medium onions, sliced
1 large lemon, sliced
12 whole cloves
6 bay leaves
6 whole black peppercorns
3 tablespoons salt
2 tablespoons sugar
2 apples, sliced

- This favorite German recipe represents an old method of tenderizing even a relatively tough rump roast. It is best known for its delicious, unusual game-like flavor. The marinating process should take at least 36 hours for a milder flavor, with 48 to 72 hours providing more adequate tenderization and a definite piquant taste. A soaking of 72 to 96 hours imparts a distinctly game-like quality, as well as a long preservation of the beef.
- The preparation is best done in a large earthen crock, which should remain covered for the entire marinating time, except for the occasional stirring of the brine and turning of the roast. Preferably, the roast should be rubbed with salt and pepper. For better handling of the roast while in the brine, and later while it is being cooked and basted, the roast should be wrapped in cheesecloth and secured with several loops of string.
- The cooking may be done in either of two ways. The first way is to brown the marinated roast in hot fat, then add 1 cup of the vinegar mixture and cook it slowly in a large covered vessel for 2 or more hours until tender. The preferable way is to bake it in a 450-degree oven for 3 or more hours, periodically turning the roast and basting it with the vinegar mixture.
- Traditionally, sauerbraten is served hot and accompanied by rotkraut (recipe follows) and mashed potatoes made with gravy made from the bastings, but it may also be eaten cold. It is easily sliced and, being so well tenderized, usually does not require a knife to divide it into individual servings.
- Yield: 10 servings.

Approx Per Serving: Cal 369; Prot 51 g; Carbo 17 g; T Fat 11 g; 27% Calories from Fat; Chol 154 mg; Fiber 1 g; Sod 2003 mg

Rotkraut (Hot Red Cabbage)

2 tablespoons vegetable oil
1 head red cabbage, shredded
2 medium apples, sliced
2/3 cup vinegar
2 cups hot water
1/2 teaspoon salt
3 tablespoons sugar

- Heat the oil in a skillet. Add the cabbage, apples, vinegar, hot water, salt and sugar. Cook until the apples are tender.
- Yield: 6 servings.

Approx Per Serving: Cal 133; Prot 2 g; Carbo 23 g; T Fat 5 g; 31% Calories from Fat; Chol 0 mg; Fiber 5 g; Sod 195 mg

A Tradition from Germany

This traditional German meal was prepared yearly at Christmas by the late H.K. Stauss, M.D. An immigrant from Germany, Dr. Stauss learned this recipe from his family. The Stauss family continues to prepare this traditional meal at Christmas.

—Faith Stauss

Beef Tips

1 (2-pound) round steak
1 (10-ounce) can cream of mushroom soup
1 envelope onion soup mix
1 cup 7-Up

- Trim steak and cut into 1¹/2-inch strips.
- Place the steak strips in a greased 2-quart casserole. Spread the soup over the steak with a spatula.
- Sprinkle with the soup mix and pour the 7-Up over the top.
- Bake, covered with foil, at 275 degrees for 4 hours. Do not open the oven door during baking.
- Serve over hot cooked rice or noodles.
- The recipe may be doubled.
- Yield: 4 servings.

Approx Per Serving: Cal 366; Prot 44 g; Carbo 16 g; T Fat 13 g; 32% Calories from Fat; Chol 113 mg; Fiber 1 g; Sod 1336 mg

—Jennifer Segrest

Tortilla Stack-Up Steak

1 (2-pound) round steak
Salt to taste
1 cup water
1 tablespoon instant bouillon granules
¹/2 cup water
1¹/2 large onions, chopped
2 hot green peppers, chopped
3 large yellow banana peppers, chopped
1 (16-ounce) can chopped tomatoes
1 tablespoon cornstarch
¹/2 cup water
1 (10-count) package medium flour tortillas
2 cups shredded low-fat Cheddar cheese

- Season the steak with salt and place it in a large skillet sprayed with nonstick cooking spray. Sauté over high heat until no longer red. Add the 1 cup water. Bring to a boil; reduce the heat to low. Cook, covered, until the steak is tender.
- Mix the bouillon granules with ¹/2 cup water in a bowl. Add the bouillon, onions, peppers and undrained tomatoes to the skillet. Return to a boil over high heat; reduce the heat to low. Simmer, covered, until the onions are clear.
- Mix the cornstarch with the remaining ¹/2 cup water in a bowl. Stir into the mixture in the skillet. Cook until the gravy is smooth, stirring constantly; remove from the heat.
- Layer 1 tortilla, some of the steak mixture and some of the cheese in an 8x8-inch baking pan sprayed with nonstick cooking spray. Repeat the layers with the remaining ingredients.
- Bake at 350 degrees just until the cheese melts. Cut into quarters.
- Serve with pretzel sticks.
- Yield: 4 servings.

Approx Per Serving: Cal 754; Prot 70 g; Carbo 70 g; T Fat 21 g; 26% Calories from Fat; Chol 142 mg; Fiber 6 g; Sod 1783 mg

—Elizabeth Helms

Pizza Round Steak

1 (2-pound) round steak
1 large onion
6 medium potatoes
2 (16-ounce) cans green beans, drained
1 (4-ounce) can mushrooms, drained
1 (16-ounce) can Italian tomatoes
1 (16-ounce) jar pizza sauce

- Brown the steak in a Dutch oven over medium-high heat.
- Slice the onion. Peel and cut the potatoes into quarters.
- Add the onion, potatoes, green beans and mushrooms to the steak.
- Pour the undrained tomatoes and pizza sauce over the top.
- Simmer, covered, for 45 minutes or until the steak and potatoes are tender.
- Yield: 6 servings.

Approx Per Serving: Cal 370; Prot 35 g; Carbo 44 g; T Fat 6 g; 15% Calories from Fat; Chol 75 mg; Fiber 5 g; Sod 1366 mg

—*Patricia Roper*

Cheese Steak Sandwich

1/4 cup (about) onion slices
1/4 cup (about) green bell pepper strips
1 (5-ounce) eye of chuck steak, very thinly sliced
2 1/2 ounces provolone or mozzarella cheese, shredded
2 tablespoons shredded lettuce
1 tomato, chopped
1 hoagie roll

- Sauté the onion and green pepper in a skillet until tender. Set aside.
- Pan-fry the steak with just enough water to moisten in a large skillet until almost done. Top with the cheese.
- Cook until the cheese is melted; remove from the heat.
- Place the sautéed onion, green pepper, lettuce and tomato on the steak. Place the steak in the roll.
- Yield: 1 serving.

Approx Per Serving: Cal 938; Prot 57 g; Carbo 91 g; T Fat 38 g; 37% Calories from Fat; Chol 107 mg; Fiber 6 g; Sod 1540 mg

—*Beverly Brimer*

Easy Lasagna

2 pounds ground beef
1 onion, chopped
1 (28-ounce) can chopped tomatoes
1 (15-ounce) can tomato sauce
2 envelopes spaghetti sauce mix
2 to 3 tablespoons minced garlic
8 ounces lasagna noodles
1 cup shredded mozzarella cheese
1 cup grated Parmesan cheese

- Brown the ground beef with the onion in a skillet, stirring until the ground beef is crumbly; drain.
- Combine the tomatoes, tomato sauce, spaghetti sauce mix and garlic in a saucepan.
- Stir in the ground beef mixture. Simmer until heated through.
- Cook the noodles using the package directions; drain.
- Layer the noodles and sauce 1/2 at a time in a greased 9x13-inch baking dish.
- Sprinkle with mozzarella cheese and Parmesan cheese.
- Bake at 350 degrees for 30 minutes.
- Yield: 10 servings.

Approx Per Serving: Cal 414; Prot 31 g; Carbo 30 g; T Fat 19 g; 41% Calories from Fat; Chol 84 mg; Fiber 3 g; Sod 1376 mg

—*Sandra Wojcik*

Baked Lasagna

1 pound ground beef
1 pound ground sausage
1 clove of garlic, minced
1 tablespoon parsley flakes
1 tablespoon basil
1 1/2 teaspoons salt
2 cups canned tomatoes
2 (6-ounce) cans Italian tomato paste
1 (10-ounce) package lasagna noodles
24 ounces large curd cottage cheese
2 eggs, beaten
2 teaspoons salt
1/2 teaspoon pepper
2 tablespoons parsley flakes
1/2 cup grated Parmesan cheese
16 ounces mozzarella cheese, sliced or shredded

- Brown the ground beef and sausage in a skillet, stirring until the ground beef is crumbly; drain. Add the garlic, 1 tablespoon parsley flakes, basil, 1 1/2 teaspoons salt, tomatoes and tomato paste. Simmer for 45 minutes to 1 hour or until thickened, stirring occasionally.
- Cook the noodles using the package directions; drain and rinse in cold water.
- Mix the cottage cheese, eggs, remaining 2 teaspoons salt, pepper, 2 tablespoons parsley flakes and Parmesan cheese in a bowl.
- Layer the noodles, cottage cheese mixture, mozzarella cheese and ground beef mixture 1/2 at a time in a 9x13-inch baking dish.
- Bake at 375 degrees for 30 minutes.
- This recipe is best when made a day or two ahead; it also freezes well.
- Yield: 8 servings.

Approx Per Serving: Cal 688; Prot 50 g; Carbo 40 g; T Fat 37 g; 48% Calories from Fat; Chol 179 mg; Fiber 4 g; Sod 2429 mg

—*Anita Sarabia*

Southern Spaghetti

1 large white onion, chopped
2 ribs celery, chopped
1 1/2 pounds lean ground sirloin, crumbled
2 cloves of garlic, minced
5 tablespoons Worcestershire sauce
Salt and pepper to taste
2 (16-ounce) cans whole tomatoes
2 bay leaves
8 ounces vermicelli

- Braise the onion and celery with a small amount of water or broth in a cast-iron skillet.
- Combine the ground sirloin, garlic, Worcestershire sauce, salt and pepper in a large skillet. Cook until the sirloin is brown and crumbly, stirring frequently. Add the onion mixture and mix well.
- Add the tomatoes and bay leaves. Bring to a boil; reduce heat. Simmer for 1 1/2 hours, stirring occasionally. Remove the bay leaves.
- Cook the vermicelli using the package directions; drain.
- Serve the sauce over the vermicelli.
- Yield: 8 servings.

Approx Per Serving: Cal 331; Prot 24 g; Carbo 30 g; T Fat 13 g; 34% Calories from Fat; Chol 63 mg; Fiber 3 g; Sod 346 mg

Reflections on Mississippi

Mississippi is genuinely the most misunder-stood and maligned state in this Union. It is likewise the best-kept secret.

As a mecca for living, the experience is rich in family values and profound lifelong friendships. The tradition in the passing of these qualities from generation to generation is a hallmark of the Mississippi experience.

My mother and father had thirteen children. The priceless memories of our simple life and the struggles of growing up in Seminary, Mississippi, has provided, and continues to provide, me a great sense of pride and satis-faction. I count myself as fortunate beyond measure to have witnessed Mississippians at their best during the Great Depression and World Wars I and II.

The stamina and courage of our people have truly been tested. Mississippi has proven itself worthy beyond the compilation of material riches. The finding of pleasure in the simple routine of our culture is a lasting legacy for all people.

—Alma Graham Conner

(Alma Graham Conner is the oldest living former first lady of Mississippi; her husband was governor from 1932 to1936. She is nearing 101 years of age.)

Mexican Spaghetti

1 pound ground beef
8 ounces mild pork sausage
1 onion, chopped
1 green bell pepper, chopped
1 (8-ounce) package small egg noodles
1 tablespoon chili powder
1 (6-ounce) can tomato sauce
1 (15-ounce) can chili with beans
1 (17-ounce) can cream-style corn
1 (4-ounce) can sliced mushrooms
Salt and pepper to taste
1/2 cup shredded Cheddar cheese

■ Combine the ground beef, sausage, onion and green pepper in a heavy skillet. Cook until the ground beef and sausage are brown and crumbly, stirring frequently; drain.
■ Cook the noodles using the package directions; drain.
■ Combine the ground beef mixture, noodles, chili powder, tomato sauce, chili, corn, mushrooms, salt and pepper in a large bowl; mix well. Spoon into a 9x13-inch baking dish. Top with the cheese.
■ Bake at 350 degrees for 20 minutes or until heated through.
■ This recipe freezes well.
■ Yield: 10 servings.

Approx Per Serving: Cal 261; Prot 21 g; Carbo 33 g; T Fat 15 g; 39% Calories from Fat; Chol 96 mg; Fiber 3 g; Sod 719 mg

—Ruby (Mrs. Woodie) Assaf

Pork Tenders in Marinade

1/2 cup soy sauce
1/2 cup vermouth
2 cloves of garlic, minced
1 tablespoon dry mustard
1 teaspoon ginger
1 teaspoon thyme
1 pound pork tenders

■ Mix the soy sauce, vermouth, garlic, mustard, ginger and thyme in a bowl or sealable plastic bag. Add the pork tenders.
■ Marinate in the refrigerator for 2 days, turning occasionally.
■ Place the tenders and marinade in a baking pan. Bake, covered, at 325 degrees for 2 1/2 to 3 hours or until cooked through, turning occasionally.
■ Yield: 4 servings.

Approx Per Serving: Cal 332; Prot 19 g; Carbo 6 g; T Fat 22 g; 61% Calories from Fat; Chol 72 mg; Fiber <1 g; Sod 2110 mg

—Gail Price, former Mrs. Mississippi

Baked Ham with Maple Pecan Glaze

1 (6-pound) fully cooked boneless ham
Maple Pecan Glaze

- Remove any wrappings from the ham. Trim if desired. Place the ham on a rack in a shallow baking pan.
- Score the top of the ham in a diamond pattern using a paring knife to make 1/4 inch cuts. Insert a meat thermometer into the center of the ham.
- Bake at 325 degrees for 1 1/4 to 2 1/2 hours or to 140 degrees on the meat thermometer, brushing the Maple Pecan Glaze over the top and sides of the ham during the last 15 minutes of baking.
- Let the ham stand at room temperature for 15 minutes or longer before slicing.
- Slice as desired and spoon any remaining Maple Pecan Glaze over the ham.
- Yield: 20 servings.

Maple Pecan Glaze

1 cup maple or maple-flavor syrup
1 cup orange marmalade
1 tablespoon margarine or butter
1/2 cup toasted pecans

- Combine the maple syrup and orange marmalade in a small saucepan. Heat until bubbly, stirring constantly.
- Add the margarine; whisk until the margarine melts. Stir in the pecans.

Approx Per Serving: Cal 318; Prot 34 g; Carbo 22 g; T Fat 10 g; 28% Calories from Fat; Chol 75 mg; Fiber <1 g; Sod 1821 mg

—*Debbie Cox*

Super Easy Ham and Mixed Vegetable Casserole

3 (16-ounce) cans mixed vegetables
1 (10-ounce) can cream of celery soup
1/2 cup mayonnaise
1/2 cup chopped onion
1 cup chopped cooked ham
2 cups saltine cracker crumbs
1/4 cup melted butter

- Drain the vegetables, reserving a small amount of the liquid.
- Combine the vegetables, soup, mayonnaise and onion in a large bowl; mix well. Add enough of the reserved vegetable liquid to make the mixture of the desired consistency.
- Stir in the ham.
- Pour into a lightly greased casserole.
- Toss the cracker crumbs with the butter in a small bowl. Spread evenly over the vegetable mixture.
- Bake at 350 degrees for 30 to 45 minutes or until the casserole is bubbly and the cracker crumbs are brown.
- Yield: 6 servings.

Approx Per Serving: Cal 506; Prot 15 g; Carbo 46 g; T Fat 30 g; 52% Calories from Fat; Chol 50 mg; Fiber 10 g; Sod 1576 mg

—*Martha Makamson*

Red Beans and Rice

1 pound dried red kidney beans
1 pound link sausage, sliced
3 bay leaves
1/2 teaspoon parsley flakes
1/2 teaspoon salt
1/4 teaspoon pepper
1 clove of garlic, minced
1 medium onion, chopped
1 green bell pepper, chopped
2 tablespoons vegetable oil
2 tablespoons flour
6 cups cooked rice

- Soak the beans in water to cover for 10 to 12 hours. Drain, rinse and sort the beans.
- Brown the sausage in a skillet; drain.
- Add the beans, bay leaves, parsley flakes, salt and pepper to the skillet. Simmer for several hours or until the beans are tender. Remove the bay leaves.
- Sauté the garlic, onion and green pepper in a skillet. Stir into the bean mixture.
- Combine the oil and flour in a skillet. Cook until very brown, stirring constantly to keep the roux from burning. Stir into the bean mixture.
- Cook for 15 minutes longer, stirring frequently.
- Serve over the rice.
- Yield: 6 servings.

Approx Per Serving: Cal 713; Prot 30 g; Carbo 109 g; T Fat 17 g; 22% Calories from Fat; Chol 30 mg; Fiber 18 g; Sod 649 mg

—Sara S. Lee

Venison Meatballs

1 pound ground venison
8 ounces ground pork
1/2 cup fine dry bread crumbs
1 egg, beaten
1/2 cup mashed potatoes
1 teaspoon seasoned salt
1/2 teaspoon brown sugar
1/4 teaspoon pepper
1/4 teaspoon ground allspice
1/4 teaspoon ground nutmeg
1/8 teaspoon ground cloves
1/8 teaspoon ground ginger
3 tablespoons butter

- Combine the venison, pork, bread crumbs, egg, mashed potatoes, seasoned salt, brown sugar, pepper, allspice, nutmeg, cloves and ginger in a bowl; mix well.
- Shape into 1-inch balls.
- Melt the butter in a skillet over low heat. Add the meatballs. Brown on all sides, shaking the skillet occasionally.
- Cover the skillet with a tightfitting lid. Cook over low heat for 15 minutes.
- Serve with wild rice and gravy, hashed brown or mashed potatoes, or white rice.
- Yield: 8 servings.

Approx Per Serving: Cal 213; Prot 20 g; Carbo 7 g; T Fat 11 g; 48% Calories from Fat; Chol 106 mg; Fiber 1 g; Sod 347 mg

—Mrs. Bill (Carroll) Waller
Former First Lady, State of Mississippi

Baked Chicken

6 chicken breasts
3 cups potato flakes
Salt and pepper to taste
1 cup vegetable oil

- Rinse the chicken and pat dry.
- Mix the potato flakes, salt and pepper in a bowl.
- Brush the chicken with the oil; drain. Coat each piece with the potato mixture.
- Place in a 10x15-inch baking pan.
- Bake at 350 degrees for 45 minutes or until the chicken is cooked through.
- Yield: 6 servings.

Approx Per Serving: Cal 542; Prot 29 g; Carbo 18 g; T Fat 40 g; 65% Calories from Fat; Chol 73 mg; Fiber 2 g; Sod 88 mg

—Lou Ella Lowery

Chicken Diable

8 chicken breast halves
1/4 cup melted butter or margarine
1/2 cup honey
1/4 cup prepared mustard
1 teaspoon salt
1 teaspoon curry powder

- Rinse the chicken and pat dry.
- Combine the butter, honey, prepared mustard, salt and curry powder in a 9x13-inch baking dish and mix well.
- Coat both sides of the chicken in the butter mixture. Arrange the chicken in a single layer bone side down in the prepared dish.
- Bake at 325 degrees for 60 to 70 minutes or until cooked through, basting with the pan juices occasionally.
- May substitute 2 fryers for chicken breasts, preferably using just the meaty pieces.
- Yield: 8 servings.

Approx Per Serving: Cal 262; Prot 27 g; Carbo 18 g; T Fat 9 g; 31% Calories from Fat; Chol 89 mg; Fiber 0 g; Sod 487 mg

—Phyllis Spearman

Yogurt Marinated Chicken

6 boneless skinless chicken breast halves
Yogurt Marinade

- Rinse the chicken and pat dry. Refrigerate the chicken while preparing the marinade.
- Pour the marinade into a shallow dish.
- Add the chicken, turning to coat with the marinade.
- Refrigerate, covered, for several hours to overnight.
- Preheat the grill or broiler.
- Drain the chicken and discard the marinade.
- Arrange the chicken on a rack over hot coals or on a rack in a broiler pan.
- Grill or broil for 3 to 4 minutes on each side or until juices run clear when the chicken is pierced with a fork.
- Yield: 6 servings.

Yogurt Marinade

1 teaspoon ground cumin
1/2 teaspoon ground coriander
1/2 teaspoon ground cayenne
1/8 teaspoon allspice
1 cup nonfat yogurt
1/2 teaspoon freshly grated lemon peel
2 tablespoons fresh lemon juice
2 teaspoons minced garlic
1/2 teaspoon salt

- Combine the cumin, coriander, cayenne and allspice in a small saucepan.
- Cook over low heat for 1 to 2 minutes or until fragrant, stirring constantly; do not allow the spices to scorch. Remove from the heat.
- Add the yogurt, lemon peel, lemon juice, garlic and salt; mix well.

Approx Per Serving: Cal 165; Prot 29 g; Carbo 3 g; T Fat 3 g; 18% Calories from Fat; Chol 74 mg; Fiber <1 g; Sod 273 mg

—Cinda Henderson

Curt's Saucy Chicken and Rice

1 (3- to 4-pound) chicken, cut up
4 slices bacon
2 cups rice
1 (10-ounce) can cream of mushroom soup
1 (10-ounce) can cream of celery soup
1 cup milk
1¹/2 cups water
Seasoned salt to taste

- Rinse the chicken and pat dry.
- Arrange the bacon in a 9x11-inch glass baking dish. Pour the rice over the bacon.
- Mix the soups, milk and water in a bowl. Pour over the rice.
- Top with the chicken. Sprinkle with the seasoned salt.
- Bake, covered, at 325 degrees for 1¹/2 hours.
- Bake, uncovered, for 30 minutes longer.
- May add additional water if the rice is too dry.
- May substitute chicken breasts for whole chicken.
- Yield: 8 servings.

Approx Per Serving: Cal 488; Prot 39 g; Carbo 44 g; T Fat 16 g; 30% Calories from Fat; Chol 112 mg; Fiber 1 g; Sod 762 mg

—*Dolores Ulmer*

Mamaw Bell's Fried Chicken

1¹/2 to 2 pounds chicken pieces, skinned
Salt to taste
1 cup water
1¹/2 to 2 cups flour
Vegetable oil for frying

- Rinse the chicken and pat dry; sprinkle with the salt. Chill for several hours.
- Dip the chicken in the water, then the flour, until well coated.
- Heat the oil to 375 degrees in a heavy skillet. Add the chicken. Cook, covered, for 25 minutes or until the oil stops bubbling and the chicken is golden brown, turning once.
- Yield: 6 servings.

Approx Per Serving: Cal 295; Prot 26 g; Carbo 32 g; T Fat 6 g; 19% Calories from Fat; Chol 67 mg; Fiber 1 g; Sod 66 mg
Nutritional information does not include oil for frying.

—*Mary Bell*

Mamaw's Sunday Chicken Dinner

When my children were growing up, we would all look forward to going to see the grandparents in the country on Sunday. It never failed for one of the children to say as we drove out of our driveway, "I sure hope Mamaw has fried chicken." She always did! They are all grown up now; she is 80 years old and they still say when going for a visit, "I sure hope Mamaw has fried chicken." And she still does!

—*Jean Berch*

Chicken Chili

4 chicken breasts
1 medium onion, chopped
1 clove of garlic, minced
1/2 teaspoon cumin
1 (15-ounce) can white navy beans
1 (15-ounce) can Great Northern beans
1 (16-ounce) can whole kernel white corn
2 (4-ounce) cans chopped green chiles

- Rinse the chicken.
- Combine the chicken with water to cover in a saucepan. Cook until the chicken is tender.
- Drain, reserving 2 cups of the broth.
- Cut the chicken into bite-size pieces.
- Sauté the onion and garlic in a skillet. Stir in the cumin.
- Combine the sautéed onion with the beans, corn, chiles, chicken and reserved broth in a large saucepan.
- Simmer for 30 minutes or longer. Serve hot.
- Garnish each serving with shredded cheese and chopped green onion.
- Yield: 8 servings.

Approx Per Serving: Cal 252; Prot 24 g;
Carbo 35 g; T Fat 3 g; 9% Calories from Fat;
Chol 37 mg; Fiber 7 g; Sod 566 mg

—*Jennifer Wilkinson*

Chicken Piccata

4 boneless skinless chicken breast halves
1 egg white
1 tablespoon lemon juice
1/4 cup flour
1/8 teaspoon paprika
1/8 teaspoon garlic powder
1/4 cup margarine
2 teaspoons instant chicken bouillon granules
1/2 cup boiling water
2 tablespoons lemon juice

- Rinse the chicken and pat dry.
- Beat the egg white with 1 tablespoon lemon juice in a small bowl. Mix the flour, paprika and garlic powder in a medium bowl.
- Dip the chicken in the egg mixture, then in the flour mixture.
- Brown the chicken in the margarine in a skillet.
- Dissolve the bouillon granules in the boiling water. Pour the bouillon and the remaining 2 tablespoons lemon juice into the skillet.
- Simmer, covered, for 20 minutes or until the chicken is cooked through.
- May spray the skillet with nonstick cooking spray and reduce the margarine to 2 tablespoons.
- Yield: 4 servings.

Approx Per Serving: Cal 283; Prot 29 g;
Carbo 8 g; T Fat 15 g; 47% Calories from Fat;
Chol 73 mg; Fiber <1 g; Sod 788 mg

—*Nan Oestmann*

Chicken Jubilee

4 boneless skinless chicken breasts
8 ounces pasta shells
1 bunch fresh broccoli
1 small onion, chopped
1 tablespoon margarine
1 (10-ounce) can cream of mushroom soup
4 cups shredded Cheddar cheese

- Rinse the chicken.
- Boil the chicken in water to cover in a stockpot until cooked through; drain, reserving the cooking liquid. Cut the chicken into small cubes and set aside.
- Cook the pasta in the reserved liquid in a stockpot; drain and set aside.
- Steam the broccoli in a small amount of water in a saucepan until tender. Sauté the onion in the margarine in a skillet.
- Combine the chicken, pasta, onion and soup in a bowl and mix well.
- Alternate layers of the chicken mixture, broccoli and cheese in a 9x12-inch baking dish until all the ingredients are used, ending with the cheese.
- Bake at 350 degrees for 30 minutes.
- Let stand for 5 minutes before serving.
- Yield: 6 servings.

Approx Per Serving: Cal 626; Prot 44 g; Carbo 37 g; T Fat 34 g; 48% Calories from Fat; Chol 129 mg; Fiber 3 g; Sod 963 mg

Party Chicken

8 chicken breasts, deboned
8 slices dried beef
4 slices bacon, cut into halves
1 cup sour cream
1 (10-ounce) can cream of mushroom soup
8 ounces wide noodles

- Rinse the chicken and pat dry. Place the chicken deboned side up on waxed paper.
- Top each chicken piece with a slice of dried beef.
- Wrap each piece with a bacon slice half; secure with a wooden pick. Place seam side down in a 9x13-inch baking pan sprayed with nonstick baking spray.
- Mix the sour cream and soup in a bowl. Pour over the chicken.
- Bake at 275 degrees for 3 hours.
- Prepare the noodles using the package directions.
- Serve the chicken over the noodles or to the side with the sauce from baking spooned over the noodles.
- Yield: 8 servings.

Approx Per Serving: Cal 268; Prot 34 g; Carbo 24 g; T Fat 15 g; 37% Calories from Fat; Chol 140 mg; Fiber <1 g; Sod 589 mg

—*Sallye M. Wilcox*

Comfort Food

I've always treasured my time sleeping. When I was younger, growing up in Eupora, Mississippi, I wanted to stay curled up in my warm bed, rather than get up to get ready for school. My mother would always say, "Get up and stir around a little bit. Have some cream of wheat and you will feel better." It always worked. As a matter of fact, it still does.

—*Amber Clanton*

Buttermilk Chicken Pie

■ ■ ■ ■ ■ ■ ■ ■ ■ ■ ■ ■ ■ ■ ■ ■ ■ ■

1 (2¹/2- to 3-pound) chicken, cut up
1 teaspoon salt
1 (16-ounce) can mixed vegetables, drained
1 (10-ounce) can cream of chicken soup
¹/2 cup melted margarine
1 cup self-rising flour
1 cup buttermilk
Salt and pepper to taste

- Rinse the chicken.
- Combine the chicken, 1 teaspoon salt and enough water to cover in a large saucepan.
- Cook until tender. Drain, reserving 2 cups broth.
- Cut the chicken into small pieces. Place the chicken in a greased 9x13-inch baking pan.
- Pour the mixed vegetables over the chicken.
- Bring the reserved broth and soup to a boil in a saucepan.
- Mix the margarine, flour, buttermilk, salt to taste and pepper in a bowl.
- Pour the broth mixture over the chicken. Spoon the flour mixture over the top.
- Bake at 425 degrees for 25 to 30 minutes or until heated through.
- Yield: 8 servings.

Approx Per Serving: Cal 403; Prot 31 g;
Carbo 22 g; T Fat 21 g; 47% Calories from Fat;
Chol 80 mg; Fiber 3 g; Sod 1281 mg

—*Elsie R. Smith*

Pineapple Chicken

■ ■ ■ ■ ■ ■ ■ ■ ■ ■ ■ ■ ■ ■ ■ ■ ■ ■

4 boneless chicken breasts
¹/2 cup flour
Salt and pepper to taste
1 (8-ounce) can pineapple chunks

- Rinse the chicken and pat dry. Spray a skillet with nonstick cooking spray and heat the skillet until hot.
- Roll the chicken in a mixture of the flour, salt and pepper. Brown 1 side of the chicken in the hot skillet.
- Remove the chicken and spray the skillet again.
- Brown the other side of the chicken in the skillet.
- Pour the undrained pineapple into the skillet.
- Cook, covered, until the chicken is cooked through.
- Yield: 4 servings.

Approx Per Serving: Cal 242 Prot 29 g;
Carbo 23 g; T Fat 3 g; 12% Calories from Fat;
Chol 73 mg; Fiber 1 g; Sod 65 mg

—*Dot Allen*

Fontayne's Chicken and Dumplings

1 (3-pound) chicken
1¹/₂ cups flour
¹/₄ cup shortening
1 teaspoon salt, or to taste
¹/₄ teaspoon baking soda
¹/₂ cup buttermilk
1 egg, beaten
³/₄ cup milk

- Rinse the chicken.
- Boil the chicken in water to cover in a saucepan until tender. Drain, reserving 4 cups broth. Debone the chicken and cut into small pieces.
- Mix the flour, shortening, salt and baking soda in a bowl. Stir in a mixture of the buttermilk and egg. Chill for 45 minutes or longer.
- Roll the dough thinly on a lightly floured surface; cut into 3-inch strips.
- Bring the broth to a boil in a saucepan. Drop in the dumplings. Cook until the dumplings are done.
- Place chicken pieces carefully on top of the dumplings.
- Simmer over low heat for 10 to 15 minutes or until the chicken is heated through; remove from the heat. Stir in the milk.
- Yield: 6 servings.

Approx Per Serving: Cal 470; Prot 42 g;
Carbo 27 g; T Fat 20 g; 40% Calories from Fat;
Chol 141 mg; Fiber 1 g; Sod 1051 mg

—*Donna Powell*

Chicken and Vegetable Casserole

4 large chicken breasts
1 medium onion, chopped
2 tablespoons butter
2 (16-ounce) cans French-style green beans, drained
1 (11-ounce) can Shoe Peg corn, drained
2 (10-ounce) cans cream of chicken soup
1 cup sour cream
1 large pimento, chopped
1 (8-ounce) can sliced water chestnuts, drained
2 cups shredded Cheddar cheese
2 tablespoons sugar
Salt and pepper to taste
1¹/₂ sleeves Waverly wafers, crushed
1 to 2 tablespoons melted butter

- Rinse the chicken.
- Boil the chicken in water to cover in a saucepan until tender. Debone the chicken and cut into small cubes.
- Cook the onion in 2 tablespoons butter in a skillet until tender. Stir in the green beans and corn.
- Combine the chicken, green bean mixture, soup, sour cream, pimento, water chestnuts, cheese, sugar, salt and pepper in a large bowl; mix well. Pour into a large baking dish.
- Sprinkle the cracker crumbs over the top. Drizzle with the melted butter.
- Bake at 350 degrees for 30 to 45 minutes or until the mixture is bubbly and the chicken is cooked through.
- Yield: 12 servings.

Approx Per Serving: Cal 476; Prot 22 g;
Carbo 38 g; T Fat 27 g; 50% Calories from Fat;
Chol 75 mg; Fiber 3 g; Sod 1094 mg

—*Fannie Lewis*

Meaders' Baked Fish with Shrimp Sauce

2 to 4 catfish fillets
Salt and coarsely ground pepper to taste
1 onion
3 ribs celery
1/4 cup margarine
2 tablespoons flour
1 (10-ounce) can cream of shrimp soup
1 (4-ounce) can shrimp, drained
1 (2-ounce) jar pimento, chopped
Paprika to taste

- Arrange the fillets in a single layer in a shallow baking dish sprayed with nonstick cooking spray. Sprinkle with salt and pepper and set aside.
- Grate the onion and celery in a blender. Melt the margarine in a saucepan. Add the celery mixture. Cook over low heat for several minutes. Stir in the flour and soup. Cook until heated through, stirring constantly until smooth. Stir in the shrimp and pimento. Spoon over the fish.
- Bake at 400 degrees for 15 minutes; do not overbake. Sprinkle with paprika.
- May substitute other fish for catfish; if fillets are thick, slice or butterfly them.
- Leftover sauce is excellent served with pasta.
- Yield: 2 servings.

Approx Per Serving: Cal 630; Prot 48 g; Carbo 25 g; T Fat 37 g; 54% Calories from Fat; Chol 210 mg; Fiber 3 g; Sod 1697 mg

—Myrtis Meaders

Elegant but Easy Redfish en Croûte

1/4 cup vermouth
Lemon pepper and seasoned salt to taste
8 redfish fillets
1/4 cup chopped onion
1 tablespoon butter
1/2 cup milk
1 (10-ounce) can cream of celery soup
1/2 (10-ounce) can cream of mushroom soup
1/4 teaspoon basil
1 (8-count) can crescent rolls
4 slices Swiss cheese, cut into halves

- Mix the vermouth, lemon pepper and seasoned salt in a bowl. Add the fish.
- Marinate in the refrigerator for several hours, turning occasionally.
- Sauté the onion in the butter in a skillet. Add the milk, cream of celery soup, cream of mushroom soup and basil; mix well. Pour into a casserole.
- Separate the crescent roll dough into triangles. Place 1 fish fillet on each triangle. Top with 1/2 cheese slice. Roll up from the wide end. Place in the prepared casserole.
- Bake at 350 degrees for 30 minutes or until the pastry is browned and the fish flakes easily.
- Yield: 8 servings.

Approx Per Serving: Cal 368; Prot 38 g; Carbo 19 g; T Fat 14 g; 35% Calories from Fat; Chol 114 mg; Fiber <1 g; Sod 879 mg

—Mrs. William T. (Jimmie) Sistrunk

Salmon Quiche

1 (1-pound) can salmon
1 cup evaporated milk
1 small onion, minced
1/4 cup butter
1/4 cup flour
1 teaspoon salt
1/4 teaspoon pepper
2 eggs, beaten
1/2 teaspoon dillweed
1 cup peas
1 unbaked (9-inch) pie shell

- Drain the salmon, reserving the liquid. Add enough water to the reserved liquid to measure 1 cup. Mix with the evaporated milk in a small bowl and set aside.
- Cook the onion in the butter in a saucepan for 2 to 3 minutes or until tender. Blend in the flour, salt and pepper. Add the evaporated milk mixture gradually, stirring constantly.
- Cook until thickened, stirring constantly. Add a small amount of the hot mixture to the eggs; stir the eggs into the hot mixture.
- Flake the salmon. Stir the salmon, dillweed and peas into the cooked mixture. Pour into the pie shell.
- Bake at 400 degrees for 30 minutes. Let stand for 10 minutes before serving.
- Yield: 8 servings.

Approx Per Serving: Cal 341; Prot 18 g; Carbo 20 g; T Fat 21 g; 55% Calories from Fat; Chol 109 mg; Fiber 2 g; Sod 812 mg

—*Linda Russo*

Crawfish Etouffée

4 medium onions, minced
3 to 4 ribs celery, minced
2 cloves of garlic, minced
3 medium green bell peppers, minced
3 to 4 cups crawfish tails
1 cup hot water
1 to 2 tablespoons cornstarch
Salt and pepper to taste
1 green onion top, finely chopped
Chopped parsley to taste

- Combine the onions, celery, garlic and green peppers in a microwave-safe bowl. Add a small amount of water.
- Microwave until tender. Add the crawfish tails.
- Blend the hot water and cornstarch. Stir into the crawfish mixture. Season with salt and pepper.
- Microwave on Simmer until the crawfish tails are tender. Stir in the green onion and parsley.
- Serve over hot cooked rice.
- May substitute Creole seasoning for salt and pepper.
- Yield: 4 servings.

Approx Per Serving: Cal 224; Prot 29 g; Carbo 19 g; T Fat 2 g; 10% Calories from Fat; Chol 215 mg; Fiber 3 g; Sod 192 mg

Mrs. Ralph Calcote

Linguini with White Clam Sauce

■ ■ ■ ■ ■ ■ ■ ■ ■ ■ ■ ■ ■ ■ ■ ■ ■ ■ ■ ■

2 (6-ounce) cans chopped or minced clams
8 ounces linguini
1½ tablespoons olive oil
½ small onion, minced
1 clove of garlic, minced
2 tablespoons flour
1 cup chicken broth
½ cup grated nonfat Parmesan cheese
1 (8-ounce) can sliced mushrooms

- Drain the clams, reserving ½ cup of the liquor.
- Cook the linguini using the package directions; drain and set aside.
- Heat the olive oil in a 10-inch heavy skillet over medium heat for 1 minute. Add the onion and garlic. Sauté for 5 minutes.
- Blend in the flour. Cook for 1 minute, stirring constantly.
- Add the reserved liquor. Cook for 2 minutes.
- Add the chicken broth. Cook for 4 minutes.
- Stir in the clams, cheese and mushrooms. Add the linguini. Cook for 1 minute or until heated through, tossing well.
- Serve with light garlic bread.
- Yield: 4 servings.

Approx Per Serving: Cal 424; Prot 29 g; Carbo 59 g; T Fat 7 g; 16% Calories from Fat; Chol 30 mg; Fiber 3 g; Sod 785 mg

Turkey Surprise!

Thanksgiving 1970 found me as a new bride of three weeks; of course, being only twenty-two years old, I was sure that I was more accomplished than any other bride had ever been before me and anxious to prove it to both my new husband and his parents. I had not yet realized the not-too-pleasant truth that I had much to learn in the culinary department! Reasoning that I had learned to cook on the elbow of my father, who was an excellent cook, I erroneously believed that I could tackle any cooking challenge—and, of course, perform in a superior manner.

With my brother-in-law playing football for Ole Miss on my first married Thanksgiving, I volunteered to cook dinner for my mother-in-law and father-in-law, suggesting that they stop back by the house when they returned from the Thanksgiving Day Ole Miss-Mississippi State rivalry, better known as the Egg Bowl. I worked diligently to prepare what I felt would be an outstanding feast to impress my in-laws and thereby establish myself as a fit companion for their eldest son.

The part of the meal which I felt the most comfortable preparing was the roasted turkey, something which I had seen prepared many times as I was growing up. So, armed with cookbooks, the turkey wrapper, and my special storehouse of turkey cooking memories, I set out to create the perfect, golden brown, tender, juicy turkey I remembered from childhood (and the Butterball ads!).

I carefully removed all the wrappings, plunging the bird under running water just as I had been taught, and finally located the neck section to be boiled for gravy broth. After I had withdrawn the neck from its hiding place, I plunged my hand further into the cavity (ick!) but could not locate what I thought I remembered—another bag of "goodies." No, it just wasn't there! Oh, well, the packers must have thrown it away. Having the bird nestled tightly into the roaster I had purchased and happily roasting in a 325-degree oven, I turned my attention to the remainder of the meal.

At the appointed time, all was ready and sitting appetizingly on my dining room table in anticipation of waves of admiring glances and verbal accolades from my in-laws for the fine job I had done as a new, inexperienced bride. Imagine my dismay when the praises turned to peals of laughter while the turkey was being carved! I had no idea that the turkey had a SECOND cavity where a small pouch could easily hide until inopportunely revealing itself as I attempted to carve the bird! Everyone had a good laugh about the "extra" treat on the Thanksgiving table—and I now am very careful to extract everything from the turkey before putting it in the oven; no more surprises for me!

—Carla Walsh

Baked Fish with Lemon Parsley Stuffing

1 (1½-pound) pan-dressed trout or bass
Lemon Parsley Stuffing
1 tablespoon fresh lemon juice

- Remove head and tail from fish. Rinse the fish and pat dry.
- Fill the cavity with Lemon Parsley Stuffing and secure with skewers.
- Place the fish in a baking dish sprayed with nonstick cooking spray. Sprinkle with the lemon juice.
- Bake at 350 degrees for 40 minutes or until the fish flakes easily.
- Yield: 4 servings.

Lemon Parsley Stuffing

¼ cup chopped onion
¼ cup chopped celery
1 clove of garlic, minced
1 tablespoon margarine
2 tablespoons chopped fresh parsley
1 tablespoon fresh lemon juice
1 tablespoon dry white wine
½ teaspoon grated lemon peel
¼ teaspoon thyme leaves, crushed
¼ teaspoon salt
⅛ teaspoon pepper
1½ cups fresh whole wheat bread crumbs

- Sauté the onion, celery and garlic in the margarine in a medium skillet for 4 minutes or until tender. Remove from heat.
- Add the parsley, lemon juice, wine, lemon peel, thyme, salt and pepper; mix well.
- Add the bread crumbs; toss until well mixed.

Approx Per Serving: Cal 282; Prot 33 g; Carbo 10 g; T Fat 12 g; 37% Calories from Fat; Chol 94 mg; Fiber 2 g; Sod 340 mg

—*Debbie Cox*

Sweet-and-Sour Shrimp with Noodles

1 cup each sliced celery and carrots
1 medium green bell pepper, cut into strips
1 tablespoon vegetable oil
1 (20-ounce) can juice-pack pineapple chunks
¼ cup cider vinegar
2 tablespoons soy sauce
2 tablespoons cornstarch
2 tablespoons sugar
1 (16-ounce) package frozen cooked peeled shrimp, thawed
Buttered Noodles

- Sauté the celery, carrots and green pepper in the oil in a large skillet for 5 minutes or until tender-crisp. Remove from the heat.
- Drain the pineapple, reserving the juice. Combine the reserved juice with the vinegar, soy sauce, cornstarch and sugar in a small bowl; mix well. Pour the mixture over the vegetables in the skillet.
- Cook the vegetables over low heat for about 3 minutes or until the sauce is clear and thickened, stirring constantly.
- Add the pineapple chunks and shrimp.
- Heat to serving temperature, stirring constantly.
- Serve the shrimp mixture over the hot Buttered Noodles.
- Yield: 4 servings.

Buttered Noodles

3 cups wide egg noodles
2 tablespoons melted margarine

- Cook the noodles using the package directions until cooked to the desired doneness.
- Drain, rinse with hot water and drain well.
- Toss the hot noodles with the margarine until coated. Keep the noodles warm while preparing the shrimp mixture.

Approx Per Serving: Cal 343; Prot 28 g; Carbo 53 g; T Fat 12 g; 24% Calories from Fat; Chol 258 mg; Fiber 2 g; Sod 873 mg

—*Laurie Mason Smith*

Italian Barbecued Shrimp

2 (16-ounce) bottles Italian salad dressing
2 pounds butter, melted
1/2 cup pepper
Juice of 4 lemons
10 pounds large unpeeled fresh shrimp

- Combine the salad dressing, butter, pepper and lemon juice in a bowl; mix well.
- Pour over the unpeeled shrimp in a large baking pan.
- Bake at 350 degrees for 45 minutes or until the shrimp turn pink.
- Serve in soup bowls with the cooking sauce.
- Serve with unbuttered French bread; bread may be dipped in sauce.
- Provide lots of napkins and a bowl for the shrimp shells and tails.
- Yield: 30 servings.

Approx Per Serving: Cal 484; Prot 26 g; Carbo 5 g; T Fat 40 g; 75% Calories from Fat; Chol 302 mg; Fiber <1 g; Sod 760 mg

—Sally (Mrs. Dick) Molpus
wife of former Secretary of State
of Mississippi

Shrimp Scampi

1 1/2 to 2 pounds medium fresh shrimp
1 cup butter
2 tablespoons minced garlic
2 tablespoons parsley flakes
2 tablespoons lemon juice
2 tablespoons Dijon mustard
Salt and pepper to taste
2 cups rice

- Cook the shrimp in boiling water in a stockpot until pink.
- Peel the shrimp and set aside on ice.
- Combine the butter, garlic, parsley flakes, lemon juice and Dijon mustard in a saucepan.
- Cook over low heat for 5 to 8 minutes or until heated through. Season with salt and pepper.
- Drain the shrimp and place them in a 9x13-inch glass baking dish. Pour the sauce over the shrimp.
- Bake at 400 degrees for 10 to 15 minutes or until the shrimp turn pink, stirring once or twice.
- Cook the rice using package directions.
- Serve the shrimp over a bed of the hot cooked rice.
- Yield: 8 servings.

Approx Per Serving: Cal 473; Prot 23 g; Carbo 38 g; T Fat 25 g; 48% Calories from Fat; Chol 239 mg; Fiber 1 g; Sod 541 mg

—Elizabeth M. Covington

Vegetables & Side Dishes

Vegetables & Side Dishes

Spinach Artichoke, 73
Asparagus Casserole, 73
Calico Beans, 74
Broccoli Casserole, 74
Broccoli and Corn Bake, 75
Glazed Carrots, 75
Julienne Walnut Carrots, 76
Corn Casserole, 76
Creamy Corn, 76
Shoe Peg Corn Casserole, 76
Green Bean and Corn Casserole, 77
Company Perfect Cheesy Onions, 77
Tamale-Stuffed Green Peppers, 78
Sliced Baked Potato Pockets, 78
Potato and Mushroom Casserole, 79
Zesty Hash Brown Potatoes Nancy, 79
Spanakopita, 80
Spinach and Shrimp Casserole, 80
Squash Casserole, 81
Sweet Potato Casserole, 81
Fried Green Tomatoes, 82
Ginger Vegetables, 82
Vegetable Medley, 83
Indian Curry, 83
Traditional Bread Stuffing, 84
Old-Fashioned Corn Bread Dressing, 84
Company Dressing, 85
Eggplant Caviar, 85
Light Fettuccini Alfredo, 86
Farfalle with Mushrooms, 86
Artichoke Rice, 87
Spanish Rice with Peas, 87
Wild Rice Casserole, 88
Pickled Peach Halves, 88

Photograph on preceding page by David Keeney. The muddy
Big Black River near West, Mississippi

Spinach Artichoke

- -

1 (16-ounce) can artichoke hearts, drained,
   cut into quarters
2 (10-ounce) packages chopped spinach,
   cooked, drained
1 (10-ounce) can cream of mushroom soup
1 (6-ounce) jar mushroom stems and pieces,
   drained
1 cup sour cream
1 cup mayonnaise
2 tablespoons lemon juice
1 (6-ounce) jar button mushrooms, drained

- Arrange the artichoke hearts in a baking
  dish.
- Combine the spinach, mushroom soup
  and mushroom stems and pieces in a bowl
  and mix well. Spoon evenly over the
  artichoke hearts.
- Combine the sour cream, mayonnaise and
  lemon juice in a bowl and mix well. Spread
  over the spinach mixture just before
  baking. Top with the button mushrooms.
- Bake at 350 degrees for 20 minutes or
  until bubbly.
- Yield: 8 servings.

Approx Per Serving: Cal 342; Prot 6 g;
Carbo 13 g; T Fat 31 g; 79% Calories from Fat;
Chol 29 mg; Fiber 3 g; Sod 899 mg

—*Becky Adams*

Asparagus Casserole

- -

1 (16-ounce) can asparagus spears
4 ounces Cheddar cheese, shredded
3 hard-cooked eggs, grated
8 ounces saltine crackers, crushed
1 (10-ounce) can cream of mushroom soup
Salt and pepper to taste
1/4 cup melted butter or margarine

- Drain the asparagus spears, reserving
  the liquid.
- Alternate layers of the asparagus spears,
  cheese, eggs and crackers in a greased
  baking pan until all the ingredients
  are used.
- Combine the soup with just enough of the
  reserved asparagus liquid until of the
  desired consistency and mix well. Stir in
  salt and pepper. Pour over the prepared
  layers. Drizzle with the butter.
- Bake at 350 degrees for 30 minutes.
- Yield: 4 servings.

Approx Per Serving: Cal 614; Prot 20 g;
Carbo 50 g; T Fat 38 g; 55% Calories from Fat;
Chol 221 mg; Fiber 3 g; Sod 2088 mg

—*Elizabeth Black*

Calico Beans

1 pound ground beef
1 pound bacon, chopped
1 large onion, chopped
3/4 cup packed brown sugar
1/2 cup catsup
2 tablespoons vinegar
1 teaspoon salt
1 (16-ounce) can pork and beans, drained
1 (16-ounce) can butter beans, drained
1 (16-ounce) can green beans, drained
1 (16-ounce) can red kidney beans, drained

- Brown the ground beef with the bacon and onion in a skillet, stirring until the ground beef is crumbly and the bacon is crisp; drain.
- Stir in the brown sugar, catsup, vinegar and salt. Add the pork and beans, butter beans, green beans and red kidney beans and mix well. Spoon into a 2 1/2-quart baking dish.
- Bake at 350 degrees for 45 minutes or until bubbly.
- Yield: 12 servings.

Approx Per Serving: Cal 315; Prot 18 g; Carbo 35 g; T Fat 12 g; 33% Calories from Fat; Chol 40 mg; Fiber 6 g; Sod 980 mg

—*Faye Bein*

Broccoli Casserole

1 onion, chopped
1/2 cup margarine
2 (10-ounce) packages frozen broccoli, cooked, drained
2 (10-ounce) cans cream of mushroom soup
1 cup cooked rice
1 (8-ounce) jar Cheez Whiz

- Sauté the onion in the margarine in a skillet. Stir in the broccoli, mushroom soup, rice and Cheez Whiz. Spoon into a baking dish.
- Bake at 350 degrees for 30 minutes or until bubbly.
- Yield: 8 servings.

Approx Per Serving: Cal 321; Prot 9 g; Carbo 21 g; T Fat 23 g; 64% Calories from Fat; Chol 16 mg; Fiber 3 g; Sod 1149 mg

Compliments from Grandmother

Grandmothers are the best cooks. To eat your grandmother's food is a wonderful treat, but to have your grandmother enjoy your cooking is the greatest compliment in the world. My grandmother says my broccoli casserole is the best she has ever eaten—and you know, grandmothers are never partial!

—*Iris Waldrop*

Broccoli and Corn Bake

■ ■

1 (10-ounce) package frozen chopped
    broccoli
1 (16-ounce) can cream-style corn
1/2 cup coarse saltine cracker crumbs
1/4 cup chopped onion
1 egg, beaten
2 tablespoons melted margarine
1/2 teaspoon salt
Pepper to taste
1/4 cup coarse saltine cracker crumbs
1 tablespoon melted margarine

- Cook the broccoli using package
  directions; drain.
- Combine the corn, broccoli, 1/2 cup
  cracker crumbs, onion, egg, 2 tablespoons
  margarine, salt and pepper in a bowl and
  mix well.
- Spoon into a 1-quart baking dish. Sprinkle
  with a mixture of 1/4 cup cracker crumbs
  and 1 tablespoon margarine.
- Bake at 350 degrees for 35 to 40 minutes or
  until brown and bubbly.
- Yield: 6 servings.

Approx Per Serving: Cal 179; Prot 5 g;
Carbo 24 g; T Fat 8 g; 38% Calories from Fat;
Chol 35 mg; Fiber 3 g; Sod 619 mg

—Sandra Wallace

Glazed Carrots

■ ■

1/2 cup butter
1/4 cup sugar
1 (16-ounce) can baby carrots, drained

- Heat the butter in a saucepan until melted.
  Stir in the sugar.
- Cook until the sugar dissolves, stirring
  constantly. Add the carrots.
- Cook until the carrots are heated through,
  stirring frequently.
- Yield: 4 servings.

Approx Per Serving: Cal 278; Prot 1 g;
Carbo 19 g; T Fat 23 g; 73% Calories from Fat;
Chol 62 mg; Fiber 2 g; Sod 506 mg

—Cathy Sparkman

Julienne Walnut Carrots

1/8 teaspoon salt
8 to 10 carrots, peeled, julienned
2 tablespoons sliced green onions
1/2 cup melted butter or margarine
1/2 to 1 cup chopped walnuts

- Pour water to measure 1 inch in a saucepan. Stir in the salt. Bring to a boil. Add the carrots and green onions and mix well; cover.
- Bring to a boil; reduce heat. Simmer for 20 minutes or until the carrots are tender; drain.
- Spoon into a serving bowl. Drizzle with the butter and sprinkle with the walnuts.
- Yield: 4 servings.

Approx Per Serving: Cal 474; Prot 6 g; Carbo 24 g; T Fat 42 g; 76% Calories from Fat; Chol 62 mg; Fiber 7 g; Sod 368 mg

—*Theresa Allen*

Corn Casserole

3 eggs
1/4 cup sugar
3 tablespoons flour
2 (15-ounce) cans cream-style corn
1/2 cup melted margarine
Salt to taste

- Beat the eggs in a bowl with a whisk. Stir in a mixture of the sugar and flour. Add the corn, margarine and salt and mix well.
- Spoon into a buttered 2-quart baking dish.
- Bake at 350 degrees for 45 minutes or until brown.
- Yield: 8 servings.

Approx Per Serving: Cal 241; Prot 5 g; Carbo 28 g; T Fat 14 g; 49% Calories from Fat; Chol 80 mg; Fiber 1 g; Sod 461 mg

—*Francis Quimby*

Creamy Corn

1 (16-ounce) can whole kernel corn
1 (8-ounce) can cream-style corn
1 (7-ounce) package corn muffin mix
1 cup sour cream
1/2 cup butter or margarine
2 eggs, beaten

- Combine the undrained whole kernel corn, cream-style corn, muffin mix, sour cream, butter and eggs in a bowl and mix well. Spoon into a lightly greased 8- or 9-inch baking dish.
- Bake at 350 degrees for 40 to 45 minutes or until brown and bubbly.
- Yield: 6 servings.

Approx Per Serving: Cal 439; Prot 7 g; Carbo 44 g; T Fat 28 g; 55% Calories from Fat; Chol 129 mg; Fiber 1 g; Sod 712 mg

—*Darlene Tenney*

Shoe Peg Corn Casserole

1 (16-ounce) can French-style green beans, drained
1 (11-ounce) can Shoe Peg corn, drained
1 (10-ounce) can cream of celery soup
1 cup sour cream
1 cup shredded Cheddar cheese
1/2 cup chopped celery
1/2 cup chopped onion
1/4 cup chopped green bell pepper
32 butter crackers, crushed
1/2 cup melted margarine

- Combine the green beans, corn, soup, sour cream, cheese, celery, onion and green pepper in a bowl and mix well. Spoon into a shallow baking dish.
- Sprinkle with the crackers; drizzle with the margarine.
- Bake at 350 degrees for 45 minutes.
- Yield: 8 servings.

Approx Per Serving: Cal 357; Prot 8 g; Carbo 23 g; T Fat 27 g; 67% Calories from Fat; Chol 32 mg; Fiber 3 g; Sod 901 mg

—*Judy Griffin*

Green Bean and Corn Casserole

■ ■ ■ ■ ■ ■ ■ ■ ■ ■ ■ ■ ■ ■ ■ ■ ■ ■ ■ ■

1 (16-ounce) can French-style green beans,
   drained
1 (11-ounce) can Shoe Peg corn, drained
1 (10-ounce) can cream of celery soup
1 cup sour cream
1 cup shredded sharp Cheddar cheese
1/2 cup chopped onion
32 butter crackers, crushed
1/2 cup melted margarine

- Combine the green beans and Shoe Peg
  corn in a bowl and mix well. Spoon into a
  baking dish.
- Combine the soup, sour cream, cheese and
  onion in a bowl and mix well. Spread over
  the vegetable layer. Sprinkle with a mixture
  of the crackers and margarine.
- Bake at 350 degrees for 30 to 45 minutes or
  until brown and bubbly.
- Yield: 8 servings.

Approx Per Serving: Cal 355; Prot 8 g;
Carbo 22 g; T Fat 27 g; 67% Calories from Fat;
Chol 32 mg; Fiber 3 g; Sod 895 mg

—Dena Howington

Company Perfect Cheesy Onions

■ ■ ■ ■ ■ ■ ■ ■ ■ ■ ■ ■ ■ ■ ■ ■ ■ ■ ■ ■

6 medium onions, sliced
3/4 teaspoon sugar
1/2 teaspoon salt
1/2 teaspoon pepper
3/4 cup margarine
3/4 cup white wine
1/2 cup shredded Cheddar cheese

- Combine the onions, sugar, salt and pepper
  in a bowl and mix gently.
- Heat the margarine in a skillet until melted.
  Add the onion mixture.
- Cook for 8 to 10 minutes or until the
  onions are tender, stirring frequently. Stir
  in the wine.
- Cook for 3 minutes, stirring frequently.
  Spoon into a serving dish; sprinkle with
  the cheese.
- Yield: 6 servings.

Approx Per Serving: Cal 305; Prot 4 g;
Carbo 11 g; T Fat 26 g; 75% Calories from Fat;
Chol 10 mg; Fiber 2 g; Sod 509 mg

—Jennifer Hane

Tamale-Stuffed Green Peppers

4 large green bell peppers, cut into halves
1/2 cup bouillon
1 onion, chopped
2 cloves of garlic, minced
1 (28-ounce) can plum tomatoes
1 tablespoon chili powder
1 teaspoon cumin
1/2 cup cornmeal
1 (16-ounce) can kidney beans, drained
1 cup fresh or frozen corn
1/4 cup sliced black olives
Paprika to taste

- Blanch the green peppers in a saucepan for 5 minutes; drain.
- Bring the bouillon, onion and garlic to a boil in a saucepan; reduce heat.
- Simmer for 5 minutes. Stir in the undrained tomatoes, chili powder and cumin. Add the cornmeal and mix well.
- Cook for 10 minutes or until thickened, stirring frequently. Stir in the beans, corn and olives. Spoon into the bell pepper halves; sprinkle with paprika.
- Place the bell peppers in a shallow baking dish. Add enough water around the bell peppers to measure 1/2 inch.
- Bake at 350 degrees for 30 minutes.
- Yield: 4 servings.

Approx Per Serving: Cal 289; Prot 12 g; Carbo 58 g; T Fat 3 g; 10% Calories from Fat; Chol 0 mg; Fiber 14 g; Sod 906 mg

—*Faye Bein*

Sliced Baked Potato Pockets

6 baking potatoes, peeled
2 medium onions, cut into 1/8-inch slices
3 tablespoons butter or margarine
Salt and pepper to taste
Garlic salt to taste
1 cup sour cream
1/2 cup shredded Cheddar cheese

- Cut foil into six 10-inch squares; spray with nonstick cooking spray.
- Place 1 potato on each sheet of foil. Cut each potato into 1/4-inch slices. Top each sliced potato with some of the onions and 1/2 tablespoon of the butter. Sprinkle with salt, pepper and garlic salt; wrap securely with foil.
- Bake at 375 degrees for 45 minutes or until the potatoes are tender.
- Open foil packets; top each with sour cream and cheese.
- Yield: 6 servings.

Approx Per Serving: Cal 298; Prot 6 g; Carbo 31 g; T Fat 17 g; 51% Calories from Fat; Chol 42 mg; Fiber 2 g; Sod 145 mg

—*Christie McBroom*

Potato and Mushroom Casserole

■ ■ ■ ■ ■ ■ ■ ■ ■ ■ ■ ■ ■ ■ ■ ■ ■ ■ ■ ■

2 medium onions, chopped
1/2 cup light butter or light margarine
2 (3-ounce) cans sliced mushrooms, drained
6 cups mashed cooked potatoes
1 cup fat-free sour cream
2 tablespoons melted butter
Paprika to taste

■ Sauté the onions in 1/2 cup light butter in a skillet until tender. Add the mushrooms. Sauté for 2 minutes.
■ Layer 1/3 of the potatoes, 1/2 of the onion mixture and 1/2 of the sour cream in a shallow 2-quart baking dish. Repeat the layers. Top with the remaining potatoes.
■ Drizzle with 2 tablespoons butter; sprinkle with paprika.
■ Bake at 350 degrees for 20 to 30 minutes or until light brown.
■ Yield: 10 servings.

Approx Per Serving: Cal 196; Prot 5 g;
Carbo 27 g; T Fat 9 g; 39% Calories from Fat;
Chol 9 mg; Fiber 3 g; Sod 550 mg

—*Helga Reed*

Zesty Hash Brown Potatoes Nancy

■ ■ ■ ■ ■ ■ ■ ■ ■ ■ ■ ■ ■ ■ ■ ■ ■ ■ ■ ■

1 (2-pound) package hash brown potatoes, thawed
1 (10-ounce) can cream of chicken soup
2 cups shredded sharp Cheddar cheese
1 cup sour cream
1 cup French onion dip
1/4 cup melted margarine
1 teaspoon salt
2 cups crushed cornflakes
1/2 cup melted margarine

■ Combine the potatoes, soup, cheese, sour cream, dip, 1/4 cup margarine and salt in a bowl and mix well.
■ Spoon into a 9x13-inch baking dish sprayed with nonstick cooking spray.
■ Top with a mixture of the cornflakes and 1/2 cup margarine.
■ Bake at 350 degrees for 1 hour.
■ Yield: 12 servings.

Approx Per Serving: Cal 392; Prot 9 g;
Carbo 29 g; T Fat 27 g; 62% Calories from Fat;
Chol 40 mg; Fiber 1 g; Sod 852 mg

—*Marietta Wilkinson*

Spanakopita

2 pounds fresh spinach
1 (1-pound) package phyllo pastry
1 onion, chopped
3 bunches green onions, chopped
2 cloves of garlic, chopped
2 tablespoons chopped fresh parsley
1/4 cup butter
1/2 cup cooked rice
Salt and pepper to taste
6 egg whites
6 egg yolks
1 pound feta cheese, crumbled
1 cup olive oil
1 cup melted butter

- Rinse the spinach and finely chop. Drain in a colander for several hours.
- Arrange 4 sheets of the phyllo pastry on a baking sheet. Bake at 250 degrees until crisp.
- Sauté the onion, green onions, garlic and parsley in 1/4 cup butter in a skillet. Stir in the spinach, rice, salt and pepper. Cook for several minutes or until of the desired consistency, stirring frequently.
- Beat the egg whites in a mixer bowl. Add the egg yolks 1 at a time, beating well after each addition. Stir in the spinach mixture. Add the feta cheese and mix well.
- Whisk the olive oil and 1 cup butter in a bowl. Line the bottom and sides of an 11x15-inch baking pan with 1/2 of the remaining phyllo pastry, brushing each pastry layer with some of the olive oil mixture and extending 4 sheets of phyllo pastry on each side of the pan. Top with 2 sheets of the baked phyllo.
- Spread the prepared layers with the spinach mixture and arrange the remaining baked phyllo over the spinach mixture. Top with the remaining phyllo pastry, brushing each pastry layer with the remaining olive oil mixture; tuck in the edges. Score the top into squares.
- Bake at 350 degrees for 55 to 60 minutes or until light brown.

- May substitute two 10-ounce packages frozen spinach for fresh spinach and may omit the rice.
- Yield: 12 servings.

Approx Per Serving: Cal 619; Prot 14 g; Carbo 30 g; T Fat 50 g; 72% Calories from Fat; Chol 191 mg; Fiber 3 g; Sod 894 mg

—*Myrtis Meaders*

Spinach and Shrimp Casserole

1 (10-ounce) package frozen chopped spinach, cooked, drained
1 cup peeled cooked shrimp
1 cup sour cream
1/2 cup catsup
1 small onion, minced
1 clove of garlic, minced
1 teaspoon prepared horseradish
Tabasco sauce to taste
1 cup bread crumbs
2 tablespoons melted butter

- Combine the spinach, shrimp, sour cream, catsup, onion, garlic, horseradish and Tabasco sauce in a bowl and mix well.
- Spoon into 8 buttered ramekins. Sprinkle with a mixture of the bread crumbs and butter.
- Bake at 450 degrees for 10 minutes.
- Yield: 8 servings.

Approx Per Serving: Cal 185; Prot 8 g; Carbo 17 g; T Fat 10 g; 47% Calories from Fat; Chol 60 mg; Fiber 2 g; Sod 406 mg

—*Dott Cannon*

Squash Casserole

3 pounds squash
3/4 cup chopped onion
1 (5-ounce) can evaporated milk
1/2 cup butter
3 eggs, beaten
3 tablespoons sugar
2 tablespoons flour
4 teaspoons salt
1 teaspoon pepper

- Combine the squash with enough water to cover in a saucepan. Cook until tender. Drain and chop.
- Combine the squash, onion, evaporated milk, butter, eggs, sugar, flour, salt and pepper in a bowl and mix well.
- Spoon into an ungreased 9x11-inch baking dish.
- Bake at 425 degrees for 30 minutes or until bubbly.
- Yield: 10 servings.

Approx Per Serving: Cal 175; Prot 5 g; Carbo 14 g; T Fat 12 g; 60% Calories from Fat; Chol 93 mg; Fiber 2 g; Sod 983 mg

—*Mary Ann Lefoldt*

Sweet Potato Casserole

3 cups (rounded) mashed cooked sweet potatoes
1 cup sugar
1/2 cup margarine
2 eggs, beaten
1 tablespoon vanilla extract
1 cup packed dark brown sugar
1/3 cup flour
1/3 cup margarine
1 cup chopped pecans

- Combine the sweet potatoes, sugar, 1/2 cup margarine, eggs and vanilla in a bowl and mix well.
- Spoon into a greased baking pan.
- Combine the brown sugar and flour in a bowl and mix well.
- Cut in 1/3 cup margarine until crumbly. Stir in the pecans. Sprinkle over the prepared layer.
- Bake at 350 degrees for 25 minutes.
- Yield: 8 servings.

Approx Per Serving: Cal 573; Prot 5 g; Carbo 73 g; T Fat 31 g; 47% Calories from Fat; Chol 53 mg; Fiber 3 g; Sod 258 mg

—*Elizabeth Black*

Fried Green Tomatoes

3 firm green tomatoes, cored
1 egg
1 tablespoon milk
1/3 cup flour
1/3 cup yellow cornmeal
1 teaspoon salt
1/4 teaspoon paprika
1/8 teaspoon cayenne
1/8 teaspoon black pepper
Vegetable oil for frying

- Cut a thin slice from the top and bottom of each tomato. Cut each tomato horizontally into 4 slices.
- Whisk the egg and milk in a bowl. Mix the flour, cornmeal, salt, paprika, cayenne and black pepper on waxed paper.
- Dip the tomato slices in the egg mixture; coat with the flour mixture.
- Add oil to a skillet to a depth of 1/4 inch. Heat until hot.
- Brown the tomatoes in batches in the hot oil for 1 to 2 minutes per side; drain on paper towels.
- Serve immediately.
- Yield: 6 servings.

Approx Per Serving: Cal 82; Prot 3 g;
Carbo 15 g; T Fat 1 g; 14% Calories from Fat;
Chol 36 mg; Fiber 2 g; Sod 375 mg
Nutritional information does not include oil
for frying.

—*Joe Anne Johnson*

Ginger Vegetables

1 cup chicken broth
1 teaspoon minced garlic
1 teaspoon grated gingerroot
1/8 teaspoon red pepper flakes
8 ounces carrots, peeled, cut into 1/2x4-inch strips
8 ounces turnips, peeled, cut into 1/2x4-inch strips
4 cups broccoli florets

- Bring 1/4 cup of the broth, garlic, gingerroot and red pepper flakes to a boil in a saucepan.
- Boil until most of the liquid evaporates. Stir in the remaining broth, carrots, turnips and broccoli.
- Cook, covered, for 4 to 6 minutes or just until the vegetables are tender-crisp.
- Yield: 4 servings.

Approx Per Serving: Cal 76; Prot 5 g;
Carbo 14 g; T Fat 1 g; 9% Calories from Fat;
Chol 0 mg; Fiber 5 g; Sod 276 mg

—*Janis Zimmerman*

Vegetable Medley

1 (10-ounce) package frozen Italian-style
  green beans, cooked, drained
2 cups sliced zucchini
1¹/₃ cups drained canned whole tomatoes
1¹/₃ cups sliced carrots
1 cup sliced onion
¹/₂ large green bell pepper, cut into strips
2 tablespoons cornstarch
2 tablespoons sugar
1 teaspoon salt
3 tablespoons butter

- Combine the green beans, zucchini,
  tomatoes, carrots, onion and green
  pepper in a bowl and mix gently. Stir in
  a mixture of the cornstarch, sugar and
  salt. Spoon into a 3-quart baking dish;
  dot with the butter.
- Bake, covered, at 350 degrees for 1¹/₄ hours.
- May substitute canned green beans for
  frozen green beans.
- Yield: 6 servings.

Approx Per Serving: Cal 123; Prot 2 g;
Carbo 17 g; T Fat 6 g; 42% Calories from Fat;
Chol 16 mg; Fiber 4 g; Sod 515 mg

—*Betty L. Johnston*

Indian Curry

2 tablespoons cornstarch
2 teaspoons beef bouillon granules
2 teaspoons curry powder, or to taste
2 potatoes, peeled, coarsely chopped
2 onions, cut into wedges
2 carrots, coarsely chopped

- Combine the cornstarch, bouillon granules
  and curry powder in a saucepan and mix
  well. Stir in just enough water to make of a
  sauce consistency. Add the potatoes,
  onions and carrots and mix well.
- Simmer until the vegetables are tender-
  crisp, stirring occasionally.
- May adjust seasonings, adding additional
  bouillon granules, soy sauce or water if
  desired.
- Use as a base for Chicken Curry, Pork
  Curry or Shrimp Curry. Add chopped
  chicken or chopped pork along with the
  vegetables; add the shrimp 15 minutes
  before serving. Spoon over hot rice;
  sprinkle with chopped peanuts, raisins,
  chutney and/or pickled onions.
- Yield: 6 servings.

Approx Per Serving: Cal 76; Prot 2 g;
Carbo 17 g; T Fat <1 g; 3% Calories from Fat;
Chol <1 mg; Fiber 2 g; Sod 300 mg

Rice Curry

*Our children grew up in Japan so their
preference in food is oriental. They developed
this taste early in their childhood. Our youngest
son loved Rice Curry during his preschool
years. When we traveled by car he would
always ask the same question, "When are we
stopping for Rice Curry?" We'd stop, he'd eat,
we'd leave and before we were ten kilometers up
the road he would again ask, "When are we
going to stop for Rice Curry?"*

—*Mrs. Ralph Calcote*

Traditional Bread Stuffing

3 tablespoons butter
3/4 cup chopped celery
1/2 cup chopped onion
3 tablespoons chopped fresh parsley
4 cups dry bread cubes
1/2 teaspoon salt
Freshly ground pepper to taste
Sage or poultry seasoning to taste

- Heat the butter in a skillet until melted. Add the celery, onion and parsley.
- Cook until the vegetables are tender, stirring frequently. Add the bread cubes.
- Cook until the bread cubes are brown, stirring constantly. Add the seasonings.
- Use to stuff the cavity of a chicken or turkey. Cooking time will vary according to the size of the chicken or turkey.
- Yield: 8 servings.

Approx Per Serving: Cal 105; Prot 2 g;
Carbo 12 g; T Fat 5 g; 45% Calories from Fat;
Chol 12 mg; Fiber 1 g; Sod 293 mg

—Roselle Brister Lefferts

Black-Eyed Peas with a Sizzle

When I was a teenager growing up in Florida, my mother, who was a teacher, spent several weeks of her summer breaks visiting with her parents in West, Mississippi. My father, sister, and I stayed behind in Florida for much of the summer.

One night I got the urge to fix supper for the three of us. I chose my menu and decided on black-eyed peas as one of the side dishes. The only problem was that I had never fixed them, so I called my mom long-distance for directions. Ever the home economics instructor, my mom gave me step-by-step directions, but left out one crucial step. I guess she thought I would know to add water, but I didn't. Not until the peas began to fry and then burn did I realize something was wrong. Needless to say, no one wanted fried peas for supper. Dad took us out to eat.

—Melanie Lefferts Stone

Old-Fashioned Corn Bread Dressing

1 (5- to 6-pound) hen
Salt to taste
1 to 2 tablespoons vegetable oil
4 cups yellow cornmeal
2 tablespoons baking powder
4 eggs
1 1/2 to 2 cups milk
3 slices dry bread
6 to 8 eggs, beaten
1 cup chopped onion
1 cup chopped celery
1/2 cup chopped green onions
4 or 5 cloves of garlic, minced
Pepper to taste
Melted butter to taste

- Rinse the hen. Combine the hen and salt with enough water to cover in a stockpot. Cook until tender. Drain, reserving the broth. Chop the hen, discarding the skin and bones and freeze for future use.
- Heat the oil in a cast-iron skillet until hot.
- Combine the cornmeal, baking powder, 4 eggs and milk in a bowl and mix well. Spoon into the prepared skillet.
- Bake at 450 degrees until brown and crisp. Let stand until cool; crumble into a bowl.
- Moisten the bread slices with water. Add to the crumbled corn bread. Stir in the 6 to 8 eggs, onion, celery, green onions, garlic, pepper and melted butter. Add enough of the reserved broth to make of a soupy consistency and mix well. May add hot water if needed to make of the desired degree of consistency.
- Spoon desired amount into a baking pan and top with a chicken or turkey. Cooking time will depend on amount of dressing and size of chicken or turkey.
- This recipe makes enough dressing to serve with 2 or 3 chickens or 2 turkeys. May freeze uncooked dressing for future use.
- Yield: variable.

Nutritional information is not available for this recipe.

—Jane Breeland

Company Dressing

1 pound pork sausage
1 onion, chopped
1 green bell pepper, chopped
1 rib celery, chopped
2 tablespoons butter
6 potatoes, peeled, cooked, chopped
2 or 3 slices bread, torn
1 cup milk
Salt and pepper to taste

- Fry the sausage in a skillet, stirring until crumbly; drain.
- Sauté the onion, green pepper and celery in the butter in a skillet. Stir in the sausage. Add the potatoes and mix well.
- Dip the bread into the milk. Add the remaining milk and bread to the sausage mixture and mix well. Season with salt and pepper. Spoon into a baking pan.
- Bake at 325 degrees for 15 to 20 minutes or until heated through.
- Yield: 6 servings.

Approx Per Serving: Cal 352; Prot 12 g; Carbo 38 g; T Fat 17 g; 43% Calories from Fat; Chol 46 mg; Fiber 3 g; Sod 602 mg

—*Margaret Jo Rose*

Eggplant Caviar

2 medium eggplant
1/2 cup chopped fresh parsley
2 cloves of garlic, crushed
2 tablespoons vinegar
1 tablespoon lemon juice
1 tablespoon mint
1 teaspoon salt
1/2 teaspoon pepper
1/4 teaspoon cinnamon

- Place the eggplant on a baking pan. Bake at 350 degrees for 1 hour or until tender. Peel and chop the eggplant.
- Combine the eggplant and parsley in a bowl and mix well. Stir in the garlic, vinegar, lemon juice, mint, salt, pepper and cinnamon.
- Let stand at room temperature for several hours before serving.
- Yield: 6 servings.

Approx Per Serving: Cal 55; Prot 2 g; Carbo 13 g; T Fat <1 g; 7% Calories from Fat; Chol 0 mg; Fiber 6 g; Sod 364 mg

—*Zahra Noe*

Fridays and Fish Sticks

I grew up in a good Catholic home and attended a Catholic school. Our school, as well as most public schools, always served fish sticks on Fridays because we did not eat meat on Fridays. They were usually prepared the same way—there is not much you can do to enhance the flavor of a fish stick! And then for supper at home on Fridays we often had fish sticks. I remember lots of fish sticks. I can not eat fish sticks to this day.

—*Jean Marie Rose*

Light Fettuccini Alfredo

1¹/₃ cups skim milk
2 tablespoons fat-free cream cheese
2 small cloves of garlic, minced
2 teaspoons flour
1 cup grated Parmesan cheese
1 tablespoon plus 2 teaspoons imitation
   butter-flavor seasoning
4 cups hot cooked fettuccini

- Whisk the skim milk, cream cheese, garlic and flour in a saucepan. Bring to a boil over high heat, whisking constantly; reduce heat.
- Simmer for 2 minutes or until thickened, whisking constantly. Stir in the Parmesan cheese. Remove from heat. Stir in the butter-flavor seasoning.
- Arrange the fettuccini on a serving platter. Top with the sauce.
- Yield: 4 servings.

Approx Per Serving: Cal 364; Prot 22 g; Carbo 48 g; T Fat 9 g; 22% Calories from Fat; Chol 24 mg; Fiber 2 g; Sod 819 mg

—*Laurie Mason Smith*

Farfalle with Mushrooms

5 shallots, chopped
¹/₂ cup butter
2 pounds fresh mushrooms with stems,
   chopped
¹/₂ to 1 cup chicken broth
1 teaspoon salt
¹/₂ teaspoon red pepper flakes
12 ounces farfalle
¹/₂ cup freshly grated Romano cheese

- Sauté the shallots in the butter in a skillet until tender. Add the mushrooms and ¹/₂ cup of the broth and mix well.
- Simmer for 45 minutes, stirring frequently. Stir in the salt and red pepper flakes. Add the remaining broth if needed for desired consistency.
- Cook for 5 minutes, stirring frequently.
- Cook the pasta in boiling water to cover in a saucepan until al dente; drain.
- Place the pasta in a large heated serving bowl. Add the cheese and mix well. Pour the mushroom sauce over the pasta and toss gently.
- Serve with additional Romano cheese.
- Yield: 6 servings.

Approx Per Serving: Cal 470; Prot 16 g; Carbo 61 g; T Fat 19 g; 36% Calories from Fat; Chol 50 mg; Fiber 4 g; Sod 759 mg

—*Holly Perkins*

Artichoke Rice

2 (6-ounce) jars marinated artichoke hearts
1/3 cup mayonnaise
1/2 teaspoon curry powder
1 (7-ounce) package chicken-flavor
    Rice-A-Roni
4 scallions, thinly sliced
1/2 green bell pepper, chopped
12 pimento-stuffed green olives, sliced

- Drain the artichokes, reserving the marinade from 1 jar; slice the artichokes.
- Combine the reserved marinade, mayonnaise and curry powder in a bowl and mix well.
- Cook the Rice-A-Roni using package directions. Stir into the mayonnaise mixture.
- Add the artichokes, scallions, green pepper and olives and mix well.
- Serve hot, cold or at room temperature.
- May add chopped cooked chicken for a delicious entrée.
- Yield: 8 servings.

Approx Per Serving: Cal 170; Prot 2 g;
Carbo 10 g; T Fat 15 g; 74% Calories from Fat;
Chol 6 mg; Fiber 2 g; Sod 698 mg

—*Patricia A. Perkins*

Spanish Rice with Peas

2 teaspoons vegetable oil
1 cup long grain rice
1 cup chopped onion
2 cups chicken broth
1 cup green peas
1 cup chopped tomato
1 teaspoon chili powder
1/4 teaspoon salt
1/4 teaspoon crushed red pepper
1/3 cup chopped fresh cilantro
1 medium avocado

- Heat the vegetable oil in a saucepan over medium heat until hot. Stir in the rice and onion.
- Sauté for 3 minutes. Add the broth, peas, tomato, chili powder, salt and red pepper and mix well; reduce heat.
- Simmer, covered, for 20 minutes or until liquid has been absorbed.
- Spoon onto 5 dinner plates; sprinkle with the cilantro.
- Cut the avocado into 10 wedges. Arrange 2 avocado wedges on each plate.
- Yield: 5 servings.

Approx Per Serving: Cal 275; Prot 8 g;
Carbo 41 g; T Fat 9 g; 29% Calories from Fat;
Chol 0 mg; Fiber 4 g; Sod 429 mg

—*Dianna Gonzalez*

Wild Rice Casserole

1/2 cup margarine
2 tablespoons flour
2 cups milk
8 ounces cream cheese
1 teaspoon salt
1 (6-ounce) package wild rice, cooked, drained
1 cup drained canned mushrooms

- Heat the margarine in a double boiler until melted. Add the flour, stirring until blended. Add the milk gradually, stirring constantly.
- Stir in the cream cheese.
- Cook until thickened and smooth, stirring constantly. Stir in the salt.
- Layer the rice, mushrooms and sauce 1/2 at a time in a buttered baking dish, ending with the sauce.
- Bake at 325 degrees for 20 to 30 minutes or until brown.
- Yield: 12 servings.

Approx Per Serving: Cal 217; Prot 5 g;
Carbo 15 g; T Fat 16 g; 64% Calories from Fat;
Chol 26 mg; Fiber <1 g; Sod 399 mg

—Jo Mathews

Pickled Peach Halves

1 (29-ounce) can peach halves
1/2 cup white vinegar
1/2 cup sugar
1 stick cinnamon
1/2 teaspoon whole cloves

- Drain the peaches, reserving 1 cup of the syrup.
- Combine the reserved syrup, vinegar, sugar, cinnamon and cloves in a saucepan.
- Simmer the mixture for 5 minutes, stirring occasionally. Add the peaches and mix well.
- Bring to a boil. Remove from heat. Let stand until cool.
- Ladle the peaches and syrup into sterilized jars, leaving 1/2 inch headspace; seal with 2-piece lids.
- Chill for 8 to 10 hours.
- Yield: 8 servings.

Approx Per Serving: Cal 126; Prot <1 g;
Carbo 34 g; T Fat <1 g; 1% Calories from Fat;
Chol 0 mg; Fiber 1 g; Sod 6 mg

—Martha Makamson

Cakes & Cookies

Cakes & Cookies

Photograph on preceding page by Gil Ford Photography. Sailing at day's end
on the peaceful Okatibbee in Meridian, Mississippi

Butterscotch Apple Cake

3 cups flour
1 teaspoon baking soda
1 teaspoon cinnamon
1/2 teaspoon salt
2 cups sugar
1 cup vegetable oil
2 eggs
3 cups chopped apples
2 teaspoons vanilla extract
1 cup chopped pecans
1 cup butterscotch chips

- Sift the flour, baking soda, cinnamon and salt together.
- Mix the sugar and oil in a large bowl. Add the eggs, apples and vanilla; mix well. Add the flour mixture gradually, mixing well after each addition.
- Stir in the pecans. Sprinkle with the butterscotch chips.
- Pour into a nonstick 9x13-inch cake pan.
- Bake at 350 degrees for 55 to 60 minutes or until the cake tests done.
- Yield: 15 servings.

Approx Per Serving: Cal 471; Prot 4 g;
Carbo 62 g; T Fat 24 g; 45% Calories from Fat;
Chol 28 mg; Fiber 2 g; Sod 146 mg

—Elsie R. Smith

Jewish Apple Cake

3 cups self-rising flour
2 cups sugar
1 teaspoon vanilla extract
4 eggs
1 cup vegetable oil
1/4 cup orange juice
3 apples, sliced
2 teaspoons cinnamon-sugar

- Mix the flour, sugar, vanilla, eggs, oil and orange juice in a bowl; the batter will be thick.
- Pour 2/3 of the batter into a nonstick bundt pan. Add half the apples and sprinkle with half the cinnamon-sugar. Pour in the remaining batter.
- Top with the remaining apples and sprinkle with the remaining cinnamon-sugar.
- Bake at 350 degrees for 1 hour to 1 hour and 15 minutes or until the cake tests done.
- Yield: 16 servings.

Approx Per Serving: Cal 336; Prot 4 g;
Carbo 47 g; T Fat 15 g; 40% Calories from Fat;
Chol 53 mg; Fiber 1 g; Sod 313 mg

—Pam Myrick-Motley

Fresh Apple Cake

2 cups flour
2 cups sugar
2 teaspoons baking soda
1 teaspoon cinnamon
1/2 teaspoon nutmeg
1/2 teaspoon salt
4 cups chopped apples
1/2 cup margarine, softened
2 eggs

- Sift the flour, sugar, baking soda, cinnamon, nutmeg and salt into a large bowl. Add the apples, margarine and eggs, stirring just until mixed; the batter will be thick. Pour into a greased 9x13-inch cake pan.
- Bake at 325 degrees for 1 hour. Cool in the pan before serving.
- Yield: 12 servings.

Approx Per Serving: Cal 310; Prot 3 g; Carbo 56 g; T Fat 9 g; 25% Calories from Fat; Chol 35 mg; Fiber 1 g; Sod 326 mg

Apples, Apples Everywhere!

Soon after becoming newlyweds, my husband and I were sent to Germany with the U.S. Air Force. I was well known for my lack of sales resistance. One day my husband came home from work to find that I had bought twenty pounds of apples from a door-to-door salesman. I had to write home to all of my friends and relatives for recipes that included apples. Fresh Apple Cake became one of our favorites.

—Sara S. Lee

Blackberry Wine Cake

1/2 cup finely chopped pecans
1 (2-layer) package white cake mix
1 (3-ounce) package blackberry gelatin
1/2 cup blackberry wine
1/2 cup vegetable oil
4 eggs
1/2 cup margarine
2 1/2 cups confectioners' sugar
1/2 cup blackberry wine

- Sprinkle the pecans in a greased and floured loaf pan.
- Combine the cake mix, gelatin, 1/2 cup wine and oil in a large bowl; mix well. Add the eggs 1 at a time, beating well after each addition. Pour the batter into the prepared pan.
- Bake at 325 degrees for 1 hour.
- Melt the margarine in a saucepan. Add the confectioners' sugar and remaining 1/2 cup wine, mixing until smooth. Cook until of glaze consistency, stirring frequently.
- Drizzle the glaze over the hot cake. Let the cake stand for 20 to 30 minutes.
- Remove to a wire rack. Cool for several hours to overnight.
- This cake freezes well.
- Yield: 12 servings.

Approx Per Serving: Cal 542; Prot 5 g; Carbo 68 g; T Fat 26 g; 43% Calories from Fat; Chol 71 mg; Fiber 1 g; Sod 413 mg

—Nell Rein

Carrot Cake

2 cups flour
2 cups sugar
2 teaspoons cinnamon
2 teaspoons baking soda
1 teaspoon salt
4 eggs, beaten
1 1/2 cups vegetable oil
3 cups grated carrots

- Combine the flour, sugar, cinnamon, baking soda and salt in a bowl; mix well.
- Add the eggs and oil; mix until smooth. Stir in the carrots.
- Pour into a nonstick 9x13-inch cake pan.
- Bake at 350 degrees for 30 to 35 minutes or until the cake tests done.
- Yield: 15 servings.

Approx Per Serving: Cal 386; Prot 4 g; Carbo 42 g; T Fat 23 g; 54% Calories from Fat; Chol 57 mg; Fiber 1 g; Sod 277 mg

—*Linda Ebbers*

Blond Fudge Cake

1/2 cup margarine, softened
1 cup sugar
1 cup flour
2 eggs
1 teaspoon almond extract
1/2 cup chopped pecans

- Mix the margarine and sugar in a bowl. Stir in the flour.
- Add the eggs 1 at a time, mixing well after each addition.
- Stir in the flavoring and pecans.
- Pour into a nonstick 8x8-inch cake pan.
- Bake at 350 degrees for 30 minutes. Cool in the pan. Cut into squares.
- Yield: 8 servings.

Approx Per Serving: Cal 324; Prot 4 g; Carbo 38 g; T Fat 18 g; 49% Calories from Fat; Chol 53 mg; Fiber 1 g; Sod 150 mg

—*Ruth Stevens*

Chocolate Cake with Frosting

1/2 cup shortening
1 1/2 cups sugar
1 cup sour milk
1 egg
1/4 cup baking cocoa
2 cups flour
1 teaspoon vanilla extract
1 teaspoon butter flavoring
1 teaspoon salt
1 teaspoon baking soda
1/2 cup hot water
2 cups confectioners' sugar
1/4 cup butter, softened
1/4 cup baking cocoa
1 teaspoon vanilla extract
1/4 teaspoon butter flavoring
1/4 to 1/2 cup light cream

- Combine the shortening, sugar, sour milk, egg, 1/4 cup baking cocoa, flour, 1 teaspoon vanilla, 1 teaspoon butter flavoring and salt in a bowl; mix well.
- Dissolve the baking soda in the hot water. Stir into the batter. Pour into a nonstick 9x13-inch cake pan.
- Bake at 350 degrees for 30 minutes. Let stand until cool.
- Combine the confectioners' sugar, butter, remaining 1/4 cup cocoa, 1 teaspoon vanilla and 1/4 teaspoon butter flavoring in a bowl; mix well. Add the cream gradually, beating well until of spreading consistency. Spread over the cooled cake.
- Yield: 15 servings.

Approx Per Serving: Cal 361; Prot 3 g;
Carbo 52 g; T Fat 17 g; 40% Calories from Fat;
Chol 38 mg; Fiber 1 g; Sod 244 mg

—Mary L. Taylor

Delicious Chocolate Pudding Cake

3/4 cup sugar
1 cup self-rising flour
2 tablespoons baking cocoa
1/2 cup milk
3 tablespoons melted margarine
1 teaspoon vanilla extract
1/2 cup sugar
1/2 cup packed brown sugar
1/4 cup baking cocoa
1 3/4 cups water

- Sift the 3/4 cup sugar, flour and 2 tablespoons cocoa into a nonstick 9x9-inch cake pan. Stir in the milk, margarine and vanilla.
- Mix the remaining 1/2 cup sugar, brown sugar and 1/4 cup cocoa in a bowl. Sprinkle over the batter. Pour the water over the batter and topping.
- Bake at 350 degrees for 45 minutes.
- Serve warm with whipped topping or ice cream.
- Yield: 8 servings.

Approx Per Serving: Cal 276; Prot 3 g;
Carbo 57 g; T Fat 5 g; 17% Calories from Fat;
Chol 2 mg; Fiber 2 g; Sod 262 mg

—Anita Sarabia

Chocolate Cookie Sheet Cake

2 cups sifted flour
2 cups sugar
1/2 teaspoon salt
1/2 cup margarine
1/2 cup shortening
1 cup water
3 tablespoons baking cocoa
2 eggs, beaten
1 teaspoon baking soda
1/2 cup buttermilk
1 teaspoon vanilla extract
Chocolate Pecan Frosting

- Sift the flour, sugar and salt into a large bowl.
- Bring the margarine, shortening, water and cocoa to a boil in a saucepan. Pour over the flour mixture.
- Mix the eggs, baking soda, buttermilk and vanilla in a medium bowl. Add to the flour mixture and mix well. Pour into a greased and floured sheet cake pan.
- Bake at 350 degrees for 20 minutes. Spread the Chocolate Pecan Frosting over the hot cake.
- Yield: 24 servings.

Chocolate Pecan Frosting

1/2 cup margarine
3 tablespoons baking cocoa
6 tablespoons milk
1 (1-pound) package confectioners' sugar
1/2 cup chopped pecans
1 teaspoon vanilla extract

- Heat the margarine, cocoa and milk in a saucepan over low heat; do not boil.
- Remove the mixture from the heat and beat in the confectioners' sugar. Stir in the pecans and vanilla.

Approx Per Serving: Cal 310; Prot 2 g;
Carbo 45 g; T Fat 14 g; 41% Calories from Fat;
Chol 18 mg; Fiber 1 g; Sod 181 mg

—Frances Parker

Basic Cake with Chocolate Icing

1/2 cup shortening
1 1/2 cups sugar
2 cups sifted self-rising flour
3/4 cup plus 2 tablespoons milk
1 teaspoon vanilla extract
3 eggs
Chocolate Icing

- Combine the shortening, sugar and flour in a large bowl. Add the milk and vanilla; mix well. Add the eggs 1 at a time, mixing well after each addition.
- Pour into a 9x13-inch nonstick cake pan or 2 nonstick round cake pans.
- Bake at 350 degrees for 25 to 30 minutes or until the cake tests done. Cool in the pan.
- Spread with the Chocolate Icing.
- Yield: 15 servings.

Chocolate Icing

2 cups sugar
3 tablespoons baking cocoa
1/2 cup milk
2 tablespoons light corn syrup
1/2 cup butter
1 teaspoon vanilla extract

- Mix the sugar and cocoa in a saucepan. Add the milk, corn syrup and butter.
- Cook over low heat until the sugar is dissolved, stirring constantly. Bring the mixture to a boil over medium heat; reduce heat. Simmer for 2 minutes.
- Add the vanilla and beat until of spreading consistency.

Approx Per Serving: Cal 390; Prot 4 g;
Carbo 62 g; T Fat 15 g; 34% Calories from Fat;
Chol 62 mg; Fiber 1 g; Sod 285 mg

—Hattie Berch

Lena's Chocolate Cake with Rocky Road Frosting

1/2 cup melted margarine
1/2 cup vegetable oil
1 cup water
3 1/2 tablespoons baking cocoa
2 eggs, beaten
2 cups sugar
1 teaspoon vanilla extract
2 cups flour
1/2 teaspoon baking soda
1/4 teaspoon salt
1/2 cup buttermilk
2 cups miniature marshmallows
Rocky Road Frosting

- Blend melted margarine, oil, water and baking cocoa in a small bowl. Set aside.
- Beat the eggs with sugar and vanilla in a large bowl.
- Add a mixture of flour, baking soda and salt alternately with the buttermilk, mixing well after each addition.
- Stir in the cocoa mixture. Mix until smooth.
- Pour into a greased and floured 9x13-inch cake pan.
- Bake at 350 degrees for 35 minutes or until the cake tests done.
- Sprinkle the marshmallows over the hot cake as soon as the cake is removed from the oven. Let stand while preparing the frosting.
- Frost with Rocky Road Frosting.
- Yield: 15 servings.

Rocky Road Frosting

1/4 cup margarine
2 tablespoons baking cocoa
3 tablespoons milk
1/2 (1-pound) package confectioners' sugar
1 teaspoon vanilla extract
1/2 cup finely chopped pecans

- Melt the margarine in a medium saucepan; remove from the heat.

- Blend in the cocoa and milk. Add the confectioners' sugar gradually, blending well.
- Add the vanilla and pecans; mix well.
- Drizzle over the hot cake.

Approx Per Serving: Cal 434; Prot 4 g;
Carbo 62 g; T Fat 20 g; 41% Calories from Fat;
Chol 29 mg; Fiber 1 g; Sod 193 mg

—Donna Powell

Turtle Cake

1 (2-layer) package German chocolate cake mix
1 (14-ounce) package caramels
6 tablespoons margarine
1/2 cup evaporated milk
1 cup chopped pecans
1 cup semisweet chocolate chips

- Prepare the cake mix using the package directions.
- Pour half the batter into a greased and floured 9x13-inch cake pan.
- Bake at 350 degrees for 15 minutes.
- Combine the caramels, margarine and evaporated milk in a medium saucepan.
- Heat over medium heat until the caramels and margarine melt and the mixture is well blended, stirring constantly.
- Drizzle the caramel mixture over the baked cake layer. Pour remaining cake batter over the caramel mixture.
- Sprinkle the pecans and chocolate chips over the top.
- Bake at 350 degrees for 20 minutes.
- Cool completely before cutting.
- Yield: 15 servings.

Approx Per Serving: Cal 468; Prot 5 g;
Carbo 58 g; T Fat 26 g; 48% Calories from Fat;
Chol 48 mg; Fiber 2 g; Sod 465 mg

—Darlene Stephens

Mississippi Mud Cake

1 cup shortening
2 cups sugar
4 eggs
1 tablespoon vanilla extract
1¹/₂ cups flour
¹/₃ cup baking cocoa
¹/₄ teaspoon salt
1 cup chopped pecans
¹/₂ (10-ounce) package miniature
    marshmallows
Rich Chocolate Icing

- Cream the shortening and sugar in a large bowl.
- Add eggs and vanilla; beat well by hand.
- Sift the flour, cocoa and salt together. Add to the creamed mixture; mix well.
- Stir in the pecans.
- Pour into a greased and floured 9x13-inch cake pan.
- Bake at 300 degrees for 35 minutes.
- Sprinkle marshmallows over the hot cake.
- Increase the oven temperature to 350 degrees.
- Bake the cake for 10 minutes longer.
- Let cake stand for 1 hour to cool.
- Frost with Rich Chocolate Icing.
- Yield: 15 servings.

Rich Chocolate Icing

1 (1-pound) package confectioners' sugar
¹/₃ cup baking cocoa
1 cup melted margarine
¹/₄ to ¹/₃ cup evaporated milk
1 teaspoon vanilla extract
1 cup chopped pecans

- Sift the confectioners' sugar and cocoa into a medium bowl.
- Add the melted margarine, blending well.
- Blend in enough evaporated milk to make of spreading consistency. Blend in vanilla.
- Add the pecans; mix well.

Approx Per Serving: Cal 672; Prot 6 g;
Carbo 80 g; T Fat 40 g; 51% Calories from Fat;
Chol 58 mg; Fiber 3 g; Sod 207 mg

—*Kathy May*

Easy Dobos Torte

1 (11-ounce) pound cake
1 cup semisweet chocolate chips
¹/₄ cup boiling water
4 egg yolks
1 teaspoon vanilla extract, brandy or rum
¹/₂ cup butter

- Use a frozen loaf pound cake or freeze the cake for easier slicing.
- Cut the cake horizontally into 6 slices. Set aside.
- Combine the chocolate chips with boiling water in a blender container. Process at high speed for 15 seconds or until smooth.
- Add the egg yolks, vanilla and butter. Process for several seconds or until smooth.
- Spread the chocolate mixture between the cake layers and over the top and sides of the cake.
- Chill in the refrigerator until chocolate mixture is firm.
- Wrap in foil and store in the freezer or refrigerator until serving time.
- Yield: 8 servings.

Approx Per Serving: Cal 385; Prot 5 g;
Carbo 33 g; T Fat 28 g; 63% Calories from Fat;
Chol 223 mg; Fiber 2 g; Sod 278 mg

—*Helga Reed*

Red Velvet Cake

2 cups flour
1 teaspoon cinnamon
1/4 teaspoon salt
1 1/2 cups sugar
1/2 cup shortening
2 eggs
1 cup buttermilk
1 teaspoon lemon extract
1 teaspoon orange extract
1/4 cup red food coloring
1 teaspoon baking soda
1 tablespoon vinegar
Red Velvet Frosting
1/4 cup flaked coconut

- Sift the flour, cinnamon and salt together.
- Cream the sugar and shortening in a mixer bowl until light and fluffy. Add the eggs; mix well. Add the flour mixture and buttermilk alternately to the creamed mixture, beating well after each addition. Stir in the flavorings and food coloring. Dissolve the baking soda in the vinegar and stir into the batter. Pour into two 9-inch nonstick cake pans.
- Bake at 350 degrees for 35 minutes. Cool in the pans for several minutes. Remove to a wire rack to cool completely.
- Spread the Red Velvet Frosting between the layers and over the top and side of the cake. Sprinkle the top of the cake with the coconut.
- Yield: 12 servings.

Red Velvet Frosting

1 cup milk
1/4 cup flour
1/4 teaspoon salt
1 cup sugar
1/2 cup margarine, softened
1/2 cup confectioners' sugar
1 teaspoon vanilla extract

- Combine the milk, flour and salt in a saucepan. Cook until thickened, stirring frequently. Pour into a bowl. Cover with plastic wrap and chill thoroughly.
- Cream the sugar, margarine, confectioners' sugar and chilled mixture in a mixer bowl until light and fluffy. Beat in the vanilla.

Approx Per Serving: Cal 453; Prot 5 g; Carbo 68 g; T Fat 19 g; 37% Calories from Fat; Chol 39 mg; Fiber 1 g; Sod 290 mg

—Marian C. Brewer

Mounds Cake

1 (2-layer) package chocolate cake mix
1 cup sugar
1 cup milk
24 large marshmallows
14 ounces flaked coconut
1 1/2 cups sugar
1/2 cup milk
1/2 cup margarine
1 1/2 cups chocolate chips

- Prepare and bake the cake mix using the package directions for a 9x13-inch cake pan.
- Combine the 1 cup sugar, 1 cup milk and marshmallows in a saucepan. Cook until the marshmallows melt, stirring constantly. Stir in the coconut. Pour over the cake and let cool.
- Combine the remaining 1 1/2 cups sugar, 1/2 cup milk, margarine and chocolate chips in a saucepan. Cook until the chocolate is melted, stirring constantly. Drizzle over the cake. Let stand to cool.
- Chill until serving time.
- Yield: 15 servings.

Approx Per Serving: Cal 609; Prot 6 g; Carbo 94 g; T Fat 27 g; 38% Calories from Fat; Chol 33 mg; Fiber 5 g; Sod 473 mg

—Linda McLain

Fruit Cocktail Cake

1 egg
1¹/2 cups sugar
2 cups flour
1¹/4 teaspoons salt
2 teaspoons baking soda
1 (12-ounce) can fruit cocktail in heavy
  syrup
¹/2 cup packed brown sugar
1 cup chopped pecans
Coconut Frosting

- Beat the egg in a large bowl. Add the sugar; mix well.
- Mix the flour, salt and baking soda together.
- Drain the fruit cocktail, reserving the syrup.
- Add the reserved fruit cocktail syrup and the flour mixture to the sugar mixture; mix well. Stir in the drained fruit cocktail.
- Pour into a buttered 9x12-inch glass cake dish. Spread to cover dish; layer will be thin. Sprinkle brown sugar and pecans over the top.
- Bake at 325 degrees for 45 minutes or until brown and a wooden pick inserted in center comes out clean.
- Poke holes in hot cake with a fork.
- Spread the hot Coconut Frosting over the top of the cake. Cool and cut into squares.
- Garnish each piece with whipped cream.
- Yield: 15 servings.

Coconut Frosting

¹/2 cup butter
1 (5-ounce) can evaporated milk
³/4 cup sugar
1 teaspoon vanilla extract
¹/2 cup coconut

- Melt the butter in a medium saucepan.
- Add evaporated milk, sugar and vanilla; blend well.
- Bring to a boil. Boil for 5 minutes, stirring frequently; remove from heat.
- Stir in the coconut.

Approx Per Serving: Cal 352; Prot 4 g;
Carbo 56 g; T Fat 14 g; 34% Calories from Fat;
Chol 34 mg; Fiber 2 g; Sod 369 mg

—*Patricia Simpson*

Orange Pineapple Cake

1 (2-layer) package orange cake mix
¹/2 cup margarine, softened
¹/2 cup sugar
2 eggs, beaten
¹/3 cup frozen orange juice concentrate,
  thawed
¹/4 teaspoon salt
1 (8-ounce) can crushed pineapple
¹/2 cup chopped pecans
¹/2 cup shredded coconut
2 cups whipping cream
Sweetener to taste

- Prepare and bake the cake mix in a tube pan using the package directions. Cool in the pan for several minutes. Invert onto a wire rack to cool.
- Cream the margarine and sugar in a large mixer bowl.
- Beat in the eggs and the orange juice concentrate. The mixture may appear to be curdled.
- Add the salt, pineapple, pecans and coconut; mix well.
- Cut the cake into 3 layers horizontally.
- Spread the pineapple mixture between cake layers and over the top of the cake.
- Beat the whipping cream until soft peaks form. Sweeten the whipped cream as desired.
- Spread the whipped cream over the top and side of cake.
- Refrigerate for 12 to 24 hours.
- Yield: 16 servings.

Approx Per Serving: Cal 441; Prot 4 g;
Carbo 41 g; T Fat 29 g; 59% Calories from Fat;
Chol 116 mg; Fiber 1 g; Sod 349 mg

—*Susan Landrum*

Three-Layer Lemon Jelly Cake

3 cups flour
1 teaspoon sugar
2 teaspoons cream of tartar
2 cups sugar
1 cup butter, softened
3/4 cup milk
4 eggs
1/4 cup milk
Lemon Filling and Frosting

- Sift the flour, 1 teaspoon sugar and cream of tartar into a mixer bowl.
- Add the remaining 2 cups sugar, butter and 3/4 cup milk. Beat for 2 minutes.
- Add the eggs and remaining 1/4 cup milk; beat for 2 minutes longer.
- Pour into 3 floured 9-inch round cake pans.
- Bake at 350 degrees for 12 to 15 minutes or until the layers test done.
- Cool in the pans for several minutes. Remove to a wire rack to cool completely. Slice each layer horizontally into 2 layers.
- Spread the Lemon Filling and Frosting between the layers and over the top and side of the cake.
- Yield: 12 servings.

Lemon Filling and Frosting

3 eggs, beaten
1 1/2 cups sugar
3 tablespoons butter
Juice and grated peel of 3 lemons

- Combine the eggs, sugar and butter in a double boiler. Stir in the lemon juice and peel.
- Cook over hot water for 30 minutes or until of spreading consistency, stirring frequently.

Approx Per Serving: Cal 563; Prot 8 g; Carbo 85 g; T Fat 22 g; 35% Calories from Fat; Chol 176 mg; Fiber 1 g; Sod 234 mg

Neshoba County Lemon Jelly Cake

I grew up with lemon jelly cake in Phila-delphia, Mississippi. This cake was served whenever we had company, especially when visiting ministers came to our church. It is also found on the tables of the Neshoba County Fair patrons when the fair is in progress in Philadelphia.

—Marjorie P. Bobington

Peanut Butter Cake

1 (2-layer) package yellow butter cake mix
1/2 cup margarine
1 cup sugar
1/2 cup peanut butter
3/4 cup milk
1 teaspoon vanilla extract
2 cups (about) confectioners' sugar
1/2 cup peanut butter

- Prepare and bake the cake mix using the package directions for 2 round cake pans.
- Cool in the pans for several minutes; remove to a wire rack to cool completely. Slice each layer horizontally into 2 layers.
- Combine the margarine, sugar, 1/2 cup peanut butter, milk and vanilla in a saucepan. Cook until thickened, stirring frequently. Let cool. Beat in the confectioners' sugar and the remaining 1/2 cup peanut butter until of spreading consistency.
- Spread between the layers and over the top and side of the cake.
- Yield: 12 servings.

Approx Per Serving: Cal 566; Prot 9 g; Carbo 79 g; T Fat 25 g; 39% Calories from Fat; Chol 42 mg; Fiber 2 g; Sod 525 mg

—Pam Myrick-Motley

Becky's Seven-Up Cake

1/2 cup margarine, softened
1/2 cup shortening
3 cups sugar
5 eggs
3 cups flour
1 cup 7-Up or Sprite
1 teaspoon vanilla extract
1 teaspoon almond or lemon extract

- Cream the margarine, shortening and sugar in a mixer bowl until light and fluffy. Beat in the eggs 1 at a time.
- Add the flour and 7-Up alternately, beating well after each addition. Stir in the flavorings. Pour into a nonstick bundt pan or tube pan.
- Bake at 325 degrees for 1 1/2 hours.
- Yield: 16 servings.

Approx Per Serving: Cal 369; Prot 4 g; Carbo 57 g; T Fat 14 g; 34% Calories from Fat; Chol 66 mg; Fiber 1 g; Sod 88 mg

—*Ruth Calcote*

Oatmeal Cake

1 1/4 cups boiling water
1/2 cup margarine
1 cup rolled oats
1 cup packed light brown sugar
1 cup sugar
1 1/4 cups flour
2 eggs
1 teaspoon baking soda
1 teaspoon cinnamon
1/2 cup margarine
3/4 cup sugar
1 teaspoon vanilla extract
1/4 cup sweetened condensed milk
1 cup chopped pecans

- Mix the boiling water, 1/2 cup margarine and oats in a medium bowl. Let stand for 20 minutes.
- Mix the brown sugar, 1 cup sugar, flour, eggs, baking soda and cinnamon in a large bowl. Stir in the oat mixture. Pour into a nonstick 8x11-inch cake pan.
- Bake at 350 degrees for 35 minutes.
- Bring the remaining 1/2 cup margarine, 3/4 cup sugar, vanilla and condensed milk to a boil in a saucepan. Stir in the pecans. Pour over the hot cake. Place the cake under the broiler and broil until the topping is bubbly and brown.
- Yield: 12 servings.

Approx Per Serving: Cal 478; Prot 5 g; Carbo 64 g; T Fat 24 g; 44% Calories from Fat; Chol 38 mg; Fiber 2 g; Sod 273 mg

—*Nell Rein*

Toasted Pecan Cake

¹/4 cup margarine
2 cups chopped pecans
1 (2-layer) package yellow cake mix
3 eggs
1¹/4 cups water
¹/4 cup vegetable oil
¹/4 cup margarine, softened
1 (1-pound) package confectioners' sugar, sifted
1 teaspoon vanilla extract
4 to 6 tablespoons evaporated milk or light cream

- Melt the ¹/4 cup margarine in a baking sheet with sides. Add the pecans in a single layer. Bake at 350 degrees for 20 to 25 minutes or until the pecans are toasted, stirring frequently.
- Combine the cake mix, eggs, water, oil and half the pecans in a bowl; mix well. Pour into 3 greased 9-inch cake pans.
- Bake at 350 degrees for 25 to 30 minutes or until the layers test done. Cool in the pans for several minutes; remove to a wire rack to cool completely.
- Cream the remaining ¹/4 cup margarine, confectioners' sugar, vanilla and evaporated milk in a mixer bowl until light and fluffy. Stir in the remaining pecans. Spread between the layers and over the top and side of the cake.
- Yield: 12 servings.

Approx Per Serving: Cal 600; Prot 6 g;
Carbo 75 g; T Fat 32 g; 47% Calories from Fat;
Chol 56 mg; Fiber 2 g; Sod 393 mg

—Sally (Mrs. Dick) Molpus
wife of former Secretary of State
of Mississippi

Chocolate Pound Cake

3 cups flour
¹/2 teaspoon salt
¹/2 teaspoon baking powder
¹/4 cup baking cocoa
1 cup butter, softened
¹/2 cup shortening
3 cups sugar
5 eggs, beaten
1 cup milk
1 teaspoon vanilla extract
Confectioners' Sugar Icing

- Sift the flour, salt, baking powder and cocoa together.
- Cream the butter, shortening and sugar in a mixer bowl until light and fluffy. Add the eggs 1 at a time, beating well after each addition. Add the flour mixture and milk alternately to the creamed mixture, beating well after each addition. Beat in the vanilla. Pour into a greased and floured tube pan.
- Bake at 325 degrees for 1 hour and 20 minutes. Cool in the pan on a wire rack for 5 minutes. Invert onto a serving plate. Spread the Confectioners' Sugar Icing over the cooled cake.
- Yield: 16 servings.

Confectioners' Sugar Icing

¹/2 cup margarine, softened
3 tablespoons baking cocoa
1 (1-pound) package confectioners' sugar
¹/4 cup (or more) hot water or hot coffee
1 teaspoon vanilla extract

- Cream the margarine, cocoa and part of the confectioners' sugar in a mixer bowl until light and fluffy. Add the remaining confectioners' sugar gradually, beating well after each addition. Stir in enough hot water to make of spreading consistency. Beat in the vanilla.

Approx Per Serving: Cal 588; Prot 6 g;
Carbo 86 g; T Fat 26 g; 39% Calories from Fat;
Chol 99 mg; Fiber 1 g; Sod 290 mg

—Marian C. Brewer

Aunt Willie's Cream Cheese Pound Cake

▪ ▪ ▪ ▪ ▪ ▪ ▪ ▪ ▪ ▪ ▪ ▪ ▪ ▪ ▪ ▪ ▪ ▪ ▪

1 cup butter, softened
1/2 cup margarine, softened
8 ounces cream cheese, softened
3 cups sugar
6 eggs
3 cups flour
1/8 teaspoon salt, or to taste
2 teaspoons vanilla extract

- Cream the butter, margarine and cream cheese in a mixer bowl until light and fluffy.
- Add the sugar and beat well. Add the eggs 1 at a time, beating well after each addition. Add the flour, salt and vanilla; beat well.
- Pour into a nonstick tube pan or bundt pan. Place the pan in a cold oven.
- Bake at 300 to 325 degrees for 1 1/2 hours or until the cake tests done. Cool in the pan for several minutes. Invert onto a serving plate.
- Yield: 16 servings.

Approx Per Serving: Cal 462; Prot 6 g; Carbo 56 g; T Fat 24 g; 47% Calories from Fat; Chol 126 mg; Fiber 1 g; Sod 267 mg

Willie and Bernice

Some of my fondest childhood memories are of visits to my two maternal great-aunts in Hickory Flat, Mississippi. They lived together in a lovely old white house which was always perfectly spotless and filled with every shade of African violet imaginable. The younger of the two, Aunt Bernice, was a stubborn, outspoken, almost formidable widow. She was quite intelligent and was a retired postmistress. She was plagued with arthritis.

The elder, Aunt Willie, was a spry, tiny little old maid with a jovial spirit and an easygoing personality. She was always busy—never stopping. They were total opposites in every way. I loved them both dearly and remember that they both laughed a lot. Both sisters were blessed with lots of talent. They were musically inclined and they sewed and crocheted. Aunt Bernice did beautiful needlepoint. Aunt Willie was the only person I ever saw tat. She was in her nineties at the time and still did beautiful work.

The two were absolutely the best cooks I have ever known. Meals weren't mere meals— they were feasts. When Aunt Bernice's health made it too difficult for her to prepare meals, she used to complain, "Willie just isn't a good cook!" Aunt Willie certainly had me (and the rest of the family) fooled!

—Melissa Melton Keeney

Grandmother's Pound Cake

3 cups sugar
1 1/2 cups butter, softened
9 eggs, at room temperature
3 cups flour
3/4 teaspoon vanilla extract
3/4 teaspoon lemon extract

- Cream the sugar and butter in a large mixer bowl until light and fluffy. Add 3 of the eggs alternately with 1 cup of the flour at a time, beating well after each addition. Beat in the flavorings. Pour into a greased and floured tube pan.
- Bake at 325 degrees for 1 hour and 15 minutes to 1 hour and 25 minutes or until the cake tests done. Cool in the pan for several minutes. Invert onto a serving plate.
- Yield: 16 servings.

Approx Per Serving: Cal 426; Prot 6 g; Carbo 56 g; T Fat 20 g; 42% Calories from Fat; Chol 166 mg; Fiber 1 g; Sod 212 mg

Summers with My Grandparents

When I was a little girl growing up in Yazoo City, Mississippi, I was surrounded by boys. I had sisters, but I also had four brothers. My parents would let me go visit my maternal grandparents in Kingsport, Tennessee, and I got to stay there all by myself—no brothers! Daddy Roberts, my grandfather, always made me feel very special. He and I were very, very close. Almost daily he would go to the fruit market, and right next door was a dairy bar where he would buy me an ice cream cone.

My grandmother worked for a living as a seamstress so I didn't get to spend as much time with her as I did with Daddy Roberts. I do remember what a wonderful cook she was. She made us special treats such as tea cakes, jam cake, and strawberry rhubarb pie. Mama Roberts' pound cake was a blue ribbon winner

at the Tennessee State Fair one year. She shared some of her recipes with me, and I even watched her prepare some of them so I would know exactly how she made them, but I still don't think they taste like hers.

—Marietta Wilkinson

Prize-Winning Pound Cake

3 1/2 cups cake flour
1/2 teaspoon baking powder
1/8 teaspoon salt
1 cup butter, softened
1/2 cup shortening
3 cups sugar
6 eggs
1 cup milk
2 teaspoons vanilla extract

- Sift the flour, baking powder and salt together.
- Cream the butter, shortening and sugar in a mixer bowl until light and fluffy. Beat in the eggs 1 at a time. Add the flour mixture and milk alternately to the creamed mixture. Beat in the vanilla. Pour into a greased and floured tube pan.
- Bake at 300 degrees for 1 1/2 hours.
- Yield: 16 servings.

Approx Per Serving: Cal 428; Prot 4 g; Carbo 52 g; T Fat 23 g; 48% Calories from Fat; Chol 113 mg; Fiber <1 g; Sod 253 mg

A Yankee Recipe Moves South

This cake won first prize at the Ledyard, Connecticut, Fair in 1966. I have been using it since 1969. For quite a long time, my mother-in-law would come to my house on Saturday with fresh milk, butter, and eggs, and we would make two cakes together—one for me, and one for her to take home. My children loved this practice because they could eat mine and then go next door to her house and help eat hers.

—Jean Berch

Sour Cream Pound Cake

■ ■ ■ ■ ■ ■ ■ ■ ■ ■ ■ ■ ■ ■ ■ ■ ■

3 cups sifted cake flour
1/4 teaspoon baking powder
1 cup butter, softened
3 cups sifted sugar
6 eggs, at room temperature
1/2 cup sour cream
1 tablespoon vanilla extract
1 teaspoon almond extract

- Spray a large bundt pan with nonstick baking spray or grease and flour the pan.
- Sift the flour and baking powder together.
- Cream the butter and sugar in a mixer bowl until light and fluffy. Add the eggs 1 at a time, beating for 1 minute after each addition. Add the flour mixture and the sour cream alternately to the creamed mixture, beating well after each addition. Fold in the flavorings. Pour into the prepared pan.
- Bake at 325 degrees for 1 1/2 hours or until a wooden pick inserted near the center comes out clean.
- Yield: 16 servings.

Approx Per Serving: Cal 359; Prot 4 g; Carbo 52 g; T Fat 15 g; 37% Calories from Fat; Chol 114 mg; Fiber <1 g; Sod 151 mg

—*Theresa Allen*

Ma Ma Coonie's Rust Cake

■ ■ ■ ■ ■ ■ ■ ■ ■ ■ ■ ■ ■ ■ ■ ■ ■

2 1/2 cups flour
2 teaspoons baking soda
1/2 teaspoon salt
1/2 teaspoon cinnamon
1/2 teaspoon ginger
1/2 cup lard
1 cup boiling water
1/2 cup sugar
1 cup molasses
1 egg, beaten
1/4 to 1/2 cup milk
1 cup sugar
Lemon extract to taste

- Sift the flour, baking soda, salt, cinnamon and ginger together.
- Mix the lard and boiling water in a large bowl. Add the sugar and molasses. Add the flour mixture; mix well. Beat in the egg. Pour into a 9x13-inch nonstick cake pan.
- Bake at 350 degrees for 25 to 30 minutes or until a wooden pick inserted near the center comes out clean.
- Bring the milk to a boil in a saucepan. Add the sugar and flavoring. Cook until of a sauce consistency, stirring constantly. Serve with the cake.
- Yield: 15 servings.

Approx Per Serving: Cal 283; Prot 3 g; Carbo 51 g; T Fat 8 g; 24% Calories from Fat; Chol 22 mg; Fiber 1 g; Sod 197 mg

Remembering Ma Ma Coonie

My grandmother, Sarah Lucretia Hutchinson, was called "Coonie" by all who knew her. Her rust cake was handed down by her to me many years ago. It has always been a favorite snack of mine. Coonie would bake, and the aroma had my taste buds going by the time her treats would come out of the oven of her old wood stove. I was always made to feel so special when served this cake warm with a cold glass of milk.

—*Mildred Myrick*

Prunella Cake

1 cup butter, softened
2 cups sugar
3 eggs, beaten
1 cup drained stewed prunes, chopped
2 1/2 cups sifted flour
1 teaspoon baking soda
1 teaspoon baking powder
1/2 teaspoon salt
1/2 teaspoon nutmeg
1/2 teaspoon allspice
1 cup buttermilk
Spiced Prune Frosting

- Cream butter and sugar in a large mixer bowl until light and fluffy. Beat in the eggs.
- Add the prunes; mix well by hand.
- Mix flour, baking soda, baking powder, salt and spices together.
- Add to the prune mixture alternately with the buttermilk, mixing well after each addition. Pour into a greased and floured tube pan or 2 layer cake pans.
- Bake at 350 degrees for 35 to 45 minutes or until cake tests done.
- Cool cake in pan for 10 to 20 minutes. Invert onto a cake plate.
- Frost with Spiced Prune Frosting.
- Yield: 16 servings.

Spiced Prune Frosting

2 tablespoons shortening
3 tablespoons prune juice
2 tablespoons lemon juice
1/2 teaspoon nutmeg
1/2 teaspoon cinnamon
1/2 teaspoon allspice
2 cups confectioners' sugar

- Combine shortening, prune juice, lemon juice and spices in a medium bowl; blend well.
- Add the confectioners' sugar; beat until creamy.

Approx Per Serving: Cal 374; Prot 4 g;
Carbo 59 g; T Fat 14 g; 34% Calories from Fat;
Chol 71 mg; Fiber 2 g; Sod 285 mg

—*Mary Helen Mayers*

Sweet Daddy Cake

3 cups sifted flour
3/4 teaspoon salt
1 tablespoon baking powder
1 1/2 teaspoons cinnamon
1 teaspoon cloves
1 1/2 teaspoons nutmeg
3/4 cup shortening
1 1/2 cups sugar
3/4 cup water
1 teaspoon baking soda
1 (10-ounce) can tomato soup
1 1/2 cups raisins
1 1/2 cups chopped pecans
6 ounces cream cheese, softened
1 egg yolk
3 cups confectioners' sugar
1/8 teaspoon salt
1 teaspoon vanilla or lemon extract

- Sift the flour, 3/4 teaspoon salt, baking powder, cinnamon, cloves and nutmeg together twice.
- Beat the shortening in a mixer bowl until light and fluffy. Add the sugar gradually, beating constantly. Beat in a mixture of the water and baking soda. Add the flour mixture and soup alternately to the creamed mixture, beginning and ending with the flour mixture and beating well after each addition. Fold in the raisins and pecans. Pour into a nonstick tube pan.
- Bake at 350 degrees for 1 hour or until the cake tests done. Cool completely.
- Blend the cream cheese, egg yolk and confectioners' sugar in a mixer bowl, adding the confectioners' sugar 1 cup at a time and beating constantly. Stir in the remaining 1/8 teaspoon salt and vanilla. Spread over the cooled cake.
- Yield: 15 servings.

Approx Per Serving: Cal 532; Prot 5 g;
Carbo 80 g; T Fat 23 g; 38% Calories from Fat;
Chol 27 mg; Fiber 2 g; Sod 423 mg

—*Edith Stewart*

Monster Cookies

12 eggs
2 cups margarine, softened
2 pounds brown sugar
4 cups sugar
3 pounds chunky peanut butter
1 tablespoon vanilla extract
1 tablespoon light corn syrup
18 cups quick-cooking oats
2 tablespoons plus 2 teaspoons baking soda
1 pound "M&M's" Chocolate Candies
1 pound chocolate chips

- Combine the eggs, margarine, brown sugar, sugar, peanut butter, vanilla and corn syrup in a large container; mix well with clean hands (or feet).
- Add the oats and baking soda; mix well. Fold in the candies and chocolate chips.
- Drop by 1/4 cupfuls onto a nonstick cookie sheet.
- Bake at 350 degrees until lightly browned.
- Yield: 75 servings.

Approx Per Serving: Cal 382; Prot 9 g; Carbo 48 g; T Fat 19 g; 43% Calories from Fat; Chol 34 mg; Fiber 4 g; Sod 255 mg

—*Mary Fair*

No-Bake Cookie Candy

2 cups sugar
1/4 cup baking cocoa
1/2 cup milk
1/2 cup margarine
1 teaspoon (or more) light or dark corn syrup
1/2 cup peanut butter
2 cups quick-cooking oats
1 cup coarsely chopped toasted pecans

- Mix the sugar, cocoa, milk and margarine in a saucepan.
- Stir in the corn syrup; the corn syrup will keep the texture smooth and not grainy.
- Bring to a boil. Boil for 2 minutes; remove from the heat.
- Add the peanut butter; mix well. Stir in the oats and pecans.
- Beat quickly with a large spoon.
- Drop by large spoonfuls onto waxed paper. Let stand to cool.
- Yield: 24 servings.

Approx Per Serving: Cal 208; Prot 3 g; Carbo 28 g; T Fat 10 g; 43% Calories from Fat; Chol 0 mg; Fiber 2 g; Sod 71 mg

—*Ruth Stevens*

Swedish Oatmeal Cookies

2 cups flour
1 teaspoon baking soda
1/4 teaspoon salt
2 cups sugar
1 cup butter, softened
1 cup margarine, softened
1 egg
4 cups quick-cooking oats

- Sift the flour, baking soda and salt together.
- Cream the sugar, butter and margarine in a mixer bowl until light and fluffy. Beat in the egg. Add the flour mixture, stirring until well blended. Stir in the oats.
- Drop by half teaspoonfuls onto a nonstick cookie sheet. Flatten with a fork.
- Bake at 350 degrees for 8 to 10 minutes or until lightly browned.
- May sift confectioners' sugar over the warm cookies.
- Yield: 60 servings.

Approx Per Serving: Cal 117; Prot 1 g; Carbo 14 g; T Fat 7 g; 50% Calories from Fat; Chol 12 mg; Fiber 1 g; Sod 91 mg

—Mrs. Ben (Phyllis) Spearman

Pecan Squares

2 eggs
2 cups packed light brown sugar
1 cup vegetable oil
1 1/2 cups flour
2 teaspoons baking powder
1 teaspoon salt
2 teaspoons vanilla extract
2 cups chopped pecans

- Beat the eggs slightly in a bowl. Add the brown sugar and oil; mix well. Add the flour, baking powder and salt; mix well. Stir in the vanilla and pecans.
- Spread the batter in a greased 9x13-inch baking pan.
- Bake at 350 degrees for 35 minutes.
- Cool and cut into squares.
- May bake in a glass baking dish at 325 degrees.
- Yield: 24 servings.

Approx Per Serving: Cal 239; Prot 2 g; Carbo 23 g; T Fat 16 g; 60% Calories from Fat; Chol 18 mg; Fiber 1 g; Sod 128 mg

—Mrs. Bill Oberschmidt

Old-Fashioned Raisin Bars

■ ■ ■ ■ ■ ■ ■ ■ ■ ■ ■ ■ ■ ■ ■ ■ ■ ■

1³/4 cups flour
1/4 teaspoon salt
1 teaspoon baking soda
1 teaspoon cinnamon
1/2 teaspoon nutmeg
1/2 teaspoon allspice
1/4 teaspoon cloves
1 cup raisins
1 cup water
1 egg, beaten
1/2 cup vegetable oil
1 cup sugar
1 cup flaked coconut
1 cup chopped pecans

- Mix the flour, salt, baking soda, cinnamon, nutmeg, allspice and cloves together.
- Bring the raisins, water and egg to a boil in a saucepan. Stir in the oil. Remove from the heat and cool to lukewarm. Stir in the sugar.
- Add the flour mixture to the raisin mixture and mix well.
- Stir in the coconut and pecans; the batter will be thin.
- Pour into a lightly greased 10x15-inch baking pan.
- Bake at 375 degrees for 12 minutes.
- Cool in the pan. Cut into bars.
- May frost as desired or sprinkle with confectioners' sugar.
- Yield: 24 servings.

Approx Per Serving: Cal 177; Prot 2 g; Carbo 23 g; T Fat 9 g; 46% Calories from Fat; Chol 9 mg; Fiber 1 g; Sod 61 mg

Raisin Bars and Graduate School

I found my recipe for Old-Fashioned Raisin Bars thirty-five years ago when my husband was in graduate school. We had three little girls and not much money. This recipe is:

- *inexpensive*
- *easy to make*
- *quick to stir up with one saucepan*
- *quick to get to the oven*
- *versatile and can be doubled easily*
- *easy to freeze*

—*Mrs. Dwight E. Waddell*

Peanut Butter Cookies

■ ■ ■ ■ ■ ■ ■ ■ ■ ■ ■ ■ ■ ■ ■ ■ ■ ■

1 cup shortening
1 cup chunky peanut butter
1 cup packed brown sugar
1 cup sugar
1 teaspoon salt
1 teaspoon vanilla extract
2 teaspoons baking soda
2 eggs, beaten
2¹/2 cups flour

- Combine the shortening, peanut butter, brown sugar, sugar, salt, vanilla, baking soda, eggs and flour in a bowl; mix well. Shape into balls. Place on a greased and lightly floured cookie sheet. Flatten the balls with a fork.
- Bake at 325 degrees for 9 minutes or until browned.
- Yield: 36 servings.

Approx Per Serving: Cal 168; Prot 3 g; Carbo 19 g; T Fat 10 g; 50% Calories from Fat; Chol 12 mg; Fiber 1 g; Sod 145 mg

—*Indy (Mrs. Charles) Whitten*

Sugar Cookies

1 cup butter or margarine, softened
1 cup sugar
1 cup confectioners' sugar
1 cup vegetable oil
2 eggs
4¹/2 cups flour
1 teaspoon cream of tartar
1 teaspoon baking soda
1 teaspoon vanilla extract
¹/2 teaspoon almond extract

- Cream the butter, sugar and confectioners' sugar in a large mixer bowl until light and fluffy. Beat in the oil and eggs. Add the flour, cream of tartar, baking soda and flavorings; beat well.
- Chill the dough for 1 hour. Drop by teaspoonfuls onto a greased cookie sheet or shape the dough into balls and flatten with a glass dipped in tinted or white sugar.
- Bake at 350 degrees for 8 to 12 minutes or until lightly browned.
- May decorate with chopped pecans.
- Yield: 72 servings.

Approx Per Serving: Cal 97; Prot 1 g;
Carbo 10 g; T Fat 6 g; 53% Calories from Fat;
Chol 13 mg; Fiber <1 g; Sod 39 mg

—*Jeanette Guice*

Hebrew Sugar Cookies

2 cups sugar
2 cups butter, softened
4 eggs
1 cup whiskey
4¹/2 to 5 cups flour
3 cups chopped pecans
Confectioners' sugar to taste
Cinnamon to taste

- Cream the sugar and butter in a large mixer bowl until light and fluffy.
- Add the eggs; beat until blended.
- Add the whiskey and flour alternately, using enough flour to make dough of desired consistency.
- For drop cookies: Add enough flour to make a soft dough that can be dropped by teaspoonfuls onto an ungreased cookie sheet.
- For shaped cookies: Add enough flour to make a medium dough that can be shaped into walnut-size balls, flattened slightly and arranged on an ungreased cookie sheet. Dough balls may also be shaped into crescents.
- For rolled cookies: Add enough flour to make a stiff dough that can be rolled to desired thickness on a lightly floured surface. Cut with cookie cutters into desired shapes or with a knife into diamond shapes. Arrange on an ungreased cookie sheet.
- Bake at 350 degrees until cookies are a very light golden color.
- Cool on the cookie sheet for 1 minute. Remove to a wire rack to cool completely.
- Sprinkle the cooled cookies with confectioners' sugar and cinnamon.
- Yield: 120 servings.

Approx Per Serving: Cal 86; Prot 1 g;
Carbo 8 g; T Fat 5 g; 54% Calories from Fat;
Chol 15 mg; Fiber <1 g; Sod 34 mg

—*Doris McDaniel*

Pies & Desserts

Pies & Desserts

Apple Custard Pies

1 (21-ounce) can apple pie filling
2 unbaked (9-inch) pie shells
Cinnamon to taste
1/2 cup packed brown sugar
5 eggs
2 cups sugar
2/3 cup margarine, softened
6 tablespoons flour
2 cups milk
2 teaspoons vanilla extract

- Arrange half the pie filling in each of the pie shells. Sprinkle with the cinnamon and brown sugar.
- Combine the eggs, sugar, margarine, flour, milk and vanilla in a blender container. Process until well mixed. Pour into the prepared pie shells.
- Bake at 350 degrees for 45 minutes or until the pies test done.
- This recipe can also be used for an apple custard; place the apples in a casserole dish and continue with the same directions.
- Yield: 16 servings.

Approx Per Serving: Cal 395; Prot 5 g; Carbo 55 g; T Fat 18 g; 41% Calories from Fat; Chol 70 mg; Fiber 1 g; Sod 265 mg

Apples in the Custard

I developed my apple custard pie recipe from an old-time custard recipe. It is a favorite of all who try it. It is especially good in the fall. One gentleman, after tasting the pie, said, "Who told this woman she could put apples in a custard pie?"

—*Sherra C. Smith*

Fresh Blueberry Pie

3/4 cup sugar
3 tablespoons (heaping) flour
6 tablespoons butter
1 cup water
1 teaspoon vanilla extract
2 cups fresh blueberries
1 (9-inch) graham cracker pie shell

- Combine the sugar, flour, butter, water and vanilla in a saucepan.
- Bring to a boil; remove from the heat and let cool.
- Fold in the blueberries. Pour into the pie shell.
- Chill until serving time. Serve with whipped topping.
- Do not substitute frozen blueberries for fresh in this recipe.
- Yield: 8 servings.

Approx Per Serving: Cal 380; Prot 2 g; Carbo 53 g; T Fat 19 g; 44% Calories from Fat; Chol 23 mg; Fiber 2 g; Sod 322 mg

—*Winifred De Jonge*

Buttermilk Pie

■ ■ ■ ■ ■ ■ ■ ■ ■ ■ ■ ■ ■ ■ ■ ■ ■ ■ ■ ■

2 eggs
1 1/3 cups sugar
1 tablespoon flour
1 1/2 cups buttermilk
1/3 cup melted butter or margarine
1 teaspoon vanilla extract
1/8 teaspoon salt, or to taste
1 unbaked (9-inch) pie shell

- Mix the eggs, sugar and flour in a bowl. Add the buttermilk and butter; mix well. Stir in the vanilla and salt. Pour into the pie shell.
- Bake at 350 degrees for 10 minutes. Reduce the oven temperature to 300 degrees. Bake for 45 minutes longer or until puffy and golden.
- Cool to room temperature before serving; the pie will fall a bit.
- Yield: 8 servings.

Approx Per Serving: Cal 356; Prot 5 g; Carbo 47 g; T Fat 17 g; 43% Calories from Fat; Chol 75 mg; Fiber <1 g; Sod 298 mg

Remembering Grandmother

My grandmother, Lou Hastings Melton, was the quintessential little old lady with a white top-knot on her head and rimless spectacles perched on her nose. She came from a fairly well-to-do family but fell in love with my Granddaddy Charlie, whom she married in 1895. He moved her to an unpainted four-room dog-trot house in the country. Her only request was that he paint her house white. Between farming and raising seven children, they never got around to painting. She never complained and always seemed to be the most contented individual on the face of the earth. My grandfather died in 1961, and she remained alone in the country in her little house, very nearly until her death at 93 in 1967.

I grew up in a large city, but I probably never belonged there. My grandmother's house was always a peaceful haven for me and my two sisters. We would rock on the porch with Grandmother, climb in the gullies with Daddy, or walk in the woods on our own. There was no running water—we bathed in washtubs on the back porch and made visits to the outhouse. We drew drinking water from the well until Mr. Murph, the rooster, fell in. There was no electricity, either. We ate supper by the light of a coal oil lamp. Nevertheless, we ate well.

There are very few recipes for most of the things Grandmother Lou prepared. I feel fortunate to have her buttermilk pie recipe. Her cookbook, for the most part, was in her head. I remember her teacakes and her wonderful homemade buttermilk biscuits. Once, her tabby cat walked across her biscuit dough, leaving paw prints. Completely unruffled, as was always her way, she simply picked the paw prints out of the dough and proceeded to cut out the biscuits. Somehow, my biscuits don't taste the same. I guess it's because I don't have the assistance of an errant gray tabby.

—Sara Melton Starns

Butter Tarts

5 tablespoons butter, softened
2 tablespoons milk or cream
1 cup packed brown sugar
1 egg, beaten
1 teaspoon vanilla extract
1/2 cup currants
4 unbaked miniature pie shells or tart shells

- Combine the butter, milk, brown sugar, egg and vanilla in a bowl.
- Stir in the currants.
- Pour the mixture into the pie shells.
- Bake at 325 degrees for 25 minutes or until set.
- Cool before serving.
- Yield: 4 servings.

Approx Per Serving: Cal 472; Prot 5 g; Carbo 67 g; T Fat 23 g; 42% Calories from Fat; Chol 93 mg; Fiber 3 g; Sod 250 mg

—*Linda Ebbers*

Bride's Pie

1 envelope unflavored gelatin
1/4 cup cold water
1 cup scalded milk
3 egg yolks, beaten
1/2 cup sugar
1/8 teaspoon salt, or to taste
1 teaspoon vanilla extract
3 egg whites, stiffly beaten
1 cup whipping cream, whipped
1 1/2 cups chocolate wafer crumbs
1/2 cup melted butter

- Soften the gelatin in the cold water. Combine the milk and egg yolks in a double boiler. Add the sugar, salt, vanilla and gelatin mixture.
- Cook over hot water until slightly thickened, stirring occasionally. Let stand until cool. Fold in the egg whites and whipped cream.
- Reserve 1/3 cup of the crumbs. Line a 9-inch pie plate with a mixture of the remaining crumbs and the butter. Pour the custard into the crumb crust. Sprinkle with the reserved crumbs. Chill in the refrigerator.
- Yield: 6 servings.

Approx Per Serving: Cal 499; Prot 8 g; Carbo 36 g; T Fat 37 g; 66% Calories from Fat; Chol 208 mg; Fiber 0 g; Sod 397 mg

Bride's Pie Revisited

Bride's Pie is my mother's recipe and was my favorite dessert when growing up. If there is too much of the custard mixture for the pie plate, chill it separately in a bowl. It is delicious with cut-up fruit.

—*Cynthia B. Harper*

Chocolate Candy Pie

1 cup sugar
1/2 cup melted butter
2 eggs
1/2 cup sifted flour
3 tablespoons baking cocoa
1 teaspoon vanilla extract
1/2 cup chopped pecans
1 unbaked (8-inch) pie shell

- Mix the sugar and butter in a bowl. Add the eggs; mix well.
- Add the flour and cocoa and blend well. Stir in the vanilla and pecans. Pour into the pie shell.
- Bake at 325 degrees for 25 minutes.
- Top with ice cream or whipped topping.
- This freezes well and is best served slightly frozen.
- Yield: 8 servings.

Approx Per Serving: Cal 403; Prot 5 g;
Carbo 43 g; T Fat 25 g; 54% Calories from Fat;
Chol 84 mg; Fiber 2 g; Sod 242 mg

—Mrs. Paul D. (Fay) Harris

Chocolate Pie

1 cup sugar
2 tablespoons self-rising flour
3 tablespoons baking cocoa
2 cups milk
3 egg yolks, lightly beaten
2 tablespoons butter
1 teaspoon vanilla extract
1 baked (9-inch) pie shell
3 egg whites
6 tablespoons sugar
1 teaspoon vanilla extract

- Mix the 1 cup sugar, flour and cocoa in a double boiler. Add enough of the milk to mix well; stir in the remaining milk and egg yolks. Add the butter.
- Cook over simmering water over medium heat until thickened. Stir in 1 teaspoon vanilla. Pour into the pie crust.
- Beat the egg whites at high speed in a mixer bowl until soft peaks form. Add the remaining 6 tablespoons sugar gradually, beating constantly until stiff peaks form. Beat in 1 teaspoon vanilla. Spread over the pie filling.
- Bake at 375 degrees until the meringue is browned.
- Yield: 8 servings.

Approx Per Serving: Cal 354; Prot 6 g;
Carbo 51 g; T Fat 15 g; 37% Calories from Fat;
Chol 96 mg; Fiber 1 g; Sod 230 mg

—Hattie Berch

Light Icebox Pie Squares

2³/4 cups graham cracker crumbs
1/4 cup melted margarine
1 (5-ounce) can evaporated skim milk
1 cup sugar
Juice of 3 lemons
1/4 cup graham cracker crumbs

- Mix the 2³/4 cups crumbs with the margarine. Press onto a baking sheet.
- Place the evaporated milk in the freezer until partially frozen. Beat in a mixer bowl until thickened. Add the sugar and lemon juice gradually. Spread over the crust. Sprinkle with the remaining 1/4 cup crumbs.
- Freeze for 2 to 3 hours or until firm. Cut into squares.
- Yield: 10 servings.

Approx Per Serving: Cal 285; Prot 4 g; Carbo 50 g; T Fat 8 g; 26% Calories from Fat; Chol 1 mg; Fiber 1 g; Sod 288 mg

—*Mildred Myrick*

Oatmeal Pie

1/2 cup margarine or butter, softened
2/3 cup sugar
3 eggs
2/3 cup light corn syrup
1 teaspoon vanilla extract
1 teaspoon almond extract
2/3 cup rolled oats
1 unbaked (9-inch) pie shell

- Combine the margarine, sugar, eggs, corn syrup and flavorings in a bowl. Stir in the oats.
- Pour into the pie shell.
- Bake at 350 degrees for 45 minutes or until browned and a knife inserted near the center comes out clean.
- May be baked in 8 miniature pie shells. Freezes well.
- Yield: 8 servings.

Approx Per Serving: Cal 416; Prot 5 g; Carbo 53 g; T Fat 22 g; 45% Calories from Fat; Chol 80 mg; Fiber 1 g; Sod 313 mg

Copiah County Oatmeal Pie

When I was Dean of Women at Copiah-Lincoln Junior College, now Copiah-Lincoln Community College, a student brought me an oatmeal pie. It was so good that I asked for the recipe. Oatmeal pie is a favorite for me to take to the sick or a new neighbor.

—*Frances McRee Oberschmidt*

Mandarin Orange Pies

1 (14-ounce) can sweetened condensed milk
1/4 cup orange-flavored breakfast drink mix
2 cups sour cream
8 ounces whipped topping
1 (16-ounce) can mandarin oranges, drained
2 (9-inch) graham cracker crumb pie shells

- Combine the condensed milk, drink mix, sour cream, whipped topping and mandarin oranges in the order listed in a bowl and mix gently.
- Spoon the mixture into the pie shells. Chill until set.
- Garnish with additional whipped topping, mandarin oranges and mint leaves.
- Yield: 12 servings.

Approx Per Serving: Cal 554; Prot 7 g; Carbo 69 g; T Fat 29 g; 46% Calories from Fat; Chol 28 mg; Fiber 1 g; Sod 379 mg

—Linda Jenkins

Peach Pie

1/2 cup margarine
1 cup milk
1 cup sugar
1 cup self-rising flour
1 (16-ounce) can peaches

- Melt the margarine in a pie plate. Mix the milk, sugar and flour in a bowl. Pour over the margarine; do not stir. Pour the peaches over the batter; do not stir.
- Bake at 350 degrees until browned.
- Yield: 8 servings.

Approx Per Serving: Cal 315; Prot 3 g; Carbo 49 g; T Fat 13 g; 35% Calories from Fat; Chol 4 mg; Fiber 1 g; Sod 351 mg

—Hazel Hogue

Caramel Pecan Pie

36 vanilla caramels
1/4 cup water
1/4 cup margarine
3/4 cup sugar
3 eggs, beaten
1/2 teaspoon vanilla extract
1/4 teaspoon salt
1 cup pecan halves
1 unbaked (9-inch) pie shell

- Combine the caramels, water and margarine in a saucepan. Cook over low heat until the caramels and margarine are melted, stirring until smooth.
- Mix the sugar, eggs, vanilla and salt in a bowl. Add the caramel sauce gradually, mixing well. Stir in the pecans. Pour into the pie shell.
- Bake at 350 degrees for 45 to 50 minutes or until a knife inserted near the center comes out clean.
- Yield: 8 servings.

Approx Per Serving: Cal 498; Prot 7 g; Carbo 60 g; T Fat 27 g; 48% Calories from Fat; Chol 82 mg; Fiber 2 g; Sod 368 mg

—Donna Evans

Mississippi Pecan Pie

1 cup light corn syrup
1 cup packed light brown sugar
1/3 cup melted butter
1/3 teaspoon salt
1 teaspoon vanilla extract
3 eggs, slightly beaten
1 unbaked (9-inch) pie shell
1 cup (heaping) pecans

- Combine the corn syrup, brown sugar, butter, salt, vanilla and eggs in a medium bowl; mix well.
- Pour into the pie shell. Sprinkle with the pecans.
- Bake at 350 degrees for 45 minutes or until the filling is set in the center.
- Yield: 6 servings.

Approx Per Serving: Cal 686; Prot 7 g; Carbo 89 g; T Fat 37 g; 46% Calories from Fat; Chol 134 mg; Fiber 2 g; Sod 495 mg

—*Louise "Peggy" Melton Bookout*

Strawberry Pie

3/4 cup sugar
2 tablespoons cornstarch
1/2 cup water
1 (3-ounce) package strawberry gelatin
2 cups strawberries
1 baked (9-inch) pie shell

- Combine the sugar, cornstarch and water in a saucepan. Cook until the mixture is clear. Stir in the gelatin.
- Arrange the strawberries in the pie crust. Pour the gelatin mixture over the strawberries. Serve with whipped topping.
- Yield: 8 servings.

Approx Per Serving: Cal 253; Prot 2 g; Carbo 43 g; T Fat 8 g; 29% Calories from Fat; Chol 0 mg; Fiber 2 g; Sod 149 mg

—*Edith Soup*

Chocolate Candy

35 to 40 soda crackers
1 cup butter or margarine
1 cup packed brown sugar
1 1/2 cups semisweet chocolate chips
1 1/2 cups chopped walnuts

- Line a 10x15-inch baking pan with foil; spray the foil with nonstick cooking spray. Arrange the crackers in rows on the foil.
- Combine the butter and brown sugar in a saucepan. Cook until the butter is melted and the sugar is dissolved. Bring to a boil. Boil for 3 minutes. Pour over the crackers and spread evenly until the crackers are completely covered.
- Bake at 350 degrees for 5 minutes. The crackers will float. Remove and turn off the oven.
- Sprinkle the chocolate chips and walnuts over the baked mixture. Return to the oven. Let stand in the oven for 5 minutes. Press down with a spatula sprayed with nonstick cooking spray. Cut while warm.
- Yield: 24 servings.

Approx Per Serving: Cal 217; Prot 2 g; Carbo 19 g; T Fat 16 g; 63% Calories from Fat; Chol 21 mg; Fiber 1 g; Sod 148 mg

Candy for Hospice

I baked my chocolate candy for the Ole Brook Festival in Brookhaven, Mississippi, to be sold at a booth where the proceeds were to benefit Hospice of Central Mississippi. We sold out, and people came back the next day asking for more!

—*Peggy Castilow*

George Washington Chocolate Bonbons

1 cup butter, softened
2 (1-pound) packages confectioners' sugar
2/3 cup sweetened condensed milk
1 teaspoon vanilla extract
1 cup chopped pecans
8 ounces unsweetened chocolate
1/3 cake paraffin

- Cream the butter, confectioners' sugar and condensed milk in a mixer bowl.
- Stir in the vanilla and 1 cup pecans.
- Chill until firm.
- Shape into balls; place on a tray.
- Chill, loosely covered, until firm.
- Melt the chocolate and the paraffin in a double boiler over hot water. Dip the chilled candy balls into the chocolate mixture to coat.
- Place on a surface lined with waxed paper. Do not allow candies to touch. Let stand until firm.
- May top with pecan halves.
- Yield: 48 servings.

Approx Per Serving: Cal 167; Prot 1 g; Carbo 23 g; T Fat 9 g; 47% Calories from Fat; Chol 12 mg; Fiber 1 g; Sod 45 mg

—Jan Szalay

Grammy's Microwave Peanut Brittle

1 1/2 cups shelled raw peanuts
1 cup sugar
1/2 cup light corn syrup
1/8 teaspoon salt, or to taste
1 tablespoon margarine
1 teaspoon vanilla extract
1 teaspoon baking soda

- Mix the peanuts, sugar, corn syrup and salt in a large glass bowl.
- Microwave on High for 7 to 9 minutes or until the mixture is bubbling and the peanuts are browned.
- Stir in the margarine and vanilla quickly.
- Microwave for 2 to 3 minutes longer or until the mixture is heated through.
- Add the baking soda quickly, stirring just until the mixture is foamy.
- Pour onto a greased baking sheet or pizza pan.
- Let cool for 15 minutes or longer.
- Break up with the back of a spoon.
- Store in an airtight container.
- Yield: 24 servings.

Approx Per Serving: Cal 108; Prot 2 g; Carbo 15 g; T Fat 5 g; 39% Calories from Fat; Chol 0 mg; Fiber 1 g; Sod 61 mg

—Lynn Manker

Frozen Almond Crunch

■ ■ ■ ■ ■ ■ ■ ■ ■ ■ ■ ■ ■ ■ ■ ■ ■ ■ ■ ■

2/3 cup sliced almonds
1/2 cup sugar
1/2 cup butter or margarine
1 tablespoon flour
2 tablespoons milk
1/2 gallon vanilla ice cream, softened

■ Combine the almonds, sugar, butter, flour and milk in a saucepan.
■ Bring to a boil over medium heat. Spread in a foil-lined 10x15-inch jelly roll pan.
■ Bake at 350 degrees for 7 minutes or until the mixture is light golden brown; do not overbake. Cool in the pan.
■ Remove from the foil and crumble. Sprinkle half the crumbs in a 10-inch springform pan.
■ Spoon ice cream evenly over the top. Sprinkle with the remaining crumbs, pressing down lightly with the back of a spoon.
■ Freeze for 8 hours or until firm.
■ Serve with a dark chocolate sauce.
■ Yield: 12 servings.

Approx Per Serving: Cal 312; Prot 4 g; Carbo 31 g; T Fat 20 g; 56% Calories from Fat; Chol 60 mg; Fiber 1 g; Sod 150 mg

—Mrs. Charles R. (Patricia) Jacobs

Quick Apple Crunch

■ ■ ■ ■ ■ ■ ■ ■ ■ ■ ■ ■ ■ ■ ■ ■ ■ ■ ■ ■

1 (21-ounce) can apple pie filling
1 (1-layer) package yellow cake mix
1/4 cup margarine

■ Spread the pie filling in a 1 1/2-quart baking dish.
■ Pour the cake mix into a bowl; stir the dry mix to reduce lumps. Cut in the margarine until crumbly.
■ Sprinkle over the pie filling.
■ Bake at 400 degrees for 20 minutes.
■ Serve hot with ice cream or whipped topping.
■ Yield: 6 servings.

Approx Per Serving: Cal 536; Prot 4 g; Carbo 93 g; T Fat 18 g; 29% Calories from Fat; Chol 2 mg; Fiber 2 g; Sod 692 mg

—Ann Catt

Apple Rice Crisp

2 cups cooked rice
1 (20-ounce) can sliced apples
1/2 cup packed brown sugar
1 tablespoon lemon juice
1/2 teaspoon cinnamon
1/4 teaspoon salt
3/4 cup flour
1/2 cup packed brown sugar
6 tablespoons butter or margarine
1/2 cup chopped pecans

- Combine the rice, apples, 1/2 cup brown sugar, lemon juice, cinnamon and salt in a buttered 7x11-inch baking dish.
- Mix the flour and remaining 1/2 cup brown sugar in a bowl. Cut in the butter until crumbly. Stir in the pecans. Sprinkle over the rice mixture.
- Bake at 350 degrees for 30 minutes.
- Serve warm.
- Yield: 12 servings.

Approx Per Serving: Cal 245; Prot 2 g; Carbo 39 g; T Fat 10 g; 34% Calories from Fat; Chol 16 mg; Fiber 2 g; Sod 111 mg

—*Mary Bell*

Apple Fritters

1 cup sifted flour
1/4 teaspoon salt
2 egg yolks
1/3 cup water
1/3 cup evaporated milk
1 tablespoon lemon juice
1 tablespoon melted butter
2 egg whites
1/8 teaspoon salt
6 medium apples, peeled, cored, cut into
    1/2-inch slices
Shortening for deep-frying
2 tablespoons cinnamon
2 tablespoons sugar

- Sift the flour and 1/4 teaspoon salt together. Beat the egg yolks, water and evaporated milk in a bowl. Add the lemon juice and butter; mix well. Stir in the flour mixture.
- Beat the egg whites with the remaining 1/8 teaspoon salt in a mixer bowl until stiff peaks form. Fold into the batter. Dip the apples into the batter.
- Heat the shortening to 350 degrees in a skillet. Add the apples. Deep-fry until apples are a delicate brown; drain on paper towels. Sprinkle the apples with a mixture of cinnamon and sugar.
- May add 2 tablespoons sugar to the flour mixture; may substitute 2/3 cup water for the 1/3 cup evaporated milk; may soak the apples for 2 hours in a mixture of lemon juice and confectioners' sugar before deep-frying; may substitute other fruits for the apples.
- Yield: 6 servings.

Approx Per Serving: Cal 250; Prot 6 g; Carbo 38 g; T Fat 9 g; 32% Calories from Fat; Chol 90 mg; Fiber 4 g; Sod 228 mg
Nutritional information does not include shortening for deep-frying.

—*Martha Jenkins*

Chocolate Coffee Frozen Dessert

■ ■ ■ ■ ■ ■ ■ ■ ■ ■ ■ ■ ■ ■ ■ ■ ■ ■ ■ ■

1³/4 cups vanilla wafer crumbs
1/4 cup melted butter
2¹/2 ounces unsweetened chocolate
1/2 cup butter
2 cups sifted confectioners' sugar
1 teaspoon vanilla extract
3 egg yolks
3 egg whites, stiffly beaten
1 cup chopped pecans
2 quarts coffee ice cream
1/4 cup vanilla wafer crumbs

■ Mix the 1³/4 cups crumbs and 1/4 cup butter in a bowl. Press into a 9x13-inch dish.
■ Combine the chocolate and remaining 1/2 cup butter in a saucepan. Cook over low heat until melted, stirring frequently; remove from the heat.
■ Add the confectioners' sugar and vanilla. Beat for 2 minutes at medium speed.
■ Add the egg yolks, beating until smooth. Fold in the egg whites.
■ Spread over the crumb mixture. Sprinkle with the pecans.
■ Spread the ice cream over the pecans.
■ Sprinkle with the remaining crumbs.
■ Freeze overnight.
■ Yield: 12 servings.

Approx Per Serving: Cal 524; Prot 7 g;
Carbo 52 g; T Fat 35 g; 57% Calories from Fat;
Chol 131 mg; Fiber 2 g; Sod 250 mg

—*Betty L. Johnston*

Chocolate Custard Tipsy Trifle

■ ■ ■ ■ ■ ■ ■ ■ ■ ■ ■ ■ ■ ■ ■ ■ ■ ■ ■ ■

1 (2-layer) package devil's food cake mix
2/3 cup sugar
1/4 cup baking cocoa
1/8 teaspoon salt
3 eggs, beaten
2 cups milk
1/4 to 1/2 cup rum
1 (21-ounce) can cherry pie filling
1 cup whipping cream
2 tablespoons confectioners' sugar
1/4 cup toasted sliced almonds

■ Prepare and bake the cake mix using the package directions. Cut the cooled cake into 1/2-inch slices.
■ Combine the sugar, cocoa and salt in the top of a double boiler. Add a mixture of the eggs and milk gradually, mixing well. Bring the water in the double boiler to a boil; reduce the heat to low. Cook the chocolate mixture over the simmering water until thickened, stirring occasionally. Let stand until cool.
■ Line the bottom of a large bowl or trifle dish with half the cake slices. Sprinkle with 2 to 4 tablespoons of the rum. Spoon half the pie filling over the cake slices. Top with half the chocolate custard. Repeat the procedure with the remaining cake, rum, pie filling and custard. Cover and chill thoroughly.
■ Beat the whipping cream in a mixer bowl until foamy. Add the confectioners' sugar gradually, beating until soft peaks form. Spread over the custard. Sprinkle with the almonds.
■ Yield: 16 servings.

Approx Per Serving: Cal 375; Prot 7 g;
Carbo 47 g; T Fat 20 g; 43% Calories from Fat;
Chol 106 mg; Fiber 1 g; Sod 332 mg

—*Gerry Ann Houston, M.D.*

Delicous Chocolate Dessert

1 cup flour
1/2 cup margarine or light butter, softened
1 cup chopped pecans
8 ounces light whipped topping
1/2 cup confectioners' sugar
8 ounces fat-free cream cheese, softened
2 (4-ounce) packages fat-free instant
  chocolate pudding mix
3 cups low-fat milk

- Cream the flour and margarine in a mixer
  bowl until light and fluffy. Stir in the
  pecans. Press into a 3-quart baking dish.
  Bake at 350 degrees for 8 to 10 minutes or
  until light brown. Let stand until cool.
- Combine 1½ cups of the whipped topping,
  confectioners' sugar and cream cheese in a
  mixer bowl. Beat until smooth. Spread over
  the baked layer.
- Mix the pudding mix with the milk in a
  bowl. Beat until thick and smooth. Spread
  over the cream cheese layer.
- Spread the remaining whipped topping
  over the pudding mixture. Garnish with
  shaved chocolate.
- Chill for 12 to 24 hours before serving.
- Yield: 10 servings.

Approx Per Serving: Cal 438; Prot 8 g;
Carbo 47 g; T Fat 25 g; 50% Calories from Fat;
Chol 9 mg; Fiber 1 g; Sod 566 mg

—*Jane Breeland*

Chocolate Mousse

2 cups semisweet chocolate chips
10 tablespoons unsalted butter
8 egg yolks
1/4 cup dark rum
8 egg whites

- Combine the chocolate chips and butter
  in a double boiler. Heat over hot water
  until melted.
- Add the egg yolks 1 at a time, mixing well
  after each addition.
- Remove from the heat and let stand for
  10 minutes.
- Stir in the rum.
- Beat the egg whites in a mixer bowl until
  stiff peaks form. Fold in the chocolate
  mixture. Spoon into a serving dish.
- Cover with foil and freeze until firm.
  Remove from the freezer to the refrigerator.
  Chill for 8 hours before serving.
- Top with whipped cream.
- Yield: 8 servings.

Approx Per Serving: Cal 422; Prot 8 g;
Carbo 28 g; T Fat 32 g; 64% Calories from Fat;
Chol 251 mg; Fiber 3 g; Sod 69 mg

—*Sally Fletcher*

Icebox Coconut Trifle

2 (4-ounce) packages instant coconut cream
  pudding mix
2³⁄₄ cups skim milk
1 teaspoon coconut extract
16 ounces light whipped topping
1 (16-ounce) angel food cake, torn into
  bite-size pieces
¹⁄₄ cup flaked coconut

- Mix the pudding mix, skim milk and
  flavoring in a bowl.
- Blend in half the whipped topping until
  thickened and smooth. Pour the pudding
  mixture over the cake pieces in a large bowl,
  stirring until all the cake is well coated.
- Pour into a 1¹⁄₂-quart decorative glass bowl.
- Top with the remaining whipped topping.
- Sprinkle with the coconut.
- Chill for 8 to 10 hours.
- Yield: 8 servings.

Approx Per Serving: Cal 478; Prot 7 g;
Carbo 76 g; T Fat 17 g; 32% Calories from Fat;
Chol 2 mg; Fiber <1 g; Sod 701 mg

—*Carla Walsh*

Crescent Delights

12 ounces cream cheese, softened
1 cup sugar
2 (8-count) cans crescent rolls, at room
  temperature
¹⁄₄ cup sugar
1 cup chopped pecans

- Mix the cream cheese and 1 cup sugar in a
  bowl until smooth. Spread half the roll
  dough in a 9x13-inch baking pan sprayed
  with nonstick cooking spray. Spread with
  the cream cheese mixture. Top with the
  remaining roll dough. Sprinkle with the
  remaining ¹⁄₄ cup sugar and the pecans.
- Bake at 325 degrees for 30 minutes.
- Yield: 15 servings.

Approx Per Serving: Cal 287; Prot 4 g;
Carbo 33 g; T Fat 17 g; 50% Calories from Fat;
Chol 28 mg; Fiber 1 g; Sod 334 mg

—*Angie Spencer*

Low-Fat Cheesecake

¹⁄₂ cup low-fat granola
2 cups low-fat cottage cheese
8 ounces light cream cheese, softened
6 tablespoons flour
1 cup plus 2 tablespoons sugar
¹⁄₄ teaspoon salt
4 egg whites
1 teaspoon vanilla extract
2 tablespoons baking cocoa
2 tablespoons sugar
1 tablespoon 1% milk

- Process the granola in a food processor
  until slightly ground.
- Spray an 8-inch springform pan with
  nonstick cooking spray. Coat the pan with
  the granola.
- Combine the cottage cheese and cream
  cheese in the food processor. Process until
  smooth.
- Add the flour, 1 cup plus 2 tablespoons
  sugar, salt, egg whites and vanilla. Process
  until smooth.
- Blend ¹⁄₃ cup of the mixture with the
  cocoa, 2 tablespoons sugar and milk in a
  small bowl.
- Pour the remaining cottage cheese mixture
  into the prepared pan.
- Spoon the chocolate mixture over the top.
  Swirl gently to marbleize.
- Place the springform pan on a baking sheet.
- Bake at 325 degrees for 50 minutes. Turn
  off oven.
- Let the cheesecake stand in the oven with
  the oven door ajar for 1 hour.
- Place the cheesecake on a wire rack to cool
  completely.
- Loosen the cheesecake from the side of the
  pan. Place on a serving plate and remove
  the side of the pan.
- Yield: 12 servings.

Approx Per Serving: Cal 196; Prot 9 g;
Carbo 30 g; T Fat 4 g; 20% Calories from Fat;
Chol 14 mg; Fiber <1 g; Sod 281 mg

—*Amy Morgan*

Daisy Roll

1/2 pound marshmallows, cut into quarters
2 tablespoons sugar
1 cup light cream
1 cup chopped pecans
3 cups chopped dates
2 1/2 cups graham cracker crumbs

- Mix the marshmallows, sugar and cream in a bowl. Let stand for 10 minutes. Add the pecans, dates and 2 cups of the crumbs; mix well with a spoon.
- Shape into a 3x3-inch log. Roll in the remaining 1/2 cup crumbs. Wrap tightly in waxed paper and chill for 24 hours.
- Cut into slices. Serve with whipped cream and cherries.
- Yield: 12 servings.

Approx Per Serving: Cal 421; Prot 4 g; Carbo 72 g; T Fat 16 g; 32% Calories from Fat; Chol 22 mg; Fiber 5 g; Sod 168 mg

—*Mrs. Jeanette N. Haag*

Peach Crepes

1/2 cup flour
1 egg
3 tablespoons amaretto-flavored nondairy creamer
1/2 cup skim milk
1/8 teaspoon ground nutmeg
1 teaspoon vanilla extract
Peach Sauce

- Place the flour in a large bowl and make a well in the center. Add the egg, creamer and skim milk, whisking constantly until the batter is smooth and free of lumps. Whisk in the nutmeg and vanilla.
- Cover and let stand for 30 minutes.
- Preheat an 8-inch nonstick crepe pan or a small heavy nonstick skillet for 1 minute over medium-high heat. Spray twice with a light vegetable oil cooking spray.
- Spoon just enough batter into the pan to form a thin layer over the bottom; tilt the pan to spread the batter evenly.

- Cook for 1 to 2 minutes or just until the edge of the crepe is firm and begins to separate from the bottom. Flip the crepe with a spatula. Cook for 1 to 2 minutes longer or until golden brown. Remove the crepe to a sheet of waxed paper.
- Continue the process until 8 crepes have been prepared.
- Lay 1 crepe on each individual serving plate. Mound 1/3 cup of the peach slices on the bottom half of each; flip the top of each crepe over. Spoon 1 tablespoon of the peach syrup over each crepe. Sprinkle with cinnamon and orange zest.
- May top each crepe with a crystallized violet and scatter a few blueberries around the crepe.
- Yield: 8 servings.

Peach Sauce

2 cups freshly squeezed orange juice
2 tablespoons orange liqueur
8 peaches, peeled, thinly sliced
1 teaspoon honey
1 teaspoon ground cinnamon
1 teaspoon orange zest

- Combine the orange juice, liqueur, peaches and honey in a medium skillet.
- Cook for 10 minutes or until the liquid is thick and syrupy.
- Partially drain the peach slices and reserve the syrup.

Approx Per Serving: Cal 143; Prot 3 g; Carbo 28 g; T Fat 2 g; 9% Calories from Fat; Chol 27 mg; Fiber 2 g; Sod 19 mg

—*Holly Perkins*

Mary Ann Mobley's Peach Cobbler

▪ ▪ ▪ ▪ ▪ ▪ ▪ ▪ ▪ ▪ ▪ ▪ ▪ ▪ ▪ ▪ ▪ ▪ ▪

1 cup sugar
6 to 8 very ripe large peaches, peeled, thinly
    sliced
1/2 cup butter
1 cup self-rising flour
1 cup sugar
1 cup milk

- Pour the 1 cup sugar over the peaches in a plastic bowl; stir well. Cover tightly and chill for 2 hours.
- Place the butter in a 3-inch-deep rectangular glass baking dish. Place in a 400-degree oven until the butter melts.
- Combine the flour, remaining 1 cup sugar and milk in a bowl; beat well with a whisk. Pour over the melted butter; do not mix. Spoon the peaches over the batter; do not mix.
- Bake at 400 degrees until the top is golden brown (the flour mixture comes up around the peaches). Serve hot.
- May substitute one 16-ounce can sliced peaches for the fresh peaches; use only a small amount of the canned peach juice.
- Yield: 8 servings.

Approx Per Serving: Cal 416; Prot 3 g;
Carbo 75 g; T Fat 13 g; 27% Calories from Fat;
Chol 35 mg; Fiber 2 g; Sod 331 mg

Southern Hospitality Made Simple

My husband, Gary Collins, and I were performing in "Cabaret" at Delta State University in Cleveland, Mississippi, several years ago. Our good friend Leon Kamien invited us to dinner and served cobbler for dessert. Being a true southerner, I immediately fell in love with the dish. Leon and his friend Charles are no longer with us, but their memories live on.

Now, if guests suddenly appear, I run in the kitchen and prepare this cobbler—people think I've been slaving. It's so simple, anyone can prepare it.

My schedule is such that I don't have time to prepare long, involved dishes, but I love to entertain and have friends over. This is a wonderful dessert I can cook in ten minutes if someone drops by.

I always have everything on hand—butter, milk, sugar, self-rising flour—and if I don't have fresh peaches, I use the canned peaches, and it tastes exactly the same.

You serve it hot. I just dish it out and put vanilla ice cream on top or serve it as it is. It's not bad cold, either!

—Mary Ann Mobley
actress, former Miss Mississippi
and Miss America

Low-Fat Frozen Tiramisù

2/3 cup sifted confectioners' sugar
8 ounces reduced-fat cream cheese, softened
1 cup reduced-calorie whipped topping
1/2 cup sugar
1/4 cup water
3 egg whites
1/2 cup hot water
1 tablespoon sugar
1 tablespoon instant espresso granules
2 tablespoons coffee-flavored liqueur
20 ladyfingers, split lengthwise
1/2 teaspoon baking cocoa

- Beat the confectioners' sugar and cream cheese at high speed in a mixer bowl until well blended. Fold in the whipped topping.
- Combine the 1/2 cup sugar, 1/4 cup water and egg whites in a double boiler over simmering water. Beat at high speed with a mixer until stiff peaks form. Fold 1/4 of the egg white mixture into the cream cheese mixture. Fold in the remaining egg white mixture and set aside.
- Combine the hot water, remaining 1 tablespoon sugar, instant espresso and liqueur in a bowl; mix well.
- Arrange 20 ladyfinger halves split side up on the bottom of an 8x8-inch dish. Drizzle with half the espresso mixture. Repeat with the remaining ladyfinger halves and espresso mixture. Spread with the cream cheese mixture. Sprinkle with the cocoa.
- Place 1 wooden pick in each corner and in the center of the dessert to keep the plastic wrap from sticking to the cream cheese mixture. Cover with plastic wrap and freeze for 2 hours before serving.
- Yield: 8 servings.

Approx Per Serving: Cal 291; Prot 7 g;
Carbo 45 g; T Fat 8 g; 26% Calories from Fat;
Chol 117 mg; Fiber <1 g; Sod 146 mg

—*Nicky Lee*

Microwave Cherry Cheesecake Cups

8 ounces cream cheese, softened
1/3 cup sugar
1 egg
1 tablespoon lemon juice
1/2 teaspoon vanilla extract
6 vanilla wafers
1 (20-ounce) can cherry pie filling

- Beat the cream cheese in a mixer bowl until light and fluffy.
- Add the sugar, egg, lemon juice and vanilla; beat until smooth and creamy.
- Line microwave-safe muffin cups with paper cupcake liners. Place a vanilla wafer in each cup.
- Spoon the cream cheese mixture into the prepared cups, filling each 2/3 full.
- Microwave on Medium for 41/2 minutes or until almost firm, turning once.
- Let stand at room temperature until cooled.
- Top with cherry pie filling.
- Yield: 6 servings.

Approx Per Serving: Cal 318; Prot 5 g;
Carbo 42 g; T Fat 15 g; 43% Calories from Fat;
Chol 79 mg; Fiber 1 g; Sod 184 mg

Loretta Ward

Men in the Kitchen

Men in the Kitchen

Photograph on preceding page by Steve Colston Photography.
A sunny summer's day in Madison County, Mississippi

Taco Soup

2 pounds ground beef
1 medium onion, chopped
1 envelope taco seasoning mix
1 envelope ranch-style salad dressing mix
2 (16-ounce) cans stewed tomatoes
1 (4-ounce) can green chiles
1 (16-ounce) can whole-kernel yellow corn
1 (16-ounce) can red kidney beans
1 (15-ounce) can jalapeño pinto beans
1 (15-ounce) can pinto beans

- Brown the ground beef with the onion in a skillet; drain. Stir in the seasoning mix and salad dressing mix. Add the undrained tomatoes, green chiles, corn and beans. Cook over low to medium heat for 30 to 60 minutes or until heated through.
- May top servings with dollops of sour cream. May chill overnight and reheat the next day for even better blending of flavors.
- Yield: 6 servings.

Approx Per Serving: Cal 640; Prot 48 g; Carbo 64 g; T Fat 23 g; 31% Calories from Fat; Chol 112 mg; Fiber 10 g; Sod 2630 mg

—*John C. Fletcher*

Beef Roast with Chili-Horseradish Glaze

2 cups dry red wine
1 cup water
1 onion, finely chopped
3 tablespoons Worcestershire sauce
2 teaspoons chili powder
1½ teaspoons dried marjoram
½ teaspoon liquid red pepper seasoning
1 (5- to 6-pound) sirloin tip roast, tied
3 tablespoons chili sauce
2 tablespoons dry red wine
1 tablespoon horseradish
½ teaspoon salt
3 tablespoons flour
⅓ cup water

- Combine the 2 cups wine, 1 cup water, onion, Worcestershire sauce, chili powder, marjoram and pepper seasoning in a large sealable plastic bag. Add the beef and seal. Place on a plate. Marinate in the refrigerator for 4 hours to overnight.
- Combine the chili sauce, remaining 2 tablespoons wine, horseradish and salt in a small dish.
- Prepare the grill with hot coals around sides. Pour the marinade from the plastic bag into the foil drip pan. Place the pan in the center of the grill. Position the grill rack 6 inches above the coals. Place the roast on the grill rack over the center of the drip pan.
- Grill, covered, for 1½ hours or until a meat thermometer inserted in the center registers 140 degrees for medium-rare. Grill for 1 hour longer.
- Brush with the Chili-Horseradish Glaze occasionally. Add briquettes to each side of the grill every 50 to 60 minutes to maintain the heat.
- Let the roast stand for 20 minutes before carving.
- Pour the drippings from the drip pan into a liquid measure. Skim off the fat. Add enough water to measure 3 cups. Pour into a saucepan. Bring to a simmer. Whisk the flour and remaining ⅓ cup water in a small bowl until smooth. Stir into the saucepan. Simmer for 3 minutes or until thickened, stirring constantly. Serve with the sliced roast.
- May add soaked mesquite chips after the first hour of cooking.
- Yield: 18 servings.

Approx Per Serving: Cal 198; Prot 26 g; Carbo 3 g; T Fat 6 g; 29% Calories from Fat; Chol 72 mg; Fiber <1 g; Sod 188 mg

—*Scott Hane*

Marinated Grilled Chicken

6 boneless skinless chicken breasts
1/2 cup pineapple juice
1/2 cup soy sauce
1/4 cup vegetable oil
1 teaspoon garlic powder
1 teaspoon dry mustard
1 tablespoon brown sugar
1/4 teaspoon ground pepper

- Rinse chicken and pat dry.
- Mix the pineapple juice, soy sauce, oil, garlic powder, mustard, brown sugar and pepper in a bowl. Add the chicken. Marinate in the refrigerator for 1 hour or longer.
- Grill over hot coals.
- Yield: 6 servings.

Approx Per Serving: Cal 254; Prot 28 g; Carbo 7 g; T Fat 12 g; 44% Calories from Fat; Chol 73 mg; Fiber <1 g; Sod 1434 mg

—Abe J. Malouf, M.D.

Deep-Fried Turkey

1 (10- to 12-pound) turkey
1 (8-ounce) bottle Italian salad dressing
1 tablespoon Tony Chachere's Creole seasoning, or to taste
5 gallons peanut oil

- Rinse the turkey and pat dry.
- Strain the salad dressing into a bowl. Inject the turkey with the salad dressing. Rub with the seasoning. Place the turkey in a sealable plastic bag. Marinate in the refrigerator for 24 hours.
- Heat the oil to 285 degrees in a deep stockpot. Place the turkey breast side down in the stockpot. Deep-fry for 3 1/2 minutes per pound; turn halfway through cooking.
- Yield: 30 servings.

Nutritional information is not available for this recipe.

—Paul Hux

Barbecue Sauce for Chicken

4 cups catsup
3/4 cup Worcestershire sauce
1 cup prepared mustard
2 to 3 teaspoons celery seeds, or to taste
1/4 cup sugar
2 tablespoons butter or vegetable oil
2 1/2 to 3 cups vinegar
1 clove of garlic, minced
Juice of 1/2 lemon
1 small onion, chopped
Hot sauce to taste

- Combine the catsup, Worcestershire sauce, mustard, celery seeds, sugar, butter, vinegar, garlic, lemon juice, onion and hot sauce in a large bowl; mix well.
- May add additional catsup to make a thicker sauce.
- Use to baste chicken during grilling.
- Yield: 30 servings.

Approx Per Serving: Cal 63; Prot 1 g; Carbo 14 g; T Fat 1 g; 17% Calories from Fat; Chol 2 mg; Fiber 1 g; Sod 567 mg

Mims Mitchell's Barbecue Sauce

Mims Mitchell from Magee, Mississippi, was well known for his many barbecues. We use one-fourth of Mims' original barbecue sauce recipe. My wife Nancy actually makes the sauce, but I cook the chicken on the grill. This is the children's favorite barbecue recipe.

—Richard M. Edmonson

Baked Barbecued Doves

8 doves
3/4 teaspoon salt
1/2 teaspoon pepper
1/4 teaspoon garlic powder
1 1/2 cups margarine
Juice and grated peel of 8 lemons
1/2 cup honey
3/4 (10-ounce) bottle steak sauce
3/4 (10-ounce) bottle Worcestershire sauce
3/4 teaspoon salt
1/2 teaspoon pepper
1/4 teaspoon garlic powder

- Rinse the doves and pat dry.
- Rub the doves with 3/4 teaspoon salt, 1/2 teaspoon pepper and 1/4 teaspoon garlic powder. Place the doves in a roasting pan with a small amount of water.
- Bake at 450 degrees until the doves are browned on both sides.
- Melt the margarine in a saucepan. Add the remaining ingredients; mix well.
- Reduce the oven temperature to 350 degrees. Bake the doves for 1 1/2 hours, basting with the sauce 4 to 5 times.
- Yield: 8 servings.

Approx Per Serving: Cal 586; Prot 38 g; Carbo 31 g; T Fat 37 g; 54% Calories from Fat; Chol 109 mg; Fiber 1 g; Sod 1450 mg

—*Bret Lee*

Slow-Baked Deer

1 cup Worcestershire sauce
4 cloves of garlic, crushed
2 tablespoons liquid smoke
2 tablespoons celery seeds
2 tablespoons onion powder
2 tablespoons pepper
1/4 cup red wine vinegar
2 (1 1/2- to 2-pound) deer loins, trimmed
1 (8-ounce) bottle Italian dressing
1/2 cup Worcestershire sauce
1 tablespoon pepper

- Combine the 1 cup Worcestershire sauce, garlic, liquid smoke, celery seeds, onion powder, 2 tablespoons pepper and vinegar in a large bowl; mix well.
- Add the deer loins. Marinate in the refrigerator for 6 to 8 hours or overnight.
- Remove the meat from the marinade and place it in a 9x13-inch baking pan.
- Add the salad dressing, remaining 1/2 cup Worcestershire sauce and 1 tablespoon pepper. Cover the pan with foil.
- Bake at 200 degrees for 5 to 6 hours or until cooked through.
- Let stand for 10 to 15 minutes before slicing.
- This only serves 4 to 5 at deer camp.
- Yield: 10 servings.

Approx Per Serving: Cal 319; Prot 33 g; Carbo 13 g; T Fat 15 g; 42% Calories from Fat; Chol 120 mg; Fiber 1 g; Sod 640 mg

—*Durwood J. (Woody) Breeland*

Grilled Deer Roast

1 (4-pound) deer roast
1 cup chopped bacon
1/4 cup minced garlic
Hot pepper to taste
1 to 2 tablespoons garlic powder, or to taste
2 to 3 teaspoons salt, or to taste
2 to 3 teaspoons black pepper, or to taste
1 to 2 teaspoons cayenne, or to taste
4 cloves of garlic, minced
2 cups red wine
1 onion, sliced
1 green or red bell pepper, chopped
1 cup water
1 cup vegetable oil
1 cup wine vinegar
2 tablespoons pickling spices
1 tablespoon cracked peppercorns
1 pound sliced bacon

- Make several cuts in the roast. Stuff the cuts with the chopped bacon, 1/4 cup garlic and hot pepper. Rub the roast liberally with the garlic powder, salt, black pepper and cayenne, pushing some into the cuts.
- Combine the 4 garlic cloves, wine, onion, green pepper, water, oil, vinegar, pickling spices and peppercorns in a large bowl; mix well. Add the roast. Marinate in the refrigerator for 8 to 10 hours.
- Remove the roast from the marinade. Brown well over a charcoal fire. Remove the roast from the fire and wrap it well with the bacon. Place the roast to one side of the coals and cover the smoker. Cook the roast partially. Turn it and cover it with the bacon again. Cover and cook slowly until the roast is cooked through; do not overcook.
- Yield: 8 servings.

Approx Per Serving: Cal 632; Prot 48 g; Carbo 9 g; T Fat 41 g; 58% Calories from Fat; Chol 167 mg; Fiber 1 g; Sod 1929 mg

—*Eddie J. Briggs, former lieutenant governor, state of Mississippi*

Deer Roast

1 (3-pound) deer roast
1 onion
1 green bell pepper
1 (10-ounce) can beef bouillon

- Rinse the roast well and place it in a slow cooker.
- Slice the onion and the green pepper. Add the sliced vegetables to the slow cooker. Pour in the bouillon.
- Cook, covered, over low heat for 8 to 10 hours or until the roast shreds easily.
- May add 1 can drained whole potatoes and 1 can drained sliced carrots.
- Yield: 6 servings.

Approx Per Serving: Cal 228; Prot 42 g; Carbo 3 g; T Fat 5 g; 19% Calories from Fat; Chol 150 mg; Fiber <1 g; Sod 419 mg

—*Ron Wojcik*

Barbecue Sauce

■ ■ ■ ■ ■ ■ ■ ■ ■ ■ ■ ■ ■ ■ ■ ■ ■ ■ ■

1/4 cup chopped onion
1 tablespoon butter
1 (14-ounce) bottle catsup
1/4 cup vinegar
1/4 cup packed brown sugar
1 tablespoon Worcestershire sauce
1 tablespoon liquid smoke
1/2 teaspoon salt
1/4 teaspoon pepper

- Sauté the onion in the butter in a small skillet until tender-crisp.
- Add the catsup, vinegar, brown sugar, Worcestershire sauce, liquid smoke, salt and pepper; mix well.
- Simmer, covered, for 20 minutes.
- Yield: 12 servings.

Approx Per Serving: Cal 60; Prot 1 g; Carbo 14 g; T Fat 1 g; 15% Calories from Fat; Chol 3 mg; Fiber 1 g; Sod 506 mg

—Carlton Evans

Grilled Corn on the Cob

■ ■ ■ ■ ■ ■ ■ ■ ■ ■ ■ ■ ■ ■ ■ ■ ■ ■ ■

6 ears of fresh corn
2 tablespoons margarine or butter
2 teaspoons lemon juice
1/4 teaspoon crushed dried thyme
Salt and pepper to taste

- Peel the husks back from the corn without removing them. Remove the silks from the corn and pull the husks back up around the corn.
- Combine the corn with enough cold water to cover in a large container. Soak for 1 hour. Drain the corn and shake it to remove excess water. Cover the corn as completely as possible with the husks, tying the tips with string if needed.
- Arrange the corn on a grill rack directly over medium coals. Grill for 25 to 30 minutes or until the corn is tender, turning several times. Remove the husks carefully to avoid burns.
- Combine the margarine, lemon juice, thyme, salt and pepper in a small saucepan. Heat until the margarine is melted. Brush over the corn.
- Yield: 6 servings.

Approx Per Serving: Cal 118; Prot 3 g; Carbo 20 g; T Fat 5 g; 33% Calories from Fat; Chol 0 mg; Fiber 4 g; Sod 58 mg

—David Keeney

Eggs in Hell

▪ ▪ ▪ ▪ ▪ ▪ ▪ ▪ ▪ ▪ ▪ ▪ ▪ ▪ ▪ ▪ ▪ ▪

1 medium onion, chopped
1 green or red bell pepper, chopped
2 ribs celery, chopped
6 to 8 cloves of garlic, sliced or chopped
3 tablespoons olive oil
2 (16-ounce) cans small tomatoes
Sugar to taste
Garlic salt to taste
1 (8-ounce) block of Parmesan cheese, cut
   into chunks
6 eggs
6 pieces toast
4 ounces Parmesan cheese, grated

- Sauté the onion, bell pepper, celery and garlic in the olive oil in a skillet until tender. Add the tomatoes, sugar, garlic salt and Parmesan cheese chunks. Cook over medium heat until the cheese begins to melt, stirring frequently; reduce the heat to low. Simmer, covered, for 1½ to 2 hours, adding water as needed. Add the eggs 1 at a time, covering with the gravy and poaching to taste.
- Serve the eggs and gravy over the toast. Sprinkle with the grated Parmesan cheese.
- Yield: 6 servings.

Approx Per Serving: Cal 534; Prot 35 g; Carbo 30 g; T Fat 31 g; 51% Calories from Fat; Chol 258 mg; Fiber 4 g; Sod 1541 mg

—*Vincent "Snow" Mechatto*

Remembering "Snow"

Vincent "Snow" Mechatto was the son of second-generation Sicilian immigrants who settled in the Mississippi Delta. Like so many immigrant families in the early part of the century, Snow's parents operated several different restaurants in the small town of Belzoni. Mamaw Mechatto's last (and most famous) eatery was Mechatto's Hut, housed in the 1950s in a World War II quonset hut (the kind with the rounded roof) at the fork of Highway 12 and Church Street.

Snow grew up around good Italian cooking as well as Delta soul food. Although he didn't go into the restaurant business, there was always something delicious and unique on the stove in the back of M&H Appliance Store on Jackson Street. Most times there was a card game going on, too, with tall tales being told all around. A lot of the old card-playing gang at M&H have passed away, but, boy, if that old formica-topped table with the chrome legs could talk...!

— *Jill Mechatto Boteler*

Pork Tenderloin in Penne Pasta

■ ■ ■ ■ ■ ■ ■ ■ ■ ■ ■ ■ ■ ■ ■ ■ ■

1 cup white wine
1/4 cup Worcestershire sauce
1/4 cup soy sauce
2 cloves of garlic, crushed
Cracked black pepper to taste
1 (3- to 4-pound) pork tenderloin
16 ounces penne pasta
1 clove of garlic, minced
1/2 small purple onion, chopped
3 tablespoons butter
1 cup white wine
2 cups half-and-half
1 teaspoon oregano
4 ounces feta cheese, crumbled

- Mix 1 cup wine, Worcestershire sauce, soy sauce, 2 cloves of garlic and pepper in a baking dish. Add the tenderloin. Marinate in the refrigerator for 4 hours.
- Bake at 350 degrees for 20 minutes or until medium-rare. Remove from the marinade and slice into medallions.
- Cook the pasta using the package directions; drain.
- Sauté the remaining garlic and onion in the butter in a skillet. Add the remaining 1 cup wine. Bring to a boil. Add the half-and-half, oregano and pork medallions. Cook until the pork is cooked through and the sauce is thickened and reduced by 1/2. Remove from the heat. Stir in the cheese. Spoon over the pasta.
- Yield: 8 servings.

Approx Per Serving: Cal 648; Prot 51 g; Carbo 49 g; T Fat 22 g; 31% Calories from Fat; Chol 158 mg; Fiber 2 g; Sod 908 mg

—John T. Snook, Jr.

Unbelievably Easy Catfish Provençale

■ ■ ■ ■ ■ ■ ■ ■ ■ ■ ■ ■ ■ ■ ■ ■ ■

1 large onion, sliced
2 tomatoes, cut into thin wedges
1 tablespoon butter
4 catfish fillets
2 sprigs of fresh oregano
Salt and pepper to taste
4 teaspoons butter
1/8 teaspoon Tabasco sauce, or to taste
1 teaspoon Worcestershire sauce, or to taste

- Sauté the onion and tomatoes lightly in 1 tablespoon butter in a skillet.
- Place the fish in a single layer in a baking pan. Sprinkle with the oregano, salt and pepper. Dot with the remaining 4 teaspoons butter. Spoon the tomato mixture over the fish.
- Bake at 350 degrees for 15 minutes. Add the Tabasco sauce and Worcestershire sauce just before serving.
- Yield: 4 servings.

Approx Per Serving: Cal 219; Prot 22 g; Carbo 6 g; T Fat 12 g; 49% Calories from Fat; Chol 84 mg; Fiber 1 g; Sod 154 mg

—Thad Cochran
United States senator, R-Mississippi

Mississippi Marinated Shrimp

■ ■

5 pounds medium shrimp
1 teaspoon salt
10 small white onions, cut into rings
2 cups vegetable oil
1 1/2 cups cider vinegar
1 (4-ounce) bottle capers
Salt and pepper to taste
3/8 teaspoon Tabasco sauce, or to taste
1 teaspoon sugar
2 tablespoons Worcestershire sauce

- Combine the shrimp, salt and water to cover in a large saucepan. Bring to a boil. Simmer for 10 minutes.
- Peel and devein the shrimp.
- Mix the onions, oil, vinegar, capers, salt, pepper, Tabasco sauce, sugar and Worcestershire sauce in a bowl. Add the shrimp. Marinate in the refrigerator for 24 hours.
- Serve on a tray with wooden picks.
- Yield: 20 servings.

Approx Per Serving: Cal 291; Prot 17 g;
Carbo 5 g; T Fat 23 g; 70% Calories from Fat;
Chol 158 mg; Fiber 1 g; Sod 426 mg

—*Trent Lott*
United States senator, R-Mississippi

Whole Stuffed Artichokes Italiano

■ ■

4 (6- to 8-ounce) artichokes
1 teaspoon salt, or to taste
1 cup Italian-seasoned bread crumbs
1 tablespoon grated Parmesan cheese
Pepper, oregano and garlic powder to taste
1 quart water
1 tablespoon olive oil, or to taste
Salt to taste

- Place an artichoke on its side and cut the bottom stem off straight so that the artichoke can sit up. Place it on its side again and cut the top part 1 inch down; discard all the small bottom leaves. Open the center of the artichoke and spread it away from the center to form a pocket. Wash and drain the artichoke. Shake the water out and sprinkle the inside with a small amount of salt. Repeat the procedure with the remaining artichokes.
- Mix the bread crumbs and cheese in a bowl. Add pepper, oregano and garlic powder. Fill the artichoke pockets completely, taking care to not pack them too tightly and placing some of the cheese mixture between some of the center leaves to use all the filling.
- Fit the artichokes snugly into a saucepan so that they will not spread out while cooking. Mix the water and olive oil in a bowl. Season with additional salt and pepper. Pour enough of the water into the saucepan to reach slightly more than halfway up the artichokes.
- Cover and bring to a boil. Simmer for 45 minutes or until a leaf can be removed easily. Remove the artichokes carefully from the water. Scrape each leaf with the teeth at the bottom. Remove the chokes upon reaching the heart.
- Yield: 4 servings.

Approx Per Serving: Cal 242; Prot 12 g;
Carbo 43 g; T Fat 5 g; 17% Calories from Fat;
Chol 2 mg; Fiber 12 g; Sod 1440 mg

—*Joseph Bonfiglio*

Versatile Eggplant Pizza

Garlic and oregano to taste
1 (14-ounce) jar pizza sauce
8 (1/2-inch) slices eggplant
Salt and pepper to taste
4 ounces mozzarella cheese, shredded
1 (3-ounce) package thinly sliced pepperoni

- Stir garlic and oregano into the pizza sauce.
- Trim each eggplant slice slightly to form an almost square shape. Place close together on a baking sheet sprayed with nonstick cooking spray. Spray the eggplant generously. Season with salt and pepper.
- Broil for 5 minutes or until slightly browned. Turn over and season with additional salt and pepper. Return to the broiler until browned; do not overcook.
- Spread half the pizza sauce over a 10x15-inch baking sheet with sides. Arrange the eggplant over the sauce; spoon the remaining sauce over the eggplant. Sprinkle with the cheese. Top with the pepperoni.
- Bake at 450 degrees until the cheese is melted.
- May add additional seasonings such as garlic powder or Cajun seasoning. May use other combinations of meats and cheeses.
- Yield: 8 servings.

Approx Per Serving: Cal 135; Prot 7 g; Carbo 8 g; T Fat 9 g; 59% Calories from Fat; Chol 20 mg; Fiber 2 g; Sod 492 mg

—*Joseph Bonfiglio*

Barley Pilaf with Wild Mushrooms

3 tablespoons butter or olive oil
1 cup pearl barley
2 tablespoons butter or olive oil
1 medium yellow onion, chopped
8 ounces fresh mushrooms, sliced, such as shiitake, portobello, crimini, button or any combination
1 cup chicken stock
Salt and pepper to taste
1 1/2 cups chicken stock
1 tablespoon chopped fresh thyme

- Melt 3 tablespoons butter in a saucepan. Add the barley. Cook until the barley is a delicate brown. Remove to a casserole and keep warm.
- Add the remaining 2 tablespoons butter to the saucepan. Sauté the onion in the butter over medium-low heat until tender. Add the mushrooms. Cook over medium heat for 2 to 3 minutes or until heated through, stirring frequently. Add the mushroom mixture and 1 cup chicken stock to the barley in the casserole. Season with salt and pepper and mix well.
- Bake, covered, at 350 degrees for 30 minutes. Add 1 cup of the remaining stock. Bake for 30 minutes longer. Add the remaining 1/2 cup stock and the thyme. Bake for 20 to 25 minutes longer or until the barley is tender and all the liquid is absorbed. Garnish with chopped parsley.
- May add additional chicken stock during baking if the barley is too dry.
- Yield: 8 servings.

Approx Per Serving: Cal 176; Prot 5 g; Carbo 22 g; T Fat 8 g; 40% Calories from Fat; Chol 19 mg; Fiber 5 g; Sod 320 mg

—*Mike Moore, attorney general state of Mississippi*

Roasted Garlic with Pita Bread

4 large whole heads garlic
1 to 2 tablespoons olive oil
4 slices pita bread
2 tablespoons olive oil
Freshly ground pepper to taste

- Brush the garlic with 1 to 2 tablespoons olive oil. Grill until well browned and tender.
- Brush both sides of the bread with the remaining 2 tablespoons olive oil. Sprinkle both sides with pepper. Grill on both sides until warm.
- Squeeze the garlic from the cloves. Spread over the bread.
- Yield: 4 servings.

Approx Per Serving: Cal 329; Prot 7 g; Carbo 43 g; T Fat 14 g; 39% Calories from Fat; Chol 0 mg; Fiber 3 g; Sod 327 mg

—Abe J. Malouf, M.D.

Bacon Cornmeal Muffins

1/2 cup self-rising flour
1/2 cup self-rising cornmeal
2 tablespoons sugar
1/2 cup bacon drippings
6 slices bacon, crisp-fried, crumbled
1 egg, beaten
1/2 cup milk

- Combine the flour, cornmeal, sugar and bacon drippings in a bowl, stirring just until moistened. Stir in the bacon. Add the egg and milk; mix well.
- Spoon the batter into greased muffin cups.
- Bake at 450 degrees for 20 to 25 minutes or until lightly browned.
- Yield: 6 servings.

Approx Per Serving: Cal 323; Prot 6 g; Carbo 22 g; T Fat 24 g; 66% Calories from Fat; Chol 63 mg; Fiber 1 g; Sod 510 mg

—Thomas Huckabee

Easy Low-Fat Blueberry Muffins

2 cups flour
1/2 cup sugar
1 tablespoon baking powder
1/2 teaspoon salt
1 cup milk
1 egg
1/4 cup melted butter
1 cup blueberries

- Whisk the flour, sugar, baking powder and salt in a large bowl.
- Combine the milk, egg and butter in a small bowl; beat well.
- Blend the milk mixture into the flour mixture. Fold in the blueberries. Pour into nonstick muffin cups.
- Bake at 425 degrees for 20 minutes.
- Yield: 12 servings.

Approx Per Serving: Cal 169; Prot 3 g; Carbo 27 g; T Fat 5 g; 28% Calories from Fat; Chol 31 mg; Fiber 1 g; Sod 227 mg

—Bart Lee

Chess Pie

■ ■

1/2 cup melted butter or margarine
1 1/2 cups sugar
3 eggs
1 teaspoon vanilla extract
1/8 teaspoon salt, or to taste
3/4 tablespoon vinegar
1 unbaked (9-inch) pie shell

■ Combine the butter and sugar in a
  saucepan. Simmer slowly for 5 minutes,
  stirring constantly. Remove from the heat
  and let cool slightly, stirring constantly.
■ Add the eggs 1 at a time, beating well after
  each addition. Add the vanilla, salt, and
  vinegar; mix well. Pour into the pie shell.
■ Bake at 400 degrees for 15 minutes. Reduce
  the oven temperature to 350 degrees. Bake
  for 20 to 30 minutes longer or until the
  center quivers slightly when the pie is
  shaken gently.
■ Keeps well in the refrigerator overnight or
  may be frozen and reheated. May be cut in
  slivers for finger desserts. Do not double
  the recipe.
■ Yield: 8 servings.

Approx Per Serving: Cal 394; Prot 4 g;
Carbo 48 g; T Fat 21 g; 48% Calories from Fat;
Chol 111 mg; Fiber <1 g; Sod 297 mg

—Kane Ditto, mayor
city of Jackson, Mississippi

Favorite Chocolate Pie

■ ■

1 1/4 cups sugar
1 tablespoon cornstarch
1/4 teaspoon salt
3 tablespoons flour
1/4 cup baking cocoa
4 egg yolks
2 1/2 cups milk
1 tablespoon margarine
1 teaspoon vanilla extract
1 baked (9-inch) pie shell
4 egg whites
1/4 teaspoon cream of tartar
7 tablespoons sugar

■ Combine 1 1/4 cups sugar, cornstarch, salt,
  flour and cocoa in a saucepan. Add the
  egg yolks and milk. Beat with a mixer
  until the mixture is smooth. Cook over low
  heat until thickened, stirring constantly.
  Remove from the heat and stir in the
  margarine and vanilla. Pour into the
  pie shell.
■ Whip the egg whites in a mixer bowl until
  frothy and stiff. Add a mixture of the cream
  of tartar and 7 tablespoons sugar 1
  tablespoon at a time, beating constantly.
  Pour over the pie filling, sealing to the edge.
■ Bake at 350 degrees until lightly browned.
■ Yield: 8 servings.

Approx Per Serving: Cal 400; Prot 8 g;
Carbo 61 g; T Fat 15 g; 32% Calories from Fat;
Chol 116 mg; Fiber 1 g; Sod 275 mg

—Congressman G.V. (Sonny) Montgomery
third district of Mississipp

Sugar-Free Carrot Raisin Cake

1¹/₂ cups rice flour
¹/₂ teaspoon baking powder
¹/₂ teaspoon baking soda
¹/₄ teaspoon salt
¹/₂ teaspoon cinnamon
3 eggs, beaten
¹/₂ cup safflower oil
2¹/₂ cups grated carrots
1 cup raisins
¹/₄ to ³/₄ cup honey

- Sift the flour, baking powder, baking soda, salt and cinnamon into a large bowl. Stir in the eggs. Add the oil, carrots, raisins and honey; mix well. Pour into a medium nonstick loaf pan.
- Bake at 350 degrees for 30 to 35 minutes or until the loaf tests done.
- Yield: 12 servings.

Approx Per Serving: Cal 287; Prot 3 g; Carbo 47 g; T Fat 11 g; 32% Calories from Fat; Chol 53 mg; Fiber 2 g; Sod 119 mg

Reflections on Our Spiritual Paths

People tend to think that each new stage of the spiritual path is marked by some sort of great awakening or accomplishment . . . but what actually happens is that you stay at a particular stage until you see the silliness of it.

—Ron DelBene

Layered Strawberry Rum Cake

1 cup butter, softened
2 cups sugar
3 eggs
2 tablespoons vanilla extract
2 cups self-rising flour
Rum Glaze
2 (10-ounce) packages frozen strawberries, thawed

- Cream the butter and sugar in a bowl until light and fluffy.
- Beat in the eggs and vanilla.
- Add the flour gradually, beating until well blended. Do not add liquid of any kind.
- Pour into 2 greased and floured 9x13-inch cake pans.
- Bake at 350 degrees for 45 minutes or until golden brown.
- Invert one layer onto a serving tray.
- Pour half the Strawberry Rum Glaze over the warm layer. Spoon half the strawberries over the glaze.
- Invert the remaining layer onto the strawberries.
- Pour the remaining glaze over the cake and top with the remaining strawberries.
- Yield: 15 servings.

Rum Glaze

1 cup sugar
2 tablespoons warm water
¹/₂ cup rum, or rum flavoring to taste

- Combine the sugar, warm water and rum in a small saucepan.
- Bring to full rolling boil. Boil until of the consistency of syrup, stirring constantly. Add additional water as necessary for the proper consistency.

Approx Per Serving: Cal 373; Prot 3 g; Carbo 56 g; T Fat 14 g; 32% Calories from Fat; Chol 76 mg; Fiber 1 g; Sod 350 mg

—Perry "Pork Chop" Florence

Celebrations

Celebrations

Photograph on preceding page by David Keeney. "Reflections," the elegant
home of Mrs. Bettie C. Cates and the late Dr. Robert T. Cates in Madison, Mississippi

Ambrosia

1 large coconut, shredded
1 (8-ounce) jar maraschino cherries, drained
Sections of 12 medium oranges, seeded, chopped
1 (20-ounce) can crushed pineapple, drained
Sugar to taste
Juice of 1 lemon

- Reserve 1/4 to 1/2 cup shredded coconut for the top. Reserve several cherries for the top.
- Combine the remaining coconut, remaining cherries, oranges, pineapple, sugar and lemon juice in a bowl and mix gently.
- Chill, covered, until serving time. Sprinkle with the reserved coconut and top with the reserved cherries just before serving.
- May omit the lemon juice.
- Yield: 15 servings.

Approx Per Serving: Cal 191; Prot 2 g;
Carbo 30 g; T Fat 8 g; 36% Calories from Fat;
Chol 0 mg; Fiber 6 g; Sod 5 mg

—*Louise Brister Melton*

Mom's Ambrosia

You cannot prove it by me, but I really do come from a long line of excellent cooks. I can cook, but I do not enjoy it. I believe that every female ancestor of mine, as well as almost every living female relative loves to cook. Most of them enjoy cooking those long, involved dishes with lots of ingredients. You should see my mom's face if she hears that someone has prepared a cake from a mix—heaven forbid! There is something sacred in the South about cooking from scratch. Nevertheless, my favorite holiday dish is the easiest that my mom prepares. There are always leftovers of those dishes with a multitude of ingredients and desserts made from scratch, but there is never even a smidgeon left of my mother's ambrosia!

—*Melissa Melton Keeney*

Festive Cherry Salad

1 (17-ounce) can pitted dark cherries
1 (16-ounce) can crushed pineapple
1 (3-ounce) package lemon gelatin
1 (3-ounce) package peach gelatin
1 1/2 cups orange juice
1 cup finely chopped celery
3/4 cup finely chopped pecans

- Drain the cherries and pineapple, reserving enough juice to measure 1 1/2 cups. Chop the cherries.
- Bring the reserved juice to a boil in a saucepan. Remove from heat.
- Add the lemon gelatin and peach gelatin, stirring until dissolved. Stir in the orange juice.
- Chill until slightly thickened. Fold in the cherries, pineapple, celery and pecans. Spoon into a lightly greased 5-cup mold.
- Chill until set.
- Yield: 10 servings.

Approx Per Serving: Cal 218; Prot 3 g;
Carbo 41 g; T Fat 6 g; 24% Calories from Fat;
Chol 0 mg; Fiber 2 g; Sod 56 mg

—*Cathy Sparkman*

Cranberry Salad

2 (3-ounce) packages cherry gelatin
2 cups boiling water
1 (16-ounce) can cranberry sauce
2 tablespoons sugar
1 1/2 cups chopped unpeeled apples
3/4 cup chopped celery
3/4 cup chopped pecans

- Dissolve the gelatin in the boiling water in a bowl and mix well.
- Stir in the cranberry sauce and sugar.
- Chill until slightly thickened.
- Fold in the apples, celery and pecans.
- Spoon into a holiday mold.
- Chill until set.
- Yield: 10 servings.

Approx Per Serving: Cal 216; Prot 2 g; Carbo 41 g; T Fat 6 g; 25% Calories from Fat; Chol 0 mg; Fiber 2 g; Sod 64 mg

—*Hallie S. Lea*

Reception Salad

2 (3-ounce) packages lemon gelatin
8 ounces cream cheese, softened
2 pimentos, chopped
1 (20-ounce) can crushed pineapple, drained
1/2 cup finely chopped celery
2/3 cup finely chopped walnuts
1/8 teaspoon salt
1 cup whipping cream, whipped

- Prepare the gelatin using package directions. Chill until slightly thickened.
- Beat the cream cheese and pimentos in a mixer bowl until smooth.
- Add to the gelatin, beating until blended. Stir in the pineapple, celery, walnuts and salt. Fold in the whipped cream.
- Spoon into a shallow dish. Chill until set.
- Cut into squares and serve on lettuce-lined salad plates.
- Yield: 8 servings.

Approx Per Serving: Cal 388; Prot 6 g; Carbo 33 g; T Fat 27 g; 61% Calories from Fat; Chol 72 mg; Fiber 2 g; Sod 192 mg

—*Rosetta Belcher*

Ribbon Salad

2 (3-ounce) packages lime gelatin
4 cups each hot and cold water
1 (3-ounce) package lemon gelatin
1 cup hot water
1/2 cup marshmallows
1 cup pineapple juice
8 ounces cream cheese
1 (20-ounce) can crushed pineapple, drained
1 cup whipping cream, whipped
1 cup mayonnaise
2 (3-ounce) packages cherry gelatin

- Combine the lime gelatin and 4 cups hot water in a bowl, stirring until the gelatin dissolves. Stir in the cold water. Pour into a shallow dish. Chill until almost set.
- Combine the lemon gelatin and 1 cup hot water in a double boiler. Cook over hot water until the gelatin dissolves, stirring constantly. Add the marshmallows.
- Cook until smooth, stirring constantly. Remove from heat. Stir in the pineapple juice and cream cheese.
- Cook over hot water until blended, stirring frequently. Stir in the pineapple. Let stand until cool. Fold in the whipped cream and mayonnaise. Chill until thickened. Spread over the lime gelatin. Chill until almost set.
- Prepare the cherry gelatin using package directions. Chill until thickened. Pour over the prepared layers.
- Chill until set.
- Yield: 24 servings.

Approx Per Serving: Cal 222; Prot 3 g; Carbo 22 g; T Fat 14 g; 57% Calories from Fat; Chol 29 mg; Fiber <1 g; Sod 130 mg

A Holiday Tradition

The Ribbon Salad is a traditional Christmas salad in my home. As a matter of fact, last year I decided not to serve it and my children said they would not come for Christmas dinner unless the salad was a part of the menu. The flavors of the gelatin may be changed for a Thanksgiving salad, using orange gelatin in place of cherry gelatin.

—*Hallie S. Lea*

Glazed Ham with Orange and Cranberry Sauce

■ ■ ■ ■ ■ ■ ■ ■ ■ ■ ■ ■ ■ ■

1 (14-pound) smoked cooked whole ham
1/2 cup red currant jelly
1 tablespoon grated orange peel
1/4 teaspoon allspice
Orange and Cranberry Sauce

- Remove the skin of the ham; trim the fat leaving 1/4 inch fat covering. Place the ham on a rack in a large roasting pan. Insert a meat thermometer into the center of the ham, being careful that the end of the thermometer does not touch the bone.
- Bake at 325 degrees for 2 1/2 hours.
- Bring the currant jelly, orange peel and allspice to a boil in a saucepan. Boil for 2 minutes, stirring occasionally. Brush the ham with some of the glaze.
- Bake for 30 to 60 minutes longer or to 140 degrees on the meat thermometer, brushing occasionally with the remaining glaze.
- Arrange the ham on a serving platter. Let stand for 20 minutes before slicing.
- Garnish with assorted fresh fruit. Serve the Orange and Cranberry Sauce hot or cold with the ham.
- Yield: 24 servings.

Orange and Cranberry Sauce

2 large oranges
12 ounces cranberries
1 1/4 cups cranberry juice cocktail
1 cup sugar
1/2 cup raisins
1/4 teaspoon ground cloves

- Grate the peel of the oranges into a bowl.
- Cut sections from the oranges between membranes over a 3-quart saucepan to collect the juice. Remove the sections to a plate as you cut; chop the sections.
- Stir the cranberries, cranberry juice cocktail, sugar, raisins and cloves into the orange juice in the saucepan.
- Bring to a boil; reduce heat. Simmer for 15 minutes or until the cranberries pop and the mixture thickens, stirring occasionally.
- Stir in the oranges and grated orange peel.

Approx Per Serving: Cal 493; Prot 67 g; Carbo 21 g; T Fat 15 g; 27% Calories from Fat; Chol 146 mg; Fiber 1 g; Sod 3511 mg

—*Cathy Britt*

Holiday Asparagus Casserole

3 tablespoons butter
1/4 cup flour
1 1/2 cups milk
1/2 cup chopped Velveeta cheese
1 (16-ounce) can asparagus spears, drained
2 hard-cooked eggs, sliced
4 slices bread, cubed
2 tablespoons melted butter
1/3 cup shredded Velveeta cheese

- Heat 3 tablespoons butter in a saucepan until melted.
- Stir in the flour until blended. Add the milk and mix well.
- Cook until thickened, stirring constantly. Add 1/2 cup cheese. Cook until blended, stirring constantly.
- Layer the asparagus, eggs and sauce 1/2 at a time in a baking dish.
- Combine the bread cubes and 2 tablespoons melted butter in a bowl and toss gently.
- Arrange over the prepared layers; sprinkle with 1/3 cup cheese.
- Bake at 350 degrees until bubbly.
- Yield: 4 servings.

Approx Per Serving: Cal 484; Prot 20 g; Carbo 28 g; T Fat 33 g; 61% Calories from Fat; Chol 192 mg; Fiber 2 g; Sod 1327 mg

—*Helen McClean Fletcher*

Sweet Potato and Raisin Casserole

3 cups mashed cooked sweet potatoes
1 cup sugar
1/2 cup margarine, softened
1/2 cup milk
1/2 cup raisins
2 eggs, beaten
1 teaspoon vanilla extract
1 cup packed brown sugar
1/3 cup flour
2 tablespoons margarine
1 cup chopped pecans

- Combine the sweet potatoes, sugar, 1/2 cup margarine, milk, raisins, eggs and vanilla in a bowl and mix well.
- Spoon into a buttered baking dish.
- Combine the brown sugar and flour in a bowl and mix well. Cut in 2 tablespoons margarine until crumbly.
- Stir in the pecans. Sprinkle over the prepared layer.
- Bake at 350 degrees for 20 minutes or until bubbly.
- Yield: 6 servings.

Approx Per Serving: Cal 754; Prot 7 g; Carbo 108 g; T Fat 35 g; 41% Calories from Fat; Chol 73 mg; Fiber 5 g; Sod 281 mg

—*Rhonda "Chellie" Williams*

Cranberry Oat Bran Muffins

∎ ∎ ∎ ∎ ∎ ∎ ∎ ∎ ∎ ∎ ∎ ∎ ∎ ∎ ∎ ∎

1¹/4 cups whole wheat flour
2 teaspoons baking powder
1 cup oat bran
1 cup sugar
2 eggs
1 cup milk
2 tablespoons melted butter
1 to 2 cups cranberries, chopped
¹/4 to ³/4 cup chopped pecans

- Sift the whole wheat flour and baking powder into a bowl and mix well. Stir in the oat bran and sugar.
- Beat the eggs in a mixer bowl until frothy. Add the milk, beating until blended. Stir in the butter.
- Add the egg mixture to the dry ingredients and mix just until moistened.
- Fold in the cranberries and pecans.
- Spoon into 12 greased muffin cups, filling ²/3 full.
- Bake at 425 degrees for 20 minutes or until golden brown.
- May substitute vegetable oil for butter.
- Yield: 12 servings.

Approx Per Serving: Cal 226; Prot 5 g;
Carbo 36 g; T Fat 9 g; 34% Calories from Fat;
Chol 43 mg; Fiber 4 g; Sod 96 mg

—*Nancy C. Edmonson*

Raisin Pecan Apple Cake

∎ ∎ ∎ ∎ ∎ ∎ ∎ ∎ ∎ ∎ ∎ ∎ ∎ ∎ ∎ ∎

1 cup raisins
1 cup sugar
1 cup vegetable oil
3 eggs, beaten
1 tablespoon vanilla extract
¹/2 teaspoon salt
2 cups flour
1 tablespoon cinnamon
1 teaspoon baking soda
2 cups sliced apples
1 cup chopped pecans

- Pour hot water over the raisins in a bowl. Let stand until plump; drain.
- Combine the sugar, oil, eggs, vanilla and salt in a bowl and mix well.
- Mix the flour, cinnamon and baking soda together. Add to the sugar mixture and mix well. Add a mixture of the raisins, apples and pecans and mix well.
- Spoon the batter into a greased and floured 9x13-inch cake pan.
- Bake at 350 degrees for 40 to 45 minutes or until the cake tests done.
- Yield: 15 servings.

Approx Per Serving: Cal 354; Prot 4 g;
Carbo 39 g; T Fat 21 g; 53% Calories from Fat;
Chol 42 mg; Fiber 2 g; Sod 140 mg

—*Martha M. Kenahan*

Belgian Cherry Tea Cakes

1 cup butter, softened
1/2 cup confectioners' sugar
1/2 teaspoon almond extract
1/2 cup finely chopped pecans
2 1/2 cups sifted cake flour
2 (4-ounce) packages candied red cherries
1 1/2 cups confectioners' sugar
2 to 3 tablespoons milk
1/2 cup shortening
1/4 cup butter, softened
1/2 teaspoon vanilla extract
1/8 teaspoon salt
2 cups sifted confectioners' sugar
1 1/2 tablespoons milk
Green food coloring to taste
Red decorating gel to taste

- Beat 1 cup butter, 1/2 cup confectioners' sugar and almond flavoring with a wooden spoon in a bowl until light and fluffy. Stir in the pecans. Add the cake flour, stirring until a soft dough forms. Shape into a ball; wrap in plastic wrap.
- Chill for several hours or until firm. Divide the dough into 4 equal portions.
- Shape each portion of the dough into a log 1 inch in diameter on a lightly floured surface with lightly floured hands, keeping remaining portions refrigerated. Cut each log into 1/2-inch slices. Turn cut side up and press a cherry into the center, enclosing the cherry. Arrange 1/2 inch apart on an ungreased cookie sheet.
- Bake at 350 degrees for 20 minutes or until light brown. Remove to a wire rack to cool completely.
- Combine 1 1/2 cups confectioners' sugar and 2 to 3 tablespoons milk in a bowl and mix well. Dip the tops of the cookies into the glaze; return to the wire rack. Let stand until the glaze sets. Place a sheet of waxed paper under the rack to catch any glaze that drips off and may be reused.

- Cream the shortening and 1/4 cup butter in a mixer bowl until light and fluffy. Add the vanilla and salt and mix well. Add 2 cups confectioners's sugar gradually, beating until smooth. Beat in 1 1/2 tablespoons milk until fluffy. Beat in desired amount of green food coloring.
- Pipe frosting in the shape of leaves on top of the cookies; dot centers with red decorating gel. Store frosting, covered, in the refrigerator when not in use.
- Yield: 48 servings.

Approx Per Serving: Cal 140; Prot 1 g; Carbo 17 g; T Fat 8 g; 50% Calories from Fat; Chol 13 mg; Fiber <1 g; Sod 55 mg

Mississippi Christmas Memories

Belgian Cherry Tea Cakes are a Christmas tradition in my family. I have always lived a long distance from my family and only visit during the Christmas holidays. When my niece and nephews living in Mississippi were small, they looked forward to helping me bake these cookies. It was the start of celebrating the season for us. We played Christmas music and spent most of the day baking and decorating these cookies. They always wanted to make extras to share with someone special. It was such a special time for me that I refused to bake these cookies at any other time. It would have made me too homesick!

—Jan Szalay

Gingerbread

■ ■ ■ ■ ■ ■ ■ ■ ■ ■ ■ ■ ■ ■ ■ ■

1/2 cup margarine, softened
1/2 cup sugar
1 cup molasses
1 egg, beaten
2 1/2 cups flour
1 1/2 teaspoons baking soda
1 teaspoon cinnamon
1 teaspoon ground cloves
1 teaspoon ginger
1/2 teaspoon salt
1 cup hot water

- Beat the margarine and sugar in a mixer bowl until light and fluffy. Add the molasses and egg, beating until blended. Add the flour, baking soda, cinnamon, cloves, ginger, salt and hot water and mix well.
- Spoon into a greased baking pan. Bake at 350 degrees for 35 to 40 minutes or until the edges pull from sides of the pan.
- Yield: 8 servings.

Approx Per Serving: Cal 411; Prot 5 g; Carbo 71 g; T Fat 13 g; 27% Calories from Fat; Chol 27 mg; Fiber 1 g; Sod 445 mg

—*Joe Anne Johnson*

Jelly Roll Cake

■ ■ ■ ■ ■ ■ ■ ■ ■ ■ ■ ■ ■ ■ ■ ■

1 1/2 to 2 cups sliced strawberries
1 to 2 tablespoons sugar
3 egg yolks
1 cup sugar
5 tablespoons water
1 teaspoon vanilla extract
1 cup flour
3/4 teaspoon baking powder
3 egg whites, stiffly beaten
1 cup whipping cream, whipped
1/4 cup confectioners' sugar

- Line a greased jelly roll pan with waxed paper; grease.
- Combine the strawberries and 1 to 2 tablespoons sugar in a bowl and mix gently. Chill in the refrigerator.
- Beat the egg yolks, 1 cup sugar, water and vanilla in a mixer bowl until pale yellow. Add the flour and baking powder. Beat with a fork until blended. Fold in the egg whites. Spread in the prepared pan.
- Bake at 400 degrees for 10 minutes or until cake tests done. Cool for 5 minutes.
- Invert onto a towel sprinkled with a small amount of confectioners' sugar; remove the waxed paper. Roll the cake in the towel as for a jelly roll. Let stand until cool.
- Unroll the cake; remove the towel. Spread with the whipped cream and sprinkle with the strawberries; reroll. Place on a serving platter; sift the 1/4 cup confectioners' sugar over the jelly roll.
- May substitute frozen strawberries that have been thawed and drained for the fresh strawberries.
- Yield: 10 servings.

Approx Per Serving: Cal 260; Prot 4 g; Carbo 38 g; T Fat 11 g; 36% Calories from Fat; Chol 96 mg; Fiber 1 g; Sod 53 mg

—*Marjorie V. Scott*

Plum Puddings

1½ tablespoons butter
2 cups chopped candied fruit
2 cups raisins
¼ cup brandy
2 tablespoons grated orange peel
2 cups chopped walnuts
1 cup finely chopped suet
1 cup flour
½ cup sugar
2 teaspoons baking powder
1 teaspoon baking soda
1 teaspoon salt
1 teaspoon cinnamon
½ teaspoon allspice
½ teaspoon ground cloves
4 eggs
2 cups applesauce
1 cup molasses
1½ cups fine bread crumbs
2 to 3 ounces brandy, heated
Holiday Pudding Sauce

- Butter three 1-pound coffee cans.
- Soak the candied fruit and raisins in ¼ cup brandy in a bowl for 30 minutes. Stir in the orange peel, walnuts and suet. Coat the mixture in ¼ cup of the flour.
- Sift the remaining flour, sugar, baking powder, baking soda, salt, cinnamon, allspice and cloves into a bowl and mix well.
- Beat the eggs in a bowl lightly. Add the applesauce and molasses and mix well. Stir in the dry ingredients. Add the candied fruit mixture and mix well. Stir in the bread crumbs.
- Spoon the batter into the prepared coffee cans. Cover each can with a double layer of waxed paper; secure with string. Place the cans on a rack in a large stockpot. Add boiling water to reach halfway up the sides of the cans.

- Steam for 2½ hours. Remove the cans to a wire rack. Let stand until cool. Remove the waxed paper. Chill, covered, in the refrigerator.
- To serve, steam the plum puddings in a water bath for 30 to 45 minutes.
- Invert the plum puddings onto a serving platter. Drizzle each with 2 to 3 ounces brandy and ignite.
- Cut into slices and serve with the Holiday Pudding Sauce.
- Yield: 24 servings.

Holiday Pudding Sauce

3 egg yolks
1 cup sugar
2 tablespoons butter, softened
3 egg whites, stiffly beaten
1 cup whipping cream, whipped
3 tablespoons brandy, or to taste

- Beat the egg yolks, sugar and butter in a mixer bowl unil thickened and pale yellow.
- Fold in the egg whites and whipped cream. Stir in the brandy.

Approx Per Serving: Cal 479; Prot 5 g; Carbo 63 g; T Fat 23 g; 41% Calories from Fat; Chol 86 mg; Fiber 2 g; Sod 307 mg

—Lee Seehaver

Rum Cake with Chocolate Cream Cheese Frosting

▪ ▪ ▪ ▪ ▪ ▪ ▪ ▪ ▪ ▪ ▪ ▪ ▪ ▪ ▪ ▪ ▪ ▪ ▪ ▪

1 (2-layer) yellow cake mix
1/3 cup light rum
3 tablespoons (or more) rum
16 ounces cream cheese, softened
1 1/2 cups white chocolate chips, melted, cooled
1 cup butter, softened

- Prepare the cake using package directions substituting 1/3 cup rum for 1/3 cup of the water. Spoon the batter into 3 greased and floured 9-inch cake pans.
- Bake at 350 degrees for 23 minutes. Cool in the pans on a wire rack for 30 minutes. Drizzle the layers with 3 tablespoons rum. Invert the layers onto a wire rack.
- Beat the cream cheese in a mixer bowl until fluffy. Add the white chocolate and butter gradually, beating constantly until of spreading consistency.
- Stack the cake layers on a cake plate, spreading 1 cup frosting between each layer. Spread the remaining frosting over the top and side of the cake.
- Garnish the cake with chocolate leaves, raspberries and/or strawberries.
- May make chocolate leaves by spreading the back of 12 rose leaves with melted tinted white chocolate. Chill in the refrigerator. Peel off and discard the rose leaves.
- Yield: 12 servings.

Approx Per Serving: Cal 624; Prot 8 g;
Carbo 52 g; T Fat 42 g; 59% Calories from Fat;
Chol 128 mg; Fiber 1 g; Sod 614 mg

—Joe Myrick

Pop's Chocolate-Covered Cherries

▪ ▪ ▪ ▪ ▪ ▪ ▪ ▪ ▪ ▪ ▪ ▪ ▪ ▪ ▪ ▪ ▪ ▪ ▪ ▪

4 (16-ounce) jars maraschino cherries with stems
1/4 cup dark rum
1 (14-ounce) can sweetened condensed milk
2 tablespoons plus 2 teaspoons light corn syrup
1/2 teaspoon almond extract
2 (1-pound) packages confectioners' sugar
1 1/2 pounds dark chocolate coating

- Line 4 baking sheets with waxed paper.
- Remove 1 tablespoon of cherry juice from each jar of cherries and discard. Add 1 tablespoon rum to each jar; cover and shake. Let stand at room temperature for 4 hours or longer. Drain the cherries in a colander; pat dry.
- Combine the condensed milk, corn syrup and almond flavoring in a bowl and mix well. Add the confectioners' sugar gradually, stirring constantly with a wooden spoon until blended. Shape by teaspoonfuls around the cherries, leaving the stems bare. Place on the prepared baking sheets.
- Chill for 20 minutes to 2 hours or until firm.
- Microwave the chocolate coating in batches in a microwave-safe dish on High until smooth, stirring every 30 seconds. Dip the cherries 1 at a time in the chocolate to coat. Return the cherries to the prepared baking sheets. Chill until firm. Store, loosely covered, at room temperature for 1 week to allow the centers to liquify. Store in the refrigerator in airtight containers until serving time.
- May substitute milk chocolate coating or white chocolate coating for the dark chocolate coating. May substitute maraschino liqueur for the rum.
- Yield: 96 servings.

Approx Per Serving: Cal 112; Prot 1 g;
Carbo 22 g; T Fat 2 g; 19% Calories from Fat;
Chol 1 mg; Fiber <1 g; Sod 6 mg

—Melody Montgomery

Mother's Divinity

2¹/₂ cups sugar
1 cup water
¹/₂ cup light corn syrup
¹/₈ teaspoon salt
3 egg whites
1 teaspoon vanilla extract

- Combine the sugar, water, corn syrup and salt in a 4-quart saucepan and mix well.
- Cook to 234 to 240 degrees on a candy thermometer, soft-ball stage. Remove from heat.
- Beat the egg whites in a mixer bowl until soft peaks form.
- Pour ¹/₂ of the hot syrup over the egg whites, beating constantly.
- Cook the remaining syrup to 270 to 290 degrees on a candy thermometer, soft-crack stage. Add to the egg white mixture gradually, beating constantly at high speed until thick. Stir in the vanilla.
- Drop by tablespoonfuls onto waxed paper or foil. Let stand until firm.
- Yield: 48 servings.

Approx Per Serving: Cal 51; Prot <1 g; Carbo 13 g; T Fat 0 g; 0% Calories from Fat; Chol 0 mg; Fiber 0 g; Sod 13 mg

—*Patty Bell*

Yuletide Kisses

4 egg whites
¹/₄ teaspoon cream of tartar
³/₄ cup confectioners' sugar
1 teaspoon vanilla extract
Red and green food coloring paste

- Combine the egg whites and cream of tartar in a mixer bowl. Beat at high speed until soft peaks form.
- Add the confectioners' sugar 2 tablespoons at a time, beating until stiff peaks form. Beat in the vanilla.
- Fit a pastry bag with a large star tip ¹/₂ inch in diameter. Brush lengthwise stripes of red and green food coloring alternately inside the pastry bag, using an artist's paintbrush and slightly less than ¹/₈ teaspoon of each food coloring paste. Spoon the meringue carefully into the pastry bag.
- Pipe into rosettes 1¹/₂ inches in diameter and 1¹/₄ inches high onto a foil-lined baking sheet, arranging 1 inch apart.
- Bake at 200 degrees for 3 hours. Turn off the oven.
- Let stand in the oven with the door closed for 30 minutes.
- Cool on the baking sheet on a wire rack.
- Loosen kisses from the foil with a metal spatula. Store in an airtight container.
- Yield: 48 servings.

Approx Per Serving: Cal 9; Prot <1 g; Carbo 2 g; T Fat <1 g; <1% Calories from Fat; Chol 0 mg; Fiber 0 g; Sod 5 mg

—*Amy Morgan*

Festive Lollipops

2 cups sugar
2/3 cup light corn syrup
1/2 cup water
1 1/2 teaspoons peppermint extract
Food coloring
Decorative candies

- Combine the sugar, corn syrup and water in a saucepan and mix well. Cook over low heat until the sugar dissolves, stirring constantly; increase heat to high.
- Bring to a boil; do not stir. Cook to 300 degrees on a candy thermometer, hard-crack stage. Remove from heat.
- Stir in the flavoring and food coloring. Pour into a glass measuring cup.
- Pour into desired shapes or 2-inch circles onto a foil-lined baking sheet. Press lollipop sticks into the different shapes with the back of a spoon immediately.
- Decorate with desired candies.
- May substitute 2 teaspoons lemon extract, 1/2 teaspoon almond extract, 1/4 teaspoon oil of cinnamon or 1 teaspoon vanilla extract for the peppermint extract.
- Yield: variable.

Nutritional information for this recipe is not available.

—*Melissa Melton Keeney*

Holiday Mints

5 1/2 tablespoons butter
3 tablespoons evaporated milk
13 drops of oil of peppermint
Food coloring
1 (1-pound) package confectioners' sugar

- Microwave the butter in a microwave-safe dish until melted. Let stand until cooled to room temperature.
- Stir in the evaporated milk, flavoring and food coloring of choice. Stir in the confectioners' sugar.
- Pinch off a small amount of dough; roll and knead in hands until smooth and shiny.
- Press into a candy mold; invert onto waxed paper.
- Repeat the process with the remaining dough.
- Yield: 72 servings.

Approx Per Serving: Cal 33; Prot <1 g;
Carbo 6 g; T Fat 1 g; 25% Calories from Fat;
Chol 3 mg; Fiber 0 g; Sod 10 mg

—*Mary M. Manning*

Sugar-Candied Peanuts

- - - - - - - - - - - - - - - - - -

4 cups raw shelled peanuts
2 cups sugar
1 cup water
1/2 teaspoon salt

- Discard any loose peanut skins.
- Combine the peanuts, sugar, water and salt in a saucepan. Bring to a boil over medium-high heat, stirring constantly.
- Boil until the liquid has been absorbed and the peanuts seem almost dry, stirring constantly.
- Spread the peanuts on a baking sheet, spreading to separate the peanuts.
- Bake at 225 degrees for 1 hour, stirring occasionally.
- Let stand until cool. Separate the peanuts if needed.
- Store in an airtight container.
- Yield: 16 servings.

Approx Per Serving: Cal 305; Prot 10 g; Carbo 31 g; T Fat 18 g; 50% Calories from Fat; Chol 0 mg; Fiber 3 g; Sod 75 mg

—David Starns

Toasted Pecans

- - - - - - - - - - - - - - - - - -

2 tablespoons margarine
2 cups pecan halves
Salt to taste

- Microwave the margarine in a microwave-safe dish until melted.
- Add the pecans, stirring to coat.
- Microwave on High for 1 1/2 minutes; stir.
- Microwave on High for 1 1/2 minutes; stir.
- Microwave on High for 2 minutes longer.
- Stir in salt.
- Drain the pecans on paper towels.
- Let stand until cool.
- Do not double this recipe. As with candy, preparing several small batches is more successful than attempting large increases when timing is critical to success.
- Yield: 8 servings.

Approx Per Serving: Cal 206; Prot 2 g; Carbo 5 g; T Fat 21 g; 87% Calories from Fat; Chol 0 mg; Fiber 2 g; Sod 34 mg

—Jennifer Wilkinson

Mama's Basic Pie

1 cup sugar
1/4 cup (heaping) flour
1 cup milk
1 cup evaporated milk
3 egg yolks, beaten
1 teaspoon vanilla extract
1/2 cup butter or margarine
1 baked (9-inch) pie shell
8 ounces whipped topping

- Combine the sugar, flour, milk and evaporated milk in a double boiler over hot water; blend well.
- Cook over the hot water until the mixture is smooth and thickened, stirring constantly.
- Stir a small amount of the hot mixture into the beaten egg yolks; stir the egg yolks into the hot mixture.
- Cook briefly just until the mixture is heated through. Blend in the vanilla.
- Whisk in the butter until melted.
- Pour the hot filling into the pie shell.
- Chill until serving time.
- Spread the whipped topping over the chilled pie just before serving.
- For Chocolate Pie, blend 1 tablespoon baking cocoa into the milk mixture before cooking and proceed as above.
- For Pineapple Pie, prepare the filling as above. Fold 1 cup well drained crushed pineapple into the filling before pouring into the pie shell.
- Yield: 8 servings.

Approx Per Serving: Cal 504; Prot 7 g; Carbo 50 g; T Fat 32 g; 56% Calories from Fat; Chol 124 mg; Fiber <1 g; Sod 298 mg

Just a Little Something My Mama Taught Me

Dessert is my favorite part of the meal. I usually eat dessert first just in case I get too full with the regular meal. While I was living alone, I didn't want to go without a good homemade pie, so I learned to make my own. When I asked my mama for her recipe, like any good southern son, she sent this to me with the postscript "and bring for Christmas." Was she surprised when I did!

—Jerry Berch

Santa's Favorite Coffee Bread

2 envelopes active dry yeast
2 cups sifted flour
3/4 cup unsweetened pineapple juice
1/2 cup water
1/2 cup shortening
1/3 cup sugar
1 1/2 teaspoons salt
2 eggs
2 teaspoons grated lemon peel
3/4 cup golden raisins
1/2 cup chopped candied pineapple
2 1/2 to 3 cups sifted flour
1/4 to 1/2 cup melted butter
1/4 to 1/2 cup sugar

- Combine the yeast and 2 cups flour in a large mixer bowl. Combine the pineapple juice, water, shortening, 1/3 cup sugar and salt in a saucepan. Heat just until warm, stirring occasionally to speed the melting of the shortening. Add to the flour mixture.
- Add the eggs and lemon peel. Beat at low speed for 1 1/2 minutes, scraping the bowl constantly. Beat at high speed for 3 minutes. Stir in the raisins and pineapple. Stir in enough of the remaining flour to make a soft to moderately stiff dough.
- Turn onto a lightly floured surface. Knead for 10 minutes or until smooth. Place in a greased bowl, turning to coat the surface. Cover and let rise in a warm place for 1 to 1 1/2 hours or until doubled in bulk. Punch the dough down. Let stand for 10 minutes.
- Pat 3/4 of the dough evenly into a greased 10-inch tube pan. Divide the remaining dough into 2 equal portions. Roll each portion into a 28-inch strand; twist the strands together. Place over the dough in the tube pan, sealing the ends. Cover and let rise for 40 to 60 minutes or until doubled in bulk.

- Bake at 375 degrees for 45 minutes. Brush with the melted butter and sprinkle with the remaining sugar.
- To make a fruit bread, divide the dough into 3 equal portions and shape each portion into a smooth ball. Place the balls on a lightly greased baking sheet with the sides just touching. Cover and let rise for 45 minutes or until doubled in bulk. Bake at 350 degrees for 35 minutes. Mix 3/4 cup sifted confectioners' sugar and 1 tablespoon milk together and spread over the cooled bread. Garnish with almonds and candied cherries.
- Yield: 12 servings.

Approx Per Serving: Cal 457; Prot 7 g;
Carbo 69 g; T Fat 18 g; 34% Calories from Fat;
Chol 56 mg; Fiber 2 g; Sod 358 mg

A Special Treat for Santa

This is an excellent treat for little ones to leave for Santa Claus on Christmas Eve. It is a tasty alternative to all of the cookies he eats. Moms, Dads and other Santa's helpers might also enjoy this little snack while taking a break from all those last minute Christmas Eve chores. It is best with a pot of fresh coffee, but don't forget to save a cup for Good Old Saint Nick!

—Sara Melton Starns

Festive Fruit Tart

¹/₂ (20-ounce) package refrigerated sugar
   cookie dough
8 ounces cream cheese, softened
¹/₄ cup sugar
¹/₄ cup pineapple juice
1 teaspoon vanilla extract
1 cup sliced strawberries
1 cup blueberries
2 kiwifruit, sliced
3 to 5 canned pineapple slices

- Press the cookie dough into an ungreased 12-inch pizza pan.
- Bake at 350 degrees for 12 to 15 minutes or until brown. Let stand until cool.
- Beat the cream cheese, sugar, pineapple juice and vanilla in a mixer bowl until light and fluffy.
- Spread over the baked layer.
- Arrange the strawberries, blueberries, kiwifruit and pineapple slices in a decorative pattern over the top.
- May use any fresh or canned fruit to top the tart.
- Yield: 12 servings.

Approx Per Serving: Cal 225; Prot 3 g;
Carbo 29 g; T Fat 12 g; 45% Calories from Fat;
Chol 28 mg; Fiber 2 g; Sod 157 mg

Thanksgiving Memories

Thanksgiving holidays were always very interesting at our house when I was growing up. For instance, there was the time I spent the night in our station wagon because we had so many relatives visiting.

My mom was famous for a green and yellow congealed salad. She made it every year and I loved it! She always saved me the extra cottage cheese and cherries and I would sit on the kitchen counter and eat to my heart's content.

The year I was eight, my brother went to the refrigerator to get the famous salad and proceeded to drop the whole thing on my grandfather.

I do not think anyone was as concerned about the mess as they were about not having the salad for Thanksgiving dinner. We did, however, salvage as much as we could by scraping it off of my grandfather.

—Nicky Lee

Baklava

■ ■ ■ ■ ■ ■ ■ ■ ■ ■ ■ ■ ■ ■ ■ ■ ■ ■ ■ ■

4 cups chopped blanched almonds
2 cups sugar
1¹/₂ teaspoons cardamom
1 (1-pound) package phyllo dough
2 cups melted unsalted butter
2 cups sugar
1 cup water
2 tablespoons rose water

■ Combine the almonds, 2 cups sugar and cardamom in a bowl and mix well.
■ Layer 3 sheets of the phyllo dough in a greased 9x13-inch baking dish, brushing each sheet with butter; cover the remaining phyllo dough with a damp cloth to prevent drying out. Spread with some of the almond mixture. Top with 1 sheet of the phyllo dough; brush with butter. Repeat this process with the remaining ingredients until all the phyllo dough and almond mixture are used, ending with 2 sheets of the phyllo dough; brush with the butter.
■ Cut the phyllo with a sharp knife to make diamond shapes. Pour the remaining butter over the top.
■ Bake at 350 degrees for 35 to 40 minutes or until brown.
■ Bring 2 cups sugar and water to a boil in a saucepan over medium heat. Boil for 20 to 25 minutes, stirring frequently. Stir in the rose water. Let stand for 30 minutes. Pour over the baked layers.
■ Let stand until cool.
■ Yield: 24 servings.

Approx Per Serving: Cal 449; Prot 6 g; Carbo 48 g; T Fat 28 g; 54% Calories from Fat; Chol 41 mg; Fiber 3 g; Sod 96 mg

Persian New Year's Memories

Baklava or "Baglava," is a traditional recipe served for Aide Noruz, the Persian New Year, which is celebrated on March 21, or the first day of spring. Each Persian housewife makes her favorite recipe with help from her friends and relatives. Part of making Baklava from

scratch is knowing just how much and which ingredients to use to get the unique flavor. The pastry, which is difficult to make, can be bought ready made, making it a lot easier to create this wonderful delicacy.

—*Zahra Noe*

Pumpkin Swirl

■ ■ ■ ■ ■ ■ ■ ■ ■ ■ ■ ■ ■ ■ ■ ■ ■ ■ ■ ■

3 eggs
1 cup sugar
²/₃ (16-ounce) can pumpkin
³/₄ cup baking mix
2 teaspoons cinnamon
1 teaspoon pumpkin pie spice
¹/₂ teaspoon nutmeg
1 cup chopped pecans
8 ounces cream cheese, softened
1 cup confectioners' sugar
6 tablespoons butter, softened
1 teaspoon vanilla extract

■ Line a greased jelly roll pan with waxed paper; grease.
■ Beat the eggs and sugar in a mixer bowl until blended. Add the pumpkin, beating until mixed. Stir in the baking mix, cinnamon, pumpkin pie spice and nutmeg. Spread evenly in the prepared pan. Sprinkle with the pecans.
■ Bake at 375 degrees for 13 to 15 minutes or until light brown.
■ Invert onto a towel sprinkled with confectioners' sugar; remove the waxed paper. Roll the cake in the towel as for a jelly roll. Place seam side down on a wire rack. Let stand until cool.
■ Beat the cream cheese, confectioners' sugar, butter and vanilla in a mixer bowl until smooth, scraping the bowl occasionally.
■ Unroll the cake; spread with the cream cheese filling; reroll.
■ Place on a serving platter. Chill, covered, until serving time.
■ Yield: 10 servings.

Approx Per Serving: Cal 413; Prot 6 g; Carbo 43 g; T Fat 26 g; 55% Calories from Fat; Chol 107 mg; Fiber 2 g; Sod 267 mg

—*Rhonda "Chellie" Williams*

Mincemeat Turnovers

²/₃ cup mincemeat
¹/₃ cup chopped peeled tart apple
1 tablespoon dark rum
1 teaspoon cinnamon
1 all ready pie pastry
1 egg yolk
2 teaspoons water

- Combine the mincemeat, apple, rum and cinnamon in a bowl and mix well.
- Open the pie pastry on a lightly floured surface. Cut into 4 wedges along the fold lines.
- Place ¹/₄ cup of the mincemeat mixture in the center of each wedge.
- Brush the cut edges with a mixture of the egg yolk and water. Fold the edges of each wedge together to form a triangle; crimp edges with a fork to seal. Place on a baking sheet.
- Cut 3 slits in the top of each turnover; brush with the remaining egg mixture.
- Bake at 425 degrees for 20 minutes or until brown. Serve warm.
- Yield: 4 servings.

Approx Per Serving: Cal 565; Prot 3 g; Carbo 62 g; T Fat 32 g; 52% Calories from Fat; Chol 84 mg; Fiber 1 g; Sod 595 mg

—Delora Woodruff

Baked Apples Deluxe

6 large baking apples
³/₄ cup granola
1 tablespoon melted butter or margarine
1 teaspoon cinnamon
Pecan Sauce

- Core the apples. Peel the top ¹/₃ of the apples. Place in a baking pan.
- Combine the granola, 1 tablespoon butter and cinnamon in a bowl and mix well. Stuff into the centers of the apples.
- Bake at 350 degrees for 45 minutes.
- Arrange the apples on a serving platter; drizzle with the Pecan Sauce.
- Yield: 6 servings.

Pecan Sauce

1 cup packed brown sugar
2 tablespoons butter or margarine
¹/₄ cup whipping cream
¹/₂ cup coarsely chopped pecans

- Combine the brown sugar and 2 tablespoons butter in a saucepan.
- Cook for 15 minutes or until the brown sugar dissolves, stirring constantly. Remove from heat.
- Whisk in the whipping cream. Add the pecans and mix well.

Approx Per Serving: Cal 453; Prot 3 g; Carbo 73 g; T Fat 19 g; 36% Calories from Fat; Chol 29 mg; Fiber 7 g; Sod 103 mg

—Beth Huckabee

Merry Gingered Fruit Compote

2 (12-ounce) packages pitted prunes
1 (12-ounce) can ginger beer
1 (8-ounce) package dried apricots
1 cup golden raisins
1 cup orange juice
1 teaspoon minced gingerroot
1 (3½-inch) cinnamon stick
1 (20-ounce) can pineapple chunks, drained
1 (16-ounce) can pear halves, drained, cut
    into halves lengthwise
½ cup light corn syrup

- Bring the prunes, ginger beer, apricots, raisins, orange juice, gingerroot and cinnamon stick to a boil in a saucepan; reduce heat to low.
- Simmer for 15 minutes or until the fruit is tender, stirring occasionally.
- Add the pineapple, pears and corn syrup and mix gently with a rubber spatula.
- Discard the cinnamon stick.
- Spoon into goblets or wine glasses. Serve warm or chilled.
- May serve as an accompaniment to roasted meats.
- May substitute ginger ale for ginger beer.
- Yield: 9 servings.

Approx Per Serving: Cal 436; Prot 4 g;
Carbo 112 g; T Fat 1 g; 1% Calories from Fat;
Chol 0 mg; Fiber 10 g; Sod 35 mg

—*Opal Smith*

Pumpkin Rice Pudding with Apple-Pecan Sauce

1 (16-ounce) can pumpkin
1 cup packed brown sugar
½ cup raisins
1 egg, beaten
1½ teaspoons cinnamon
1 teaspoon vanilla extract
½ teaspoon ginger
¼ teaspoon salt
⅛ teaspoon ground cloves
1 (12-ounce) can evaporated milk
3 cups cooked rice
Apple-Pecan Sauce

- Combine the pumpkin, 1 cup brown sugar, raisins, egg, cinnamon, vanilla, ginger, salt and cloves in a bowl and mix well. Stir in the evaporated milk. Add the rice and mix well.
- Spoon into a buttered 2½-quart baking dish. Bake at 350 degrees for 35 to 40 minutes or until the pudding tests done.
- Serve warm pudding with warm Apple-Pecan Sauce.
- Yield: 10 servings.

Apple-Pecan Sauce

1 cup apple juice
¼ cup packed brown sugar
1 tablespoon cornstarch
½ cup chopped pecans
1 tablespoon margarine

- Bring the apple juice, ¼ cup brown sugar and cornstarch to a boil in a saucepan; reduce heat.
- Simmer for 1 minute, stirring constantly. Stir in the pecans and margarine.

Approx Per Serving: Cal 248; Prot 4 g;
Carbo 42 g; T Fat 8 g; 29% Calories from Fat;
Chol 31 mg; Fiber 2 g; Sod 122 mg

—*Cathie Young*

Aunt Ella's Bread Pudding

3 slices bread
1 cup sugar
2 eggs
2 cups milk
1/4 cup butter
1/4 to 1/2 teaspoon vanilla extract
Nutmeg or cinnamon to taste

- Tear the bread into bite-size pieces.
- Combine the bread, sugar, eggs, milk, butter, vanilla and nutmeg in a bowl; mix well. Spoon into a nonstick baking dish.
- Bake at 300 to 325 degrees for 45 minutes or until a knife inserted near the center comes out clean.
- May add 1/2 cup raisins before baking.
- Yield: 8 servings.

Approx Per Serving: Cal 232; Prot 5 g; Carbo 33 g; T Fat 9 g; 36% Calories from Fat; Chol 77 mg; Fiber <1 g; Sod 158 mg

—*Bob Burst*

Homemade Ice Cream

5 eggs
1 cup sugar
1 (14-ounce) can sweetened condensed milk
1 (12-ounce) can evaporated milk
1 1/2 tablespoons vanilla extract
Milk

- Combine the eggs and sugar in a mixer bowl. Beat for 5 to 7 minutes.
- Add the condensed milk, evaporated milk and vanilla. Beat until blended.
- Pour into an ice cream freezer container.
- Add whole, low-fat or skim milk to the fill line.
- Process using manufacturer's directions.
- Editor's Note: Because this recipe does not cook the eggs, for food safety, you may wish to try the recipe substituting pasteurized egg substitute for whole eggs.
- Yield: variable

Nutritional information is not available for this recipe.

—*William E. (Scott) Scott*

Eggs Benedict

1/4 cup butter
1 tablespoon lemon juice
2 egg yolks, beaten
2 tablespoons light cream
1/2 teaspoon dry mustard
1/4 teaspoon salt
Dash of Tabasco sauce
4 English muffins, split, toasted
8 slices cooked ham or Canadian bacon, warmed
8 eggs, poached

- Microwave the butter in a 2-cup glass measure on High for 1 minute or until melted. Stir in the lemon juice, egg yolks, cream, mustard, salt and Tabasco sauce; mix well. Microwave on High for 1 minute longer, stirring every 15 seconds. Whisk until smooth.
- Place 1 toasted English muffin half on each of 8 serving plates. Layer 1 slice ham and 1 poached egg on each muffin half. Spoon hot sauce over the top.
- Yield: 8 servings.

Approx Per Serving: Cal 264; Prot 16 g; Carbo 14 g; T Fat 15 g; 53% Calories from Fat; Chol 300 mg; Fiber 1 g; Sod 699 mg

A Christmas Tradition

We have a tradition at our house that we have Eggs Benedict every Christmas morning. My wife Nancy and I both cook, for it takes two people to coordinate everything being done at the same time.

—*Richard Edmonson*

Tennessee Cranberry Frappé

2 cups cranberries
2 cups water
2 cups sugar
1 (3-inch) cinnamon stick
8 whole cloves
1 quart (or more) ginger ale
2 cups pineapple juice
1 cup lemon juice
1/2 teaspoon red food coloring

- Combine the cranberries, water, sugar and cinnamon stick in a saucepan.
- Cook until the cranberries are tender, stirring occasionally.
- Strain into a freezer container, discarding the cranberries and cinnamon stick.
- Let stand until cool.
- Freeze, covered, until firm.
- Place the frozen cranberry mixture in a chilled punch bowl just before serving.
- Pour the ginger ale, pineapple juice and lemon juice over the top and mix gently. Stir in the food coloring.
- Yield: 35 servings.

Approx Per Serving: Cal 66; Prot <1 g;
Carbo 17 g; T Fat <1 g; <1% Calories from Fat;
Chol 0 mg; Fiber <1 g; Sod 2 mg

Manhattan New Year's Memories

In the sixties, I was missioned in New York City where approximately twelve sisters worked in the various offices of the Catholic charities in Harlem, Lower East Side, Upper Manhattan, and the Bronx.

We lived in an old six-story brownstone donated by the late Barbara Hutton. It was located one block off 5th Avenue, across from the Metropolitan Museum of Art.

Every New Year's Day we entertained with an open house for family and friends. My aunt, Mrs. Chris Menzler of Nashville, Tennessee, sent me this recipe, and Tennessee Cranberry Frappé thus became an annual New Year's treat in Manhattan.

—Sister June Pemberton

A Little
Something
Extra

Equivalents

WHEN THE RECIPE CALLS FOR	USE

Baking

1/2 cup butter	4 ounces
2 cups butter	1 pound
4 cups all-purpose flour	1 pound
41/2 to 5 cups sifted cake flour	1 pound
1 square chocolate	1 ounce
1 cup semisweet chocolate chips	6 ounces
4 cups marshmallows	1 pound
21/4 cups packed brown sugar	1 pound
4 cups confectioners' sugar	1 pound
2 cups granulated sugar	1 pound

Cereal-Bread

1 cup fine dry bread crumbs	4 to 5 slices
1 cup soft bread crumbs	2 slices
1 cup small bread cubes	2 slices
1 cup fine cracker crumbs	28 saltines
1 cup fine graham cracker crumbs	15 crackers
1 cup vanilla wafer crumbs	22 wafers
1 cup crushed cornflakes	3 cups uncrushed
4 cups cooked macaroni	8 ounces uncooked
31/2 cups cooked rice	1 cup uncooked

Dairy

1 cup shredded cheese	4 ounces
1 cup cottage cheese	8 ounces
1 cup sour cream	8 ounces
1 cup whipped cream	1/2 cup heavy cream
2/3 cup evaporated milk	1 small can
12/3 cups evaporated milk	1 (13-ounce) can

Fruit

4 cups sliced or chopped apples	4 medium
1 cup mashed bananas	3 medium
2 cups pitted cherries	4 cups unpitted
21/2 cups shredded coconut	8 ounces
4 cups cranberries	1 pound
1 cup pitted dates	1 (8-ounce) package
1 cup candied fruit	1 (8-ounce) package
3 to 4 tablespoons lemon juice plus 1 tablespoon grated lemon rind	1 lemon
1/3 cup orange juice plus 2 teaspoons grated orange rind	1 orange
4 cups sliced peaches	8 medium
2 cups pitted prunes	1 (12-ounce) package
3 cups raisins	1 (15-ounce) package

Equivalents

WHEN THE RECIPE CALLS FOR   **USE**

Meats
4 cups chopped cooked chicken . . . . 1 (5-pound) chicken
3 cups chopped cooked meat . . . . 1 pound, cooked
2 cups cooked ground meat . . . . 1 pound, cooked

Nuts
1 cup chopped nuts . . . . 4 ounces shelled
                                                         1 pound unshelled

Vegetables
2 cups cooked green beans . . . . 1/2 pound fresh or
                                                         1 (16-ounce) can
2 1/2 cups lima beans or red beans . . . . 1 cup dried, cooked
4 cups shredded cabbage . . . . 1 pound
1 cup grated carrot . . . . 1 large
8 ounces fresh mushrooms . . . . 1 (4-ounce) can
1 cup chopped onion . . . . 1 large
4 cups sliced or chopped potatoes . . . . 4 medium
2 cups canned tomatoes . . . . 1 (16-ounce) can

Measurement Equivalents

1 tablespoon = 3 teaspoons
2 tablespoons = 1 ounce
4 tablespoons = 1/4 cup
5 1/3 tablespoons = 1/3 cup
8 tablespoons = 1/2 cup
12 tablespoons = 3/4 cup
16 tablespoons = 1 cup
1 cup = 8 ounces or 1/2 pint
4 cups = 1 quart
4 quarts = 1 gallon

1 (6 1/2- to 8-ounce) can = 1 cup
1 (10 1/2- to 12-ounce) can = 1 1/4 cups
1 (14- to 16-ounce) can = 1 3/4 cups
1 (16- to 17-ounce) can = 2 cups
1 (18- to 20-ounce) can = 2 1/2 cups
1 (29-ounce) can = 3 1/2 cups
1 (46- to 51-ounce) can = 5 3/4 cups
1 (6 1/2- to 7 1/2-pound) can or
   Number 10 = 12 to 13 cups

Metric Equivalents

Liquid
1 teaspoon = 5 milliliters
1 tablespoon = 15 milliliters
1 fluid ounce = 30 milliliters
1 cup = 250 milliliters
1 pint = 500 milliliters

Dry
1 quart = 1 liter
1 ounce = 30 grams
1 pound = 450 grams
2.2 pounds = 1 kilogram

*NOTE: The metric measures are approximate benchmarks
for purposes of home food preparation.*

Substitutions

INSTEAD OF	USE
Baking	
1 teaspoon baking powder	$1/4$ teaspoon baking soda plus $1/2$ teaspoon cream of tartar
1 tablespoon cornstarch (for thickening)	2 tablespoons flour or 1 tablespoon tapioca
1 cup sifted all-purpose flour	1 cup plus 2 tablespoons sifted cake flour
1 cup sifted cake flour	1 cup minus 2 tablespoons sifted all-purpose flour
Bread Crumbs	
1 cup dry bread crumbs	$3/4$ cup cracker crumbs
Dairy	
1 cup buttermilk	1 cup sour milk or 1 cup yogurt
1 cup heavy cream	$3/4$ cup milk plus $1/3$ cup butter
1 cup light cream	$7/8$ cup skim milk plus 3 tablespoons butter
1 cup sour cream	$7/8$ cup sour milk plus 3 tablespoons butter
1 cup sour milk	1 cup milk plus 1 tablespoon vinegar or lemon juice or 1 cup buttermilk
Seasoning	
1 teaspoon allspice	$1/2$ teaspoon cinnamon plus $1/8$ teaspoon cloves
1 cup catsup	1 cup tomato sauce plus $1/2$ cup sugar plus 2 tablespoons vinegar
1 clove of garlic	$1/8$ teaspoon garlic powder or $1/8$ teaspoon instant minced garlic
1 teaspoon Italian spice	$1/4$ teaspoon each oregano, basil, thyme, rosemary plus dash of cayenne
1 teaspoon lemon juice	$1/2$ teaspoon vinegar
1 tablespoon mustard	1 teaspoon dry mustard
1 medium onion	1 tablespoon dried minced onion or 1 teaspoon onion powder
Sweet	
1 (1-ounce) square chocolate	$1/4$ cup cocoa plus 1 teaspoon shortening
$1^{2/3}$ ounces semisweet chocolate	1 ounce unsweetened chocolate plus 4 teaspoons granulated sugar
1 cup honey	1 to $1^{1/4}$ cups sugar plus $1/4$ cup liquid or 1 cup corn syrup or molasses
1 cup granulated sugar	1 cup packed brown sugar or 1 cup corn syrup, molasses or honey minus $1/4$ cup liquid

No-Salt Seasoning

Salt is an acquired taste and can be significantly reduced in the diet by learning to use herbs and spices instead. When using fresh herbs, use 3 times the amount of dried herbs. Begin with small amounts to determine your favorite tastes. A dash of fresh lemon or lime juice can also wake up your taste buds.

Herb Blends to Replace Salt

Combine all ingredients in small airtight container. Add several grains of rice to prevent caking.

- **No-Salt Surprise Seasoning**—2 teaspoons garlic powder and 1 teaspoon each of dried basil, oregano and dehydrated lemon juice.
- **Pungent Salt Substitute**—1 tablespoon dried basil, 2 teaspoons each of summer savory, celery seeds, cumin seeds, sage and marjoram, and 1 teaspoon lemon thyme; crush with mortar and pestle.
- **Spicy No-Salt Seasoning**—1 teaspoon each cloves, pepper and coriander, 2 teaspoons paprika and 1 tablespoon dried rosemary; crush with mortar and pestle.

Herb Complements

- **Beef** — bay leaf, chives, cumin, garlic, hot pepper, marjoram, rosemary
- **Pork** — coriander, cumin, garlic, ginger, hot pepper, savory, thyme
- **Poultry** — garlic, oregano, rosemary, savory, sage
- **Cheese** — basil, chives, curry, dill, marjoram, oregano, parsley, sage, thyme
- **Fish** — chives, coriander, dill, garlic, tarragon, thyme
- **Fruit** — cinnamon, coriander, cloves, ginger, mint
- **Bread** — caraway, marjoram, oregano, poppy seeds, rosemary, thyme
- **Salads** — basil, chives, tarragon, parsley, sorrel
- **Vegetables** — basil, chives, dill, tarragon, marjoram, mint, parsley, pepper

Basic Herb Butter

Combine 1 stick unsalted butter, 1 to 3 tablespoons dried herbs or twice that amount of minced fresh herbs of choice, 1/2 teaspoon lemon juice and white pepper to taste. Let stand for 1 hour or longer before using.

Basic Herb Vinegar

Heat vinegar of choice in saucepan; do not boil. Pour into bottle; add 1 or more herbs of choice and seal bottle. Let stand for 2 weeks before using.

Herbs and Spices

- **Allspice** — Pungent aromatic spice, whole or in powdered form. It is excellent in marinades, particularly in game marinade, or in curries.
- **Basil** — Can be chopped and added to cold poultry salads. If the recipe calls for tomatoes or tomato sauce, add a touch of basil to bring out a rich flavor.
- **Bay leaf** — The basis of many French seasonings. It is added to soups, stews, marinades and stuffings.
- **Bouquet garni** — A must in many Creole cuisine recipes. It is a bundle of herbs, spices and bay leaf tied together and added to soups, stews or sauces.
- **Celery seeds** — From wild celery rather than domestic celery. It adds pleasant flavor to bouillon or a stock base.
- **Chervil** — One of the traditional fines herbes used in French-derived cooking. (The others are tarragon, parsley and chives.) It is good in omelets or soups.
- **Chives** — Available fresh, dried or frozen, chives can be substituted for raw onion or shallot in any poultry recipe.
- **Cinnamon** — Ground from the bark of the cinnamon tree, it is important in desserts as well as savory dishes.
- **Coriander** — Adds an unusual flavor to soups, stews, chili dishes, curries and some desserts.
- **Cumin** — A staple spice in Mexican cooking. To use, rub seeds together and let them fall into the dish just before serving. Cumin also comes in powdered form.
- **Garlic** — One of the oldest herbs in the world, it must be carefully handled. For best results, press or crush garlic clove.
- **Marjoram** — An aromatic herb of the mint family, it is good in soups, sauces, stuffings and stews.
- **Mustard (dry)** — Brings a sharp bite to sauces. Sprinkle just a touch over roast chicken for a delightful flavor treat.
- **Oregano** — A staple herb in Italian, Spanish and Mexican cuisines. It is very good in dishes with a tomato foundation; it adds an excellent savory taste.
- **Paprika** — A mild pepper that adds color to many dishes. The very best paprika is imported from Hungary.
- **Rosemary** — A tasty herb important in seasoning stuffing for duck, partridge, capon and other poultry.
- **Sage** — A perennial favorite with all kinds of poultry and stuffings. It is particularly good with goose.
- **Tarragon** — One of the fines herbes. Goes well with all poultry dishes whether hot or cold.
- **Thyme** — Usually used in combination with bay leaf in soups, stews and sauces.

Herbs and Spices

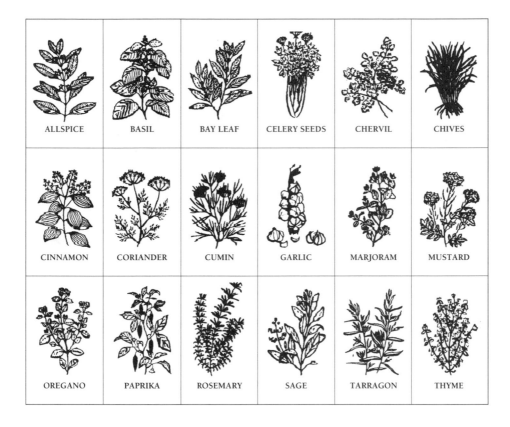

ALLSPICE	BASIL	BAY LEAF	CELERY SEEDS	CHERVIL	CHIVES
CINNAMON	CORIANDER	CUMIN	GARLIC	MARJORAM	MUSTARD
OREGANO	PAPRIKA	ROSEMARY	SAGE	TARRAGON	THYME

Food Guide Pyramid

A GUIDE TO DAILY FOOD CHOICES

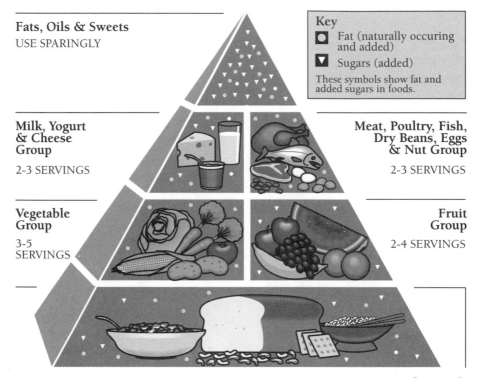

Fats, Oils & Sweets
USE SPARINGLY

Key
◯ Fat (naturally occuring and added)
▼ Sugars (added)
These symbols show fat and added sugars in foods.

Milk, Yogurt & Cheese Group
2-3 SERVINGS

Meat, Poultry, Fish, Dry Beans, Eggs & Nut Group
2-3 SERVINGS

Vegetable Group
3-5 SERVINGS

Fruit Group
2-4 SERVINGS

Source: U.S. Department of Agriculture/U.S. Department of Health and Human Services

Bread, Cereal, Rice & Pasta Group
6-11 SERVINGS

Use the Food Guide Pyramid to help you eat better every day . . . the Dietary Guidelines way. Start with plenty of Breads, Cereals, Rice, and Pasta; Vegetables; and Fruits. Add two to three servings from the Milk group and two to three servings from the Meat group.

Each of these food groups provides some, but not all, of the nutrients you need. No one food group is more important than another—for good health you need them all. Go easy on fats, oils, and sweets, the foods in the small tip of the Pyramid.

What Constitutes a Serving?

Bread group servings:
1 slice of bread
1 ounce of ready-to-eat cereal
1/2 cup cooked cereal, rice or pasta
1/2 English muffin or hamburger bun

Vegetable group servings:
1 cup of raw, leafy green vegetables
1/2 cup cooked vegetables
1/2 cup chopped raw vegetables
3/4 cup vegetable juice

Fruit group servings:
3/4 cup fruit juice
1 medium apple or orange
1 small banana
1/2 large grapefruit
11/2 cups raw, cooked or canned
   fruit

Milk group servings:
1 cup whole, 2% or skim milk
1/2 cup evaporated milk
1 cup plain or flavored yogurt
11/2 ounces natural cheese
2 ounces processed cheese

Meat group servings:
2 to 3 ounces of cooked lean meat, fish or poultry
1 egg, 1/2 cup cooked beans or
2 tablespoons peanut butter may be substituted for 1 ounce of meat

Individuals differ in their nutrient and caloric needs as shown by the range in numbers of servings. A teenage boy should eat more servings from the bread group than the 65-year-old woman. And, with the exception of the milk group, young children should eat the lower number of servings and smaller serving sizes. If you eat a larger portion, count it as more than one serving. For example, a dinner-size portion of spaghetti (1 to 11/2 cups) counts as two to three servings from the bread group.

Fats and sweets have a group of their own at the tip of the pyramid. Many of our favorite foods—desserts, snacks and spreads and beverages—are high in sugars and fats or oils but low in nutrients. The fat (o) and added sugar (▼) symbols are found throughout the other food groups. By choosing foods from each food group that are low in fat and sugar and by limiting added fats and sweets, you can have a diet that supplies needed vitamins and minerals without too many calories.

Food Safety

What we think is the flu can sometimes be caused by harmful bacteria that may be in food. Bacteria on food can grow and make you sick. You can't always see, smell or taste if food is contaminated with bacteria—so it's important to buy safe food and keep it safe when you get home.

These are some foods that bacteria like best: milk and other dairy products; eggs; meat; poultry and seafood. When buying, storing and preparing foods, it's important to use safe food handling practices. Here are some tips to follow:

At the Store:

- Buy cans and jars that look perfect. Don't buy dented, rusted cans or cans with bulging ends. Check the carton of eggs to see if any are broken or cracked.
- Keep dripping meat juices away from other foods. Put raw meat, poultry and seafood into plastic bags before they go into your cart.
- Pick up milk and other cold foods last. This gives food less time to warm up before you get home.
- Pick up hot chicken and other hot foods just before you go to the checkout lane. This will give hot food less time to cool off before you get home.

Storing Food:

- Return home as soon as you can after shopping for food. Put food into the refrigerator or freezer right away. Eggs always go in the refrigerator.

Preparing Food:

- Wash your hands with warm water and soap before and after you handle food. Wash anything that comes in contact with food, such as utensils, counters, equipment, etc. Use paper towels to wipe up cupboard spills, especially meat juices.
- If you use a dishcloth, use one that has been freshly laundered and dried in your dryer. Rinse with hot soapy water after each use and hang to dry. Change dishcloths frequently. A dirty dishcloth can add more bacteria than it removes.

Food Safety

- Rinse fresh fruits and vegetables under running water to wash away dirt. Do not use dish detergent or hand soap to wash fruits and vegetables.
- Keep raw meat, poultry, and seafood and their juices away from other foods. These foods can spread bacteria in your kitchen.
- Keep meat, poultry, and seafood cold while they thaw. Thaw them:
  - In the refrigerator, 1 to 2 days before you will cook the food.
  - In the microwave, use the "defrost" setting. Then cook the food right away.
- Cook raw meat, poultry, seafood, and eggs until they are done. Use an oven temperature of at least 325 degrees F. to destroy bacteria.
  - Cook red meat, especially ground meat, until it looks brown inside and the juices look clear, not pink.
  - Poke cooked chicken with a fork. The juices should look clear, not pink.
  - Stick a fork into cooked fish. The fish should flake.
  - Cook eggs until whites and yolks are firm, not runny.

Handling Leftovers:

- Store leftovers in the refrigerator or freezer as soon as you finish eating. If food is left out for 2 or more hours, bacteria can grow. Put leftovers in shallow dishes so they cool faster.
- Eat leftovers in the next two days.
- IF IN DOUBT, THROW IT OUT!

Source: Alice Henneman, M.S.R.D., Lancaster County Extension Educator and Julie Albrecht, Ph.D.R.D., Associate Professor, Extension Food Specialist, University of Nebraska. Adapted from: *Keep Your Food Safe*, FDA, 1991.

Index

■ ■

Order Form

I would like to order additional copies of *Mississippi Reflections*.

❐ FOR MYSELF, QUANTITY _____   ❐ AS A GIFT, QUANTITY _____

MAIL TO: NAME _____

ADDRESS _____

CITY/STATE/ZIP _____

IF GIFT, GIFT CARD SHOULD READ_____

_____

ENCLOSED IS MY CHECK FOR $16.95 PLUS $3.00 FOR
SHIPPING AND HANDLING.

Mail to:
Hospice of Central Mississippi
Mississippi Reflections
2600 Insurance Center Dr., Suite B-120
Jackson, Mississippi 39216-4911
or call (601) 366-9881 or 1-800-273-7724
or FAX (601) 981-0150

Order Form

I would like to order additional copies of *Mississippi Reflections*.

❐ FOR MYSELF, QUANTITY _____   ❐ AS A GIFT, QUANTITY _____

MAIL TO: NAME _____

ADDRESS _____

CITY/STATE/ZIP _____

IF GIFT, GIFT CARD SHOULD READ_____

_____

ENCLOSED IS MY CHECK FOR $16.95 PLUS $3.00 FOR
SHIPPING AND HANDLING.

Mail to:
Hospice of Central Mississippi
Mississippi Reflections
2600 Insurance Center Dr., Suite B-120
Jackson, Mississippi 39216-4911
or call (601) 366-9881 or 1-800-273-7724
or FAX (601) 981-0150